Investing in China through Free Trade Zones

Lorenzo Riccardi

Investing in China through Free Trade Zones

Springer

Lorenzo Riccardi
RsA asia
Shanghai, China

ISBN 978-3-662-51627-0 ISBN 978-3-662-47354-2 (eBook)
DOI 10.1007/978-3-662-47354-2

Springer Heidelberg New York Dordrecht London

Softcover reprint of the hardcover 1st edition 2016

Printed on acid-free paper

Springer-Verlag GmbH Berlin Heidelberg is part of Springer Science+Business Media (www.springer.com)

for Gala and the Art Deco Elegance of Shanghai

Contents

Chapter 1
Introduction

China has recently become the second global economy after the United States of America and differently from the other developed countries in the last decade. China has always experienced high growth rate every year. Its access to the World Trade Organization (WTO) in 2001 was saluted as a clear signal of openness toward the world economy, and Beijing is expected to play a key role in international trade. Nevertheless, Central Party preserved an important sphere of influence in economic affairs, resulting unwillingness to definitely unleash China to become a market-economy model.

Even though Beijing reacted better than Western countries to the financial crisis, the downturn has led toward staggering export growth rate during last years. This coupled with the slowdown in domestic demand has yielded an overall downsizing effect on GDP. Furthermore, China has gradually lost its low labor cost advantage over emerging countries, meaning that now the economic policies have to shift from an industrial focus to a more technology and service intensive model. Finally, developing countries gathered in a series of multilateral trading agreement (i.e. and ASEAN) are putting ever more pressure on international competitiveness of China.

All these aspects clearly underline to what extent China urges a profound and thought intervention aimed at improving its competitive position, by lowering central control over economy and letting a more sustainable economic growth. According to the large part of experts, such measures should be enacted through deregulation, market liberalization, the flourishing of a more mature capital market, and the enforcement of a reliable legal system. For the previous results to be achieved, the suggested way imposes a deeper engagement in the tertiary sector in which results still underdeveloped (compared to leading global economies), and a better country's receptiveness of Foreign Direct Investments (FDI), also allowing the facilitating conditions to let companies carry on their business in the best possible way.

The Chinese State Council is seriously evaluating to transform China in an open economy to seek new challenges for growth opportunities, but is still reluctant to abandon a strong centralized system in a very short period. The Chinese Government

L. Riccardi, *Investing in China through Free Trade Zones*,
DOI 10.1007/978-3-662-47354-2_1

is conscious about the risk of loosing control of the current system to an open driven economy. For these reason, local authority worked to create a new Free Trade Zone with a pilot basis in the area of Shanghai, unifying four previous free trade zones and elaborating a new regulation to be specifically implemented in this new special zone. The aim of the Chinese State Council is the creation of an experimenting area to prove new policies regarding financial innovations, investment liberalization, customs relaxation, tax incentives, new administration systems, and trade liberalization. Chinese administration committee will analyze by the time the results and the effects of adopting this kind of policies in order to decide if it is recommended to open the economy system also in the rest of China, with a lower control by the government and a more openness to foreign investors.

This new free trade zone is called New China (Shanghai) Pilot Free Trade Zone and has been established in September 2013 by the Chinese State Council. The aim of this book guide is providing especially to non-Chinese investors a complete view of the new economic environment that the central government, with the collaboration of the Shanghai municipality, is gradually implementing in the mentioned area. Main interest is to evaluate benefits for companies (both domestic and foreign) that decide to be located in the Shanghai Free Trade Zone. The book chapters expose different programs that policy makers are implementing. Main reforms regarding financial sector, customs supervision, the establishing of the Negative List to define which are the industries promoted for foreign enterprises, transportation, safety and environment, administration simplification with approval relaxation, transparency, and disclosure. Chinese authorities are enforcing all the plans already approved with a step-by-step approach and often investors claim about uncertainty in the current regulation, referring to plans already been implemented and for future execution. There are doubts about the timeline of execution and also referring to the real intent of introducing part of the new policies. During our analysis the process of introducing new regulation and extending the concept of the Pilot Free Trade Zone is also rapidly changing and may vary in the short term. The book chapters include facts and trends on rules under implementation procedure or discussion by local officers.

The guide provides a complete scenario on present and future elements adopted to promote the China Free Trade Zone, including a general overview on the rapid changes that impacted the economy of the country during the last decades. It is useful to focus on key points in the China Transition to a more open economy, such as the access to the World Trade Organization in 2001, the signature of regional agreements to promote intra-asia economic transactions and the creation of associations and institutions to promote international cooperation with western economies. To better show progresses in the Chinese economy, data and statistics are reported and analyzed.

The guide highlights different practices, structures, and options for foreign investors entering China. A number of factors shall be considered in order to assess the factual investment attractiveness for foreign capitals and the preferred location where to establish Headquarters (HQs) in the region. Groups shall consider not only where firms and subsidiaries operate or make profits, but also where and how to coordinate operations related to regional and Chinese market. In this case, the main purpose will consist of examining which drivers lead managers to choose the best gateway to China. Notably Shanghai, Singapore, and Hong Kong have emerged as the best places where to establish regional HQs for Chinese market, and each alternative carries on specific advantages and disadvantages. Although Shanghai can afford a strategic position in the Mainland, Singapore and Hong Kong deploy overall advantages in terms of transparency and political, legal, and regulatory environment. It is crucial to understand which are the main factors to consider when deciding the location of the corporate headquarter, and it is significant that the comparison between Shanghai, Singapore, and Hong Kong highlights their related advantages and disadvantages. The chapters focus on how investment decisions are made with regard to China and what is the role of free trade zones.

In particular is important to understand how China, through the establishment of the new China (Shanghai) Pilot Free Trade Zone, is trying to cancel the gap with other regional headquarters that attracts investors with fiscal advantages and financial reforms.

The book provides a focus on the new China (Shanghai) Pilot Free Trade Zone with the support of institutional notices and circulars that the State Council is experimenting with this project, in order to provide Shanghai with a new competitive and attractive positioning to struggle with others location for headquarters. The intent is to encourage capital entry in China and simplify procedures to set up new enterprises according to the international standards. Firstly the guide defines the new area concerning the free trade zone and then analyzes the fields of intervention. New China (Shanghai) Pilot Free Trade Zone is based on four main issues which are financial reform, investment liberalization, government authority, and trade liberalization. The Framework Plan for the new China (Shanghai) Pilot Free Trade Zone deals with the internationalization of RMB, the opening up of most of the sectors to foreign investors with the Negative List approach, a strong simplification in red tape switching in many cases from approval procedures to filing procedures finalized to reduce time losses, tax incentives, new systems for custom supervision, improvements in transportation and connections with the Shanghai area and financial innovations regarding currency exchange, cross border financing and investing, free trade accounts for both companies and individuals, interest liberalization, cross border cash pooling, and E-business. After defining all the parts of this ambitious plan, the book describes what has already been implemented, what is taking off, and what persists to be only written on some institutional notices. In fact as mentioned previously, there is still uncertainty about the implementation of the whole Framework Plan approved by the State Council but main enterprises have already relocated in the new China (Shanghai) Pilot Free Trade Zone to take advantage of the new environment.

The guide focuses also on other changes that the central Chinese government of Beijing is planning to implement in the whole country. Consequently, investors interested in the new China (Shanghai) Pilot Free Trade Zone must add to the opportunities offered by the Pilot Program, the consequences and advantages that could derive from other reforms implemented or going to be implemented in overall

China. The most interesting reform concerns the New Company Law that applies since March 1st 2014. Other issues that have been currently managed by the Chinese State Council concern the deepening of the Central Fiscal Reform, the Competition Policy Reform, the Financial System Reform, the Foreign Trade and Investment Reform, the State-owned Enterprise Reform, the Land Policy Rationalization, the Labor and Welfare Reform, the Environmental Policy Reform, and the Innovation Policy Reform.

The book analyzes deeply the sectors undergoing structural change with the implementation of the China (Shanghai) Pilot Free Trade Zone. Future economical development is mainly related to the services area and on the regional cooperation starting from the creation of the Shanghai Free Trade Zone with other areas and special zones that enjoy the benefits and the experience of Shanghai.

The appendixes include the main documents useful to define the new policy with regulations, circulars, opinions, and notices on implementations, released by government authorities (State Council, People's Bank of China, Shanghai Municipal Government, etc.).

Chapter 2
Fact Sheets

China has seen its global trade figures increase substantially since joining the World Trade Organization in 2001, but while the emerging Asian nation's imports and exports continue to grow, it is also becoming increasingly more involved in WTO disputes, both as a complainant and as a respondent.

In 2000, prior to joining the WTO, China's total trade with the world totaled USD 474.3 billion. By 2009, that number had climbed to an impressive USD 2.21 trillion, even after experiencing a slight fall due to the Global Financial Crisis.

China World Trade Statistics

Year	Exports (US$ bn)	Imports (US$ bn)	Total trade (US$ bn)	WTO cases Involving China
2000	249.2	225.1	474.3	n/a*
2001	266.1	243.6	509.7	0
2002	325.6	295.2	620.8	0
2003	438.2	412.8	851.0	1
2004	593.3	561.2	1,154.6	0
2005	762.0	660.0	1,421.9	2
2006	969.0	791.5	1,760.4	0
2007	1,220.5	956.1	2,176.6	2
2008	1,430.7	1,132.6	2,563.6	5
2009	1,201.0	1,005.6	2,207.2	6

*China joined WTO in 2001
Source: PRC National Bureau of Statistics, PRC General Administration of Customs

China's joining of the WTO only occurred in November 2001. Analysts consider a pre-WTO China, and a post-WTO China, and the two situations have proven to be significantly different. The pre-WTO China had to negotiate for an astonishing 15 years to obtain membership of the WTO. The country was considered backward, communist, largely untrustworthy, and internally incapable of dealing with disputes under international law.

L. Riccardi, *Investing in China through Free Trade Zones*,
DOI 10.1007/978-3-662-47354-2_2

Having to have its membership ratified by reaching agreements with every single member of the WTO individually was a significant effort. The technicalities of the bilateral and multilateral negotiations were by no means simple. China was too advanced in some sectors for WTO member countries to be comfortable giving it developing country status, which brings with it loose timetables and "differential and more favorable treatment" for meeting WTO obligations. But China was also not a developed economy by most measures, as its delegation insisted.

Main actors during that complex phase were the Premier Zhu Rongji together with the President Jiang Zemin; Zhu contended with resistance of central power to promote the move of China into what was seen as an irreversible position of reform. Elements not just overseas, but also within China struggled to accept that China really could change. Debates, uncertainty, and foot-dragging within China about the benefits of changing to fit the norms of international capitalism were additional reasons why the process of joining took so long.

The roots of opposition were tied to the very beginnings of reform. In 1978, China had no foreign investment and very little trade. Contrast that with the present, where China has been the largest recipient of direct foreign investment in the developing world since 1992 and is among the top three trading countries in the world. Although the reforms that opened China to international markets were gradual, by the mid-1990s foreign invested enterprises began to gain serious market share.

Fast Facts

Pre-WTO: China's GDP in 2001 at time of WTO entry: USD 509.8 billion, growth of 7.5 %

Post WTO: China's GDP in 2008: USD 4.42 trillion, growth of 9 %

In 2010 in only 2 months there is the same trade volume than in the whole 2001 year.

2.1 Pre-reform Trade Regime

Up through the 1970s, Chinese trade took place within the context of a planned economy and therefore nearly all trade was subject to very exacting quantitative guidelines. The State Planning Commission's import plan covered more than 90 % of all imports. The export plan was similarly comprehensive, specifying the physical quantities of more than 3,000 individual commodities. Prior to 1978, a handful of foreign trade corporations owned and controlled by the Ministry of Foreign Trade were responsible for carrying out the import and export plans. In this context, neither exports nor imports were sensitive to exchange rates or relative prices.

Furthermore, the composition of Chinese trade had little connection to Chinese comparative advantage, with capital-intensive goods, including refined petroleum products, playing a large role in Chinese exports well into the early 1980s. As a consequence, the volume of Chinese trade, relative to world trade, declined sharply from 1.5 % in 1953 to 0.6 % in 1977.

2.2 Trade Liberalization

China gradually reformed its trade regime over the 1980s and 1990s. However, progress was neither simple nor straightforward. As the authorities phased out the direct quantitative planning of imports and exports, they began to rely more heavily on a complicated welter of alternative trade policies, including conventional tools such as tariffs and quotas, and less conventional instruments, limiting trading rights and tougher commodity inspection requirements. The government actually raised import tariffs on most commodities in the early years of the reform period. By 1982, the average statutory tariff rate was a relatively high 56 %. The government reduced this level throughout the next 7 years, to roughly 15 % on the eve of WTO accession. In addition to tariffs, the government restricted trade in a wide range of commodities by quotas and import licenses. This range of commodities actually expanded over the course of the 1980s, and by the end of the decade nearly half of Chinese imports were regulated by licenses or quotas. However, these restrictions were also dramatically cut in the 1990s. The share of imports they regulated fell to about 18 % by 1992, and by 2001 it had fallen further to about 8.45 %.

Throughout the reform period, the government restricted the right to engage in foreign trade. Nevertheless, there was a rapid and substantial expansion in the number of domestic firms granted trading rights, as show in the following table.

Growth in companies authorized to conduct foreign trade

Year	Number of companies
1978	12
1985	800
1986	1,200
1988	5,000
1996	12,000
1997	15,000
1998	23,000
1999	29,528
2000	31,000
2001	35,000

Sources: Nicholas R. Lardy, Foreign Trade and Economic Reform in China, 1978–1990

From the initial 12 firms directly controlled by the Ministry of Foreign Trade, this expanded to 35,000 by 2001. With such a large number of potential suppliers of trading services, it is likely that the market for such services had become reasonably competitive by the mid-1990s.

2.3 Trade Regime

China's openness to imports expanded even faster than the decline in formal barriers might suggest. A major reason has to do with the special privileges extended to firms involved in export processing, which were set up in 1979. Initially, this legal framework provided various incentives for the processing of raw materials for export and the assembly of imported goods to produce finished goods for export. In 1987, the government expanded these incentives to provide for duty-free import of all raw materials, parts, and components used in the production of goods for export. Also joint ventures and wholly foreign-owned companies have generally been allowed to import capital goods duty-free throughout the reform period. As an increasingly open FDI regime brought in more foreign investment, this allowed a larger and larger fraction of China's imports to escape the formal trade barriers. Finally, in the second half of the 1990s, the Chinese government began to exempt certain categories of domestic firms and other organizations from import duties. By the first half of 2000, less than 40 % of imports were subject to any tariff. Thus, actual tariff revenues have been far lower than the average statutory rates would suggest. As shown in the following graph, tariff revenues as a share of the value of imports peaked in the 1980s at about 16 % of import values and fell steadily thereafter, reaching a low of about 3 % by 1994.

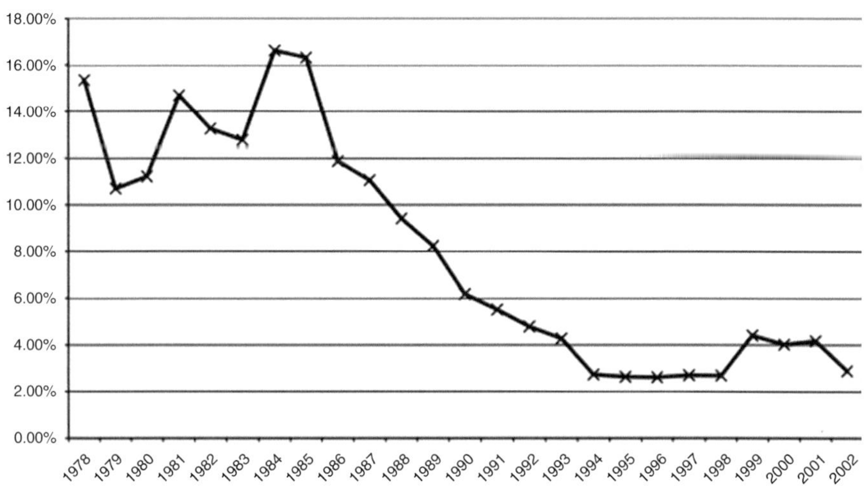

Sources: Xinhua News Service; Guoji Shangbao (International Business Daily)

Tariff revenues as a fraction of import value, 1978–2002

A substantial portion of this decline reflects the enormous expansion of foreign direct investment, the increasing importance of export processing, and the exemption of selected industries and organizations from import tariffs altogether. It also reflects widespread violations of Chinese trade laws.

2.4 China's Porous Protectionism in the Nineties

In principle, by the mid-1980s, China had two trade regimes – a very open one for foreign firms and domestic enterprises engaged in export processing, and a more restrictive trade regime for all other enterprises. Feenstra (1998) called China's trade regime an example of "one country, two systems," and claimed that the maintenance of special privileges for export processing firms was contrary to both the letter and the spirit of WTO rules.

A dualistic trade regime of this type could, in principle, generate two sets of problems. The first is akin to the problem of "trade diversion" in the economic analysis of customs unions. Domestic Chinese enterprises in some industries might have a comparative advantage at exporting a particular commodity or producing a certain good for the domestic market with imported components. In theory, welfare is reduced relative to what would have prevailed under a more even-handed trade regime, even one with a higher level of overall effective protection, because production is undertaken by a set of producers with higher social costs. The second potential problem is that a large segment of the Chinese economy could remain effectively protected from foreign competition, but this is masked by the overall trade statistics, which largely reflect the success of the export-processing regime. The notion that large swathes of the Chinese economy were effectively closed off to foreign competition provided the intellectual foundation for the belief that credible implementation of China's WTO commitments would generate destabilizing shocks. In practice, it is clear that the authorities have never been able to separate China's two trade regimes as completely as the letter of the law would suggest. Substantial quantities of parts and components imported on a duty-free basis have been illegally sold in the domestic market, and there have been substantial illegal sales in the domestic market of goods embodying duty-free imports. In addition to "leakage" into the domestic market of goods imported under the export-processing regime, there has been a significant degree of outright smuggling, much of it via Hong Kong. Between 1995 and 2000, what the Ministry of Commerce classifies as ordinary imports grew 130 %, from USD 43.7 billion to USD 100.08 billion. Over the same period, the sum of imports of duty free parts and components used in processing and the duty-free imports of capital goods of joint venture firms grew only 37 %, from USD 78.33 billion to USD 107.32 billion. Growth in ordinary imports has continued to be quite rapid since WTO accession, although it may slow in coming years, as the current unsustainable investment boom subsides. Growing linkages between firms engaged in export processing and local firms caused the ratio of value added in export processing to double over the 1990s. This reflected both the displacement of imported parts and components by locally produced parts and rising wages. This suggests that the view of the export sector as an enclave with little connection to the local economy became increasingly out of date by the eve of China's accession to the WTO.

2.5 Foreign Exchange Reform and Tax Policy

The expansion of foreign trade was also abetted by changes in foreign exchange and tax policy. Prior to reform, the regime maintained an overvalued exchange rate in order to subsidize the import of capital goods that could not be produced domestically. Overvaluation led to excess demand for foreign exchange, necessitating an extensive system of rigid exchange controls. Key elements of this control system included a 100 % foreign exchange surrender requirement for exporters, tight limitations on the rights of individuals to hold foreign currency, and strict controls on the outflow of foreign capital.

Over the course of the reform period, the government relaxed all of these restrictions. The authorities devalued the official exchange rate in stages, from RMB 1.5 to the dollar in 1981 to 8.7 in 1994. Following a modest appreciation, the government effectively fixed the exchange rate at RMB 8.3 to the dollar in 1995, a rate that was not changed until the summer of 2005. The IMF estimates that the Chinese currency lost about 70 % of its value against the dollar in real terms over the period from 1980 to 1995, substantially enhancing the international competitiveness of China-based export operations. In addition to substantial real devaluation, Chinese exporters were allowed to retain part of their foreign exchange earnings, individuals were allowed to hold foreign exchange, and capital outflow restrictions were relaxed. Over the course of the reform period, China has come to increasingly rely on indirect taxes to fund government expenditures. The World Trade Organization allows the rebate of indirect taxes to exporters, in order to eliminate the disadvantage exporters in such countries face relative to those based in countries that rely on direct taxes on income. The system of indirect taxes in the 1980s was complex and a rebate program for exporters was correspondingly difficult to administer effectively. As the value-added tax, which had only two basic rates, became more important as a revenue source, the export tax rebate became easier to administer in some respects, but the government still encountered difficulties.

The system was subject to extensive fraud as firms claimed rebates for goods that were never exported. In addition, the government lacked the revenue to rebate all taxes and fell considerably behind in rebate payments to exporting firms. The central government clamped down on corruption and cut the rebate rates for exporters in 1995 and 1996. The exports lowdown experienced in the wake of the Asian financial crisis prompted the government to reverse course, raising the amount of the tax rebated to 100 % for some commodities and accelerating the actual payment of rebates due. This arguably helped promote the extremely high rates of export growth recorded after the Asian crisis began to abate, but it exacerbated the central government's financial problems.

2.6 The Opening to FDI Prior to WTO Accession

Despite rising interest in foreign direct investment in China after the 1972 visit of U.S. President Richard Nixon, a number of severe restrictions on FDI remained in place – including a ban on external financing of FDI projects – such that there was very little inward investment until policies were dramatically changed in 1979. In that year a new Law on Joint Ventures was passed, providing a basic framework under which foreign firms were allowed to operate.

Restrictions on external debt and equity finance were relaxed, and, as has been already indicated, restrictions on foreign trade were reduced. Provincial and local governments were allowed considerable freedom in regulating the joint ventures that were established within their jurisdictions. In the same year, four "special economic zones" were established in which foreign firms were offered preferential tax and administrative treatment and given an unusually free handing their operations. These "experiments" in attracting foreign direct investment were quite successful.

A major regulatory change in FDI came in 1986 and it represented a major liberalization that applied throughout China. "Foreign invested enterprises" were made eligible for reduced business income tax rates regardless of location and were given increased managerial autonomy. Tight controls on the remittance of profit in foreign currencies were lifted.

2.7 Growth Drivers in the 1990s

The rapid growth of Chinese exports in the decade prior to WTO accession, the relatively large share of GDP the export sector has come to represent, and the persistent and growing trade imbalance with the United States might suggest that net exports, and the FDI that contributed to it, has been an important driving factor in Chinese economic growth in the 1990s.

First, it's our aim to analyze FDI growth and in a second moment we will focus on trade growth.

According to the Chinese Statistical Yearbook, between 1999 and 2006, some 79,600 new Equity Joint Ventures were established, whereas 178,500 MNEs entered China through own subsidiaries. Data for 2013 report 4,476 new Joint Ventures and 18,125 further subsidiaries.

Tables 2.1 and 2.2 compare China's reception of FDI during last years (2008–2012) with U.S. and other BRICs. The emerging result from Table 2.1 deals with the steady state of Chinese growth trend, far above the other countries taken into account. Moreover, Chinese economy showed a higher resilience to the financial crisis occurred in 2008. Capital inflows in 2009 drop relatively slighter than the U.S. and other emerging nations. In 2010, we can appreciate a full recovery to the precrisis levels. This better overall attractiveness of Chinese market, even within the downturn period, led China to become the first emerging country (among BRICs) for FDI stock and the second worldwide just behind U.S. (Table 2.2).

Table 2.1 Foreign direct investment inflows US billion (%GDP)

Country	2008	2009	2010	2011	2012	2013
U.S.	310.2 (2.2 %)	50.4 (1.1 %)	5.9 (1.4 %)	30.2 (1.5 %)	66.4 (1 %)	6.5
Brazil	45.1 (2.7 %)	5.9 (1.6 %)	8.5 (2.3 %)	6.7 (2.7 %)	5.3 (2.9 %)	0.1
Russia	75.9 (4.6 %)	7.8 (2.3 %)	1.7 (2.1 %)	6.9 (1.9 %)	0.2 (1.5 %)	7.1
India	43.4 (3.4 %)	5.6 (2.6 %)	7.4 (1.7 %)	6.5 (1.9 %)	4.0 (1.3 %)	3.7
China	171.5 (3.8 %)	31.1 (2.6 %)	43.7 (4.1 %)	80.0 (3.8 %)	53.4 (3.1 %)	14.6

Source: OECD International Direct Investment Database, IMF

Table 2.2 Foreign direct investment stock in US billion (%GDP)

Country	2008	2009	2010	2011	2012
U.S.	2,397.4 (16 %)	2,398.2 (17.3 %)	2,623.6 (18.2 %)	2,879.5 (19.2 %)	3,057.3 (18.8 %)
Brazil	287.7 (17.4 %)	400.8 (24.7 %)	682.3 (31.8 %)	695.1 (28.1 %)	718.9 (31.9 %)
Russia	215.8 (13.0 %)	378.8 (31.0 %)	490.6 (32.2 %)	454.9 (24.0 %)	497.8 (24.5 %)
India	125.2 (9.8 %)	171.4 (12.7 %)	205.6 (12.6 %)	206.5 (11.0 %)	226.4 (12.3 %)
China	915.5 (20.3 %)	1,314.8 (26.3 %)	1,569.6 (26.5 %)	1,906.9 (26.1 %)	2,159.6 (26.3 %)

Source: OECD International Direct Investment Database, IMF

Table 2.3 shows the evolution of the number of Multinational Enterprises (MNEs) and the Practical Foreign Capital Utilized to run their operation (bn US dollar). In the last decade, new FDIs witness a clear trend underlining the reduction of new MNEs, coupled with the increased value of Practical Foreign Capital Utilized. Apart from the sharp decrease occurred in the world downturn years, data lead to the conclusion that foreign companies entering China have become bigger in order to address a higher competition. The last latter consideration can underpin the belief that China is becoming a mature market.

Table 2.4 breakdowns the Practical Foreign Capital Utilized for 2012 according to Home areas of investors. It is worthwhile to notice how the major locations to launch investments in the Mainland are represented by countries nearby China where investors enjoy a greater extent of advantages in terms of taxation, transparency, and law enforcement. Additionally they host a big number of foreign-Chinese population. Letting aside the overwhelming relevance related to the closeness, these 10 economies account for around the 91.4 % of overall foreign capital utilization in 2012.

To sum up, above figures show how China still preserves an overall huge degree of attractiveness to MNEs. But at the same time, foreign companies are reshaping their strategies to enter the Chinese market, to deal with an increasing competition.

Table 2.3 Latest development of FDI in China

Year	Number of new MNEs	Practical foreign capital utilization (Billion US dollars)
2003	41,081	53,505
2004	43,664	60,630
2005	44,019	72,406
2006	41,485	69,468
2007	37,888	82,658
2008	27,514	92,395
2009	23,435	90,033
2010	27,406	105,735
2011	27,712	116,011
2012	24,925	111,716
2013	22,773	117,586

Source: Chinese Statistical Yearbook

Table 2.4 Top 10 home areas for FDI in Mainland China in 2012

Country	Practical Foreign Capital Utilization (billion US dollars)
Hong Kong	71.289
Japan	7.380
Singapore	6.539
Taiwan	6.183
USA	3.130
South Korea	3.066
Germany	1.471
Netherlands	1.144
UK	1.031
Switzerland	0.878

Source: Chinese Statistical Yearbook

The main trends occurring are the increased dimension of MNEs while entering China and the placement of capitals in favorable environments close to the mainland. By the same token, China is rapidly evolving from a developing economy to a developed market, and this new feature might require the Government Authority to adequate the regulatory system in near future.

In a narrow growth accounting sense, it is simply not true that net exports have been a consistently important driver of growth in the 1990s, as is illustrated in the following figure, using components of the national income and product accounts taken from IMF International Financial Statistics data.

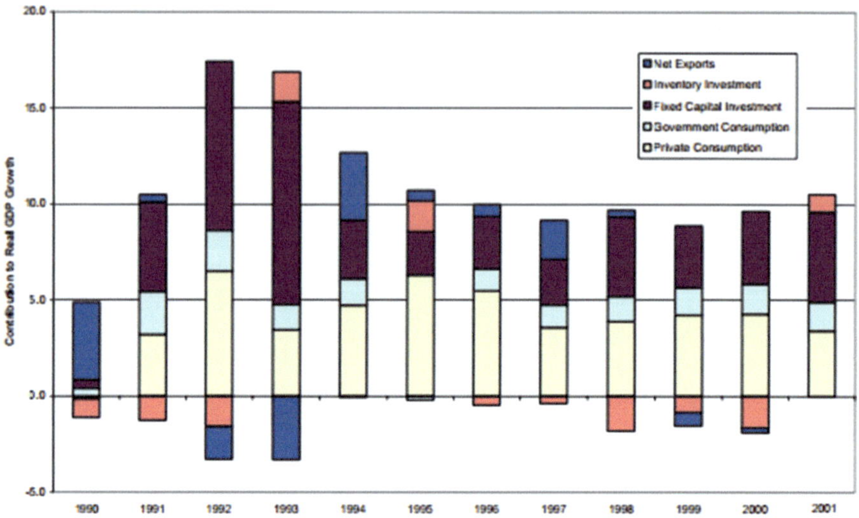

The components of real GDP growth, 1991–2000 (Source: International Monetary Fund)

Growth in imports has broadly kept pace with growth in exports. In the 11 years shown in this chart, net exports contributed positively to GDP growth in 7 years and detracted from it in four, but with a few exceptions, the net impact was modest compared either to capital investment or to private consumption. FDI, much of it export-related, has contributed to capital formation, but as we have already noted, that contribution has also been relatively modest, declining from a peak of 17 % in 1994 to about 7 % in 2003. Recognition of these facts helps place useful bounds both on the degree to which recent growth can be ascribed to trade and to the prospects for further "trade-driven" growth.

That being said, there is no question that expanding trade and FDI have contributed to Chinese living standards since the reform period began and particularly in the last decade.

Chinese consumers have benefited from price declines and an increase in the quality and variety of goods consumed, and China has been able to alter its pattern of industrial production to conform to its comparative advantage. These are the static gains stressed by classical trade theory.

While difficult to quantify with precision, they are certainly substantial. Moreover, these gains are shared with China's trading partners, who have also benefited from cheaper imports, export sales to China, and returns from investment in Chinese enterprises.

China's increasing openness to trade and FDI also has fostered a much greater degree of competition in Chinese product (and, increasingly, service) markets than would have otherwise existed. This has provided a powerful disciplining force constraining the expansion of inefficient enterprises, even when such enterprises received extensive support from other features of the institutional environment, such as the problematic banking system. As foreign producers have been allowed steadily greater freedom to operate in the Chinese market, this competitive pressure has intensified, increasing the likelihood that market share gains are concentrated in the most efficient firms. This, in turn, arguably raises the marginal productivity of capital and labor throughout the economy, although it is clearly difficult to quantify this impact.

China has arguably gained in other dimensions as well, although these benefits are also difficult to quantify. The ability to import technology embodied in capital goods and components has certainly contributed to output expansion.

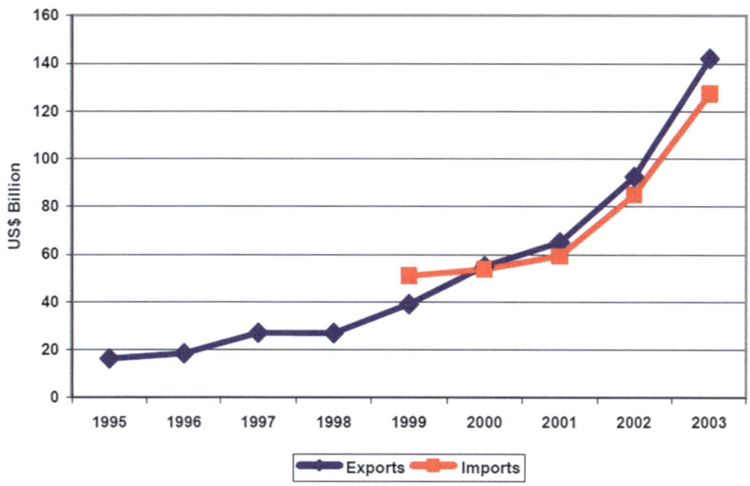

Exports and imports of high-tech products (Sources: Chinese Ministry of Information Industries, China General Customs Administration)

Chinese workers and managers have also benefited from training in foreign technology and management practices. While the Chinese economy as a whole does not appear to exhibit exceptional performance in terms of total factor productivity growth, it is clear that the relative labor productivity of Chinese workers has increased substantially, particularly in the export sector. This has been partially reflected in wage increases and will be eventually reflected in an appreciation of the real exchange rate. Given the level of China's openness to trade, the improvement in terms of trade that would result from such an appreciation would confer nontrivial welfare effects. The fundamental attractors of a large, low-cost labor force, relatively good export infrastructure, and the ability to purchase inputs at world prices, would still exist under this counterfactual scenario. In addition, China's internal market might, if anything, be even more attractive, and growing even more rapidly, under a counterfactual scenario in which the financial system was not burdened by a large stock of nonperforming loans to state-owned enterprises. Despite recent rapid growth in the size, investment, and legal recognition of the private sector in China, FIEs continue to play an important role in mediating China's foreign trade. We expect this to continue, at least in the short-to-medium run.

2.8 Structure of China Exports

At present date, China is the world's second largest trading nation behind the US – leading the world in exports and coming in second for imports. From 2009 to 2011 its trade to GDP ratio was 53.1 %, while its trade per capita was USD 2,413.

Since its accession into the WTO in 2001, China's share in global trade has doubled – accounting for 10.38 % of the world's merchandise trade exports and 9.43 % of merchandise trade imports.

For many countries around the world, China is rapidly becoming their most important bilateral trade partner. In 2011, they were the largest exporting/importing partner for 32 and 34 countries respectively.

However, there have been concerns over large trade imbalances between China and the rest of the world. The US in particular has the largest trade deficit in the world with China at $315 billion, more than three times what it was a decade ago.

There have also been a growing number of trade disputes brought against, mainly for dumping, unfair subsidies by the Chinese government, intellectual property and the valuation of the yuan. Nonetheless its WTO entry ensures that the country will remain a key figure in international trade.

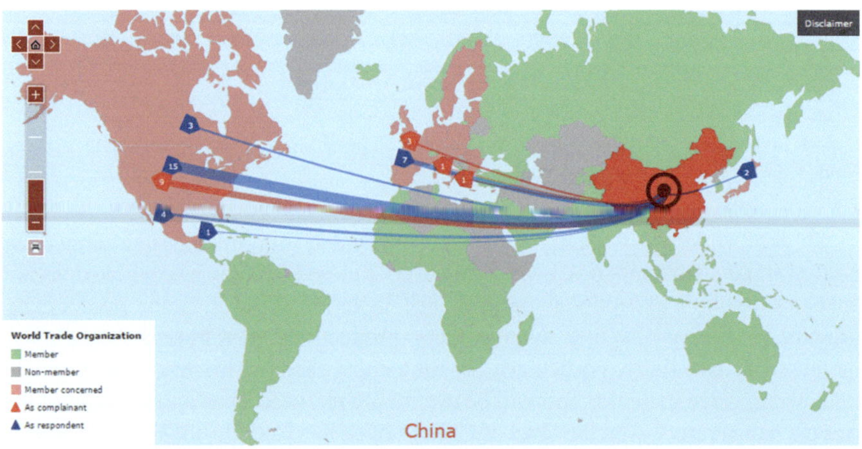

Source:wto.org

From 2001 to the end of 2005, China was involved in just three cases in WTO courts. By 2009, China was involved in 6 of the 14 total trade disputes filed that year. Nations are becoming increasingly willing to make China play by the rules, and China is proving that it is more than ready to fight back.

In 2014, China has been so far involved only in one case, as a respondent against Canada's accusation of anti-dumping on imports of cellulose pulp from Canada.

Domestically, the Chinese government has been keen to reduce the economy's reliance on exports and focus on internal consumption. In March 2013, China's new leadership announced that they would move to recalibrate the economy, acknowledging that there is a "growing conflict between downward pressure on economic growth and excess production capacity."

Extracted from the World Bank database, the following charts show Chinese trade volume in 2013 compared to that of the year previous to China's accession to WTO:

	2000	2013
Exports (US $)	249,203	2,209,007
No of products	4,493	4,436
No of partners	152	122
World ranking of top exporters	9th (3 %)	1st (12 % of share)
Imports (US $)	225,094	1,949,992
No of products	4,084	4,161
No of partners	154	189
World ranking of top importers	4th (6 %)	2nd (7 %)
GDP	1,198,475	9,240,270

China went from being 9th world biggest exporter in the world to number one in only 13 years.

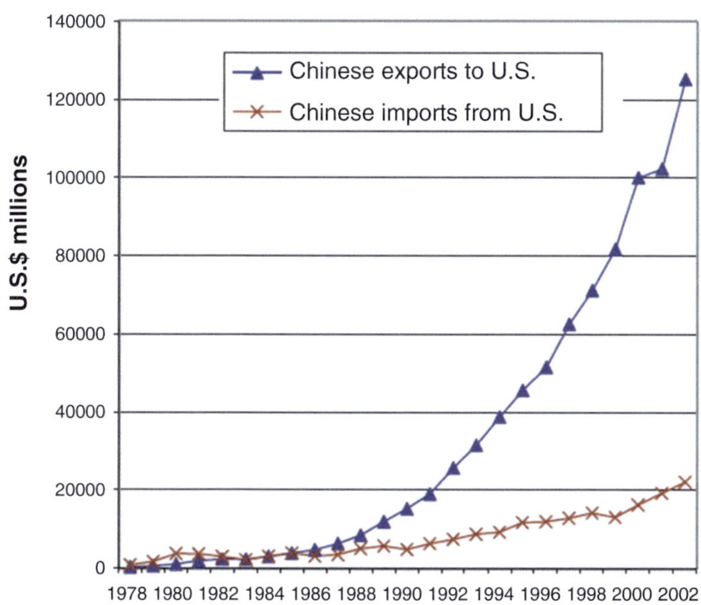

China bilateral trade imbalance (Source: Ministry of Commerce, People's Republic of China)

2.9 WTO Accession: What Has Actually Changed

While negotiations over China's WTO entry were ongoing in the late 1990s, a number of studies were conducted estimating the impact of WTO accession on Chinese trade, employment and growth. Some predicted that China would incur significant restructuring costs in meeting its WTO commitments. Other studies forecast fairly dramatic increases in imports as import tariffs were reduced. There was a tendency for these studies to overestimate the impact of WTO, because many were based on conditions that existed in the mid-1990s, and did not take into account the dramatic acceleration of reform in the years immediately preceding China's WTO entry. Important changes already occurred regime even prior to formal WTO accession, such as tariffs cut, enhancement of trading rights, liberalization; Chinese government also launched a major effort to restructure state-owned manufacturing industries and substantially cut the prices for wheat and corn in 1999 driving prices toward international levels two years before WTO accession. That being said, the combination of China's pre-WTO and post-WTO reforms is making it arguably the most open large developing economy. China's FDI regime is one of the most open and welcoming of any country in the world, and China has made liberalization commitments in all of the service industries covered by the WTO General Agreement on Trade in Services. Only a handful of members come close to meeting this standard. Former U.S. Trade Representative Charlene Barshefsky described China's commitment to liberalize its distribution system as "broader actually than any World Trade Organization member has made" relatively strong commitments to liberalize financial and telecommunications services. This high degree of openness is evidenced by the sharp increase in Chinese imports in recent years, which, in turn, has had an increasingly powerful impact on the East Asian regional economy and, indeed, on the global economy. However, important macroeconomic imbalances, clearly not sustainable in the long run, are also playing an important role in driving this growth.

References

Statistical Data. National Bureau of Statistics of China. N.p., n.d. Web. 18 June 2015

Feenstra RC (1998) One country, two systems: implications of WTO entry for China. Institute of Governmental Affairs, University of California, Davis

Chapter 3
How to Enter China

3.1 Investing in the Free Trade Zones

In late 1990s, the real significance of Special Economic Zones (SEZs) became effective. At that time, eight kinds of SEZs were focused on the implementation of economic reforms introduced during the next three decades after 1970s. Meanwhile, these zones have become the most attractive regions for foreign investments in Mainland China because importing and exporting goods are not as strictly regulated by customs and provides a tax heaven for firms who are involved in the Asia Pacific. Specifically, 15 bonded zones that aimed at driving regional development and optimizing soft environment of investment in China have been set up across the country. These SEZs share the characteristics of enjoying the most beneficial economic policies regime as well as the highest level of market liberalization, which are virtual factors of gaining acceptance from global trading partners of China. This model triggered the economic growth of China in the aftermath of the WTO accession, reflecting the procedure of China's exploration to stimulate domestic economy, while stepping into the global trade. A key feature shown from the very beginning was the high engagement in trade and manufacture sectors. In fact, services carry with them the nonphysical feature; this has always resulted into a biased view that services were both non-storable and non-tradable, and finally constraining the entire system to an effective service development. In the attempt to address the difference underlying the types of SEZs, Economic and Technological Development Areas, Bonded Zones, and Free Trade Zones (FTZs) will be discussed.

Economic and Technological Development Areas, Development Zones for short, have the main purposes of increasing GDP by attracting FDI, experienced management and accelerating industrial structural reforms. It began in 1978 in three cities and has since expanded into 49 cities. Usually these areas are located in inland regions, in a specific environment fostering manufacturing and exporting activities. The issue of foreign exchange management seldom appears. Companies are encouraged to establish in these development zones with incentives such as limited

L. Riccardi, *Investing in China through Free Trade Zones*,
DOI 10.1007/978-3-662-47354-2_3

Corporate Income Tax (CIT fixed at 15 %) for production-related firms, waiver from building tax, tax return, and export rebates.

Bonded Zoned have different goals. The key drivers are the stimulation of regional economic growth and the optimization of the investment environment. In this second case, the most suitable location is embedded in coastline centers associated with ports. Bonded Zones features the following activities: export processing, engagement in the global trading, and bonded warehousing and exhibition. The business environment here presents a greater degree of openness. Although business branches are not allowed to operate cross-border payments as they run their business in RMB, foreign banks can manage offshore financial services along with cross-border financing operations. Furthermore, pricing and account settlement in Chinese Yuan is permitted within the bonded zone. With regard to tax incentives, the 15 % CIT is still recognized in addition to bonded raw materials, exemption from export tariff and VAT within the zone.

Free Trade Zones (FTZs) are endorsed with the governmental function to transform the economic system, lifting the market liberalization and leading to a global financial center. The targeted areas to establish a FTZ can be seaport and airport areas but also bonded zones. Following the long-standing effort to shift the Chinese economy from manufacture-bases to a deeper tertiary involvement, FTZs combine the basic bonded zones' functions in addition to financial and IT services. The greatest amendment to the general system is the financial regulatory system. In FTZs, RMB exchange of capital items is allowed, whereas interest rates and cross-border payments are both liberalized. Foreign-founded companies operating in FTZs are entitled to conduct international trading, manufacturing, processing, warehousing, logistics, and exhibition of bonded commodities. Moreover foreign-owned companies are also entitled to conduct trade related services, such as testing and maintenance. When it comes to operating incentives, all those activities run within the zone are generally exempt from VAT, while goods leaving the zone to domestic location are deemed as import. For goods entering the zone there is no provision of VAT refund. Finally, trading activities between entities within the zone are exempt from turnover taxes.

From their early adoption, to the latest definition of FTZs, these initiatives have always been a tool to explore the way of gaining a more liberalized market. As it continues to grow, these economically developing tools have embraced various functions and evolved their characteristics from single trade liberalization to multiple directions. The first-stage advantage is the limited scope of trade liberalization, which allows the government to experiment with economic policies without the risks of applying them to the economy as a whole. For this reason, a FTZ can function as an economic laboratory, enabling a government to learn what will be of the most benefit to the economy over the long-term. The important aspect is the future option to extend the measures adopted in FTZ also at a nationwide level. Therefore, a FTZ can be seen as a behavior of a sovereign nation rather than a market with no barriers. Another way to look at it is that it is politically established but economically driven. Because of this, the actual success of a FTZ relies on a set of preconditions. First of all, the choice of location is crucial. A port with an outstanding harbor and wealthy hinterland is more likely to grow into an international transportation and trading center. Second, a FTZ is expected to provide more advanced infrastructures than the others regions of the hosting country, as it is a major condition to attract investments. Just as important as physical conditions, a stable and liberalized market incorporated with a developed economy is also attractive. Relatively, regulatory environment and taxation incentives are either restrictions or attractions especially for foreign capitals.

A number of different types of areas exist under special Customs supervision, which can be briefly summarized below:

- *Export Processing Zone (EPZ)*: This is a type of FTZ, typically set up in developing countries by their governments to promote industrial and commercial exports. It offers tax benefits and business regulation exemptions. It serves for as an area for export processing, bonded logistics, R&D, testing and inspection, and repair and maintenance. It is also known as a "development economic zone" or "special economic zone."
- *Bonded Logistics Park (BLP)*: This is a type of special economic zone, similar to a bonded warehouse but over a specific geographic area. It may have international port capabilities. It serves as an area for warehousing, simple circulative processing and value-added services, international sourcing and distribution, import and export trading (including entrepôt trade), international transit, inspection and repair, exhibition, and other business approved by the Customs. BLPs have similar regulations to FTZ except for export VAT refund, which is eligible once goods enter the zone.
- *Bonded Port (BP)*: A BP serves as an area for warehousing, export processing, international sourcing and distribution, import and export trading (including entrepôt trade), international transit, inspection and repair, exhibition, and other business approved by the Customs.
- *Comprehensive Bonded Zone (CBZ)*: It operates under special customs supervision.
- *Cross-Border Industrial Zone (CBIZ)*: It is similar to EPZ and FTZ, but less common in China. There are more political aspects involved.

To some extent, the agreement on trade in services (GATS) became a guideline for China to optimize its services market. However, all the promises of removing specific entry barriers that were supposed to be done by the end of 2007 could be a challenging task for China under the temporal economic situation. Using the U.S. as a benchmark, the employment percentage of the tertiary industry accounted for more than 70 % in the late 1990s while that of China amounted for only 26.9 %. People who were occupied in the primary industry still dominated the labor force with a proportion of 50 %. Main reason of the unbalanced development of the industrial structure was a preferential policy regime on the second industry, and as Mayes and Wang (2003) identified, there were non-tariff barriers in Chinese agriculture trade policies. Other askew structures existing in the openness level of different provinces were due to a strong support of the eastern coast cities from the central government.

Chinese employment composition from 1996 to 2000

Year	Primary industry	Secondary industry	Tertiary industry
1996	50.50 %	23.50 %	26.00 %
1997	49.90 %	23.70 %	26.40 %
1998	49.80 %	23.50 %	26.70 %
1999	50.10 %	23.00 %	26.90 %
2000	50.00 %	22.50 %	27.50 %

Source: China Statistical Yearbook

China signed the GATS to break the unhealthy developing pattern and endeavored to integrate into the world trade network for gaining a sustainable economic growth. At the beginning of its accession, China tended to import land-intensive goods and export labor-intensive goods in the primary industry while the striking competitive advantages in manufacturing industries were developed mainly based on a large supply of cheap labor (Mayes and Wang, 2003). In regards to the trade in services that had been strictly protected, it was relatively under-developed and embraced a minimal level of foreign penetration with 0.2 % of foreign direct investment (FDI) in the finance and insurance sector, while only eight foreign investment joint-share companies accounted for 0.04 % of the total foreign investment enterprises (China Statistical Yearbook, 2001).

Eleven years have passed since the last time when China decided to open its market to the world on her WTO accession. China economy steps on a node with a stagnant status domestically while being rejecting by the U.S. to join its world trade agreements. The rapid economic development that has been contributed by the WTO accession gives central government the confidence to go one step further, Shanghai pilot FTZ program has been designed using the GATS as an reference to guide a step further in opening Chinese market, especially services sector, to settle the same problems that China faced before her WTO accession.

The future spread (传播) of Chinese FTZs would be based on the success of Shanghai pilot program. For the early stage, the FTZ would conceive in cities associated with sea ports to further assess the administrative measures adopted in Shanghai pilot FTZ and therefore enhance the feasibility for operating cross the country, which followed by FTZ operating in a mode of combination of several inland regions to maximize the utility of inland market as well as to achieve a synergy effect. In general, the FTZ would spread with Shanghai as a starting point along with the coast and then extend to southeast cities. Considering the geographical skewed of economy development in China as well as the limitations on trading partners, the FTZ mode of remote regions such as Xingjian needs more investigation.

As Shanghai FTZ is in its initial phase of development, this paper provides a macroscopically view of shanghai FTZ with an emphasis of the pilot program's special characteristics. A prospection of tendency of Chinese FTZs has been presented to provide reference. However, the lack of qualitative methods for the FTZ performance assessment results in a vague opinion about the zone's economic impact. Future studies could rest on particular benefits that Shanghai FTZ bring to its registered enterprises, from which the improvement in practice can be gained.

Moreover, studies on the effects that FTZ has on its neighbor regions and city dwells could be carried from a microscopic view while the wealth effectiveness that Shanghai FTZ acting on the whole national economic could be assessed macroscopically. From an empirical view of point, a questionnaire has been designed to elicit opinions and suggestions from the registered enterprises.

3.2 Reasons for Establishing a Headquarter in Asia-Pacific

MNEs (Multinational Enterprises) for decades have been looking to the Asia-Pacific market with an increasing interest. Reasons such as higher growth rate of GDP, expanding markets, and tax exemptions (corporate and personal) often support strategies to penetrate these countries. As usually remarked, China plays a crucial role in making decisions on how to go abroad in Asia-Pacific region so that no company can overlook it. What changes among managerial choices is how to approach China, namely the way to leverage at the same time the different opportunities arising from the entire area. According to the European Chamber's study conducted in 2011, amid the majority of managers who decided to establish a China/Asia-Pacific Headquarter (HQ), the main drivers leading to that decision were straightforwardly related to the proximity to the clients/markets, and a favorable overall system environment (legal and regulatory system, political system, business and tax environment). Other secondary reasons considered are the access to human capital, cost advantage in operations, transparency, ease (减轻) of access to target markets, and proximity to distribution facilities and distribution channels.

Gathering all this information, the results yield Shanghai, Hong Kong, and Singapore as the three best performers in line with the previous criteria. Remaining places are kept by Mainland China cities like Beijing (in this case the closer position to the Party's offices are determinant, Guangzhou and Shenzhen regarded as major emerging markets. Focusing our analysis on the top-three, a great extent of different characteristics shapes the locations' environment, leading to various considerations.

3.2.1 Reduction in Tax Rates

Tax heavens are known for no or nominal tax, lack of effective exchange of information and transparency and with no substantial activities (Organization for Economic Cooperation and Development 2009). They are also known as an offshore financial center. Tax reduction by using tax heaven has always been a heated issue in the tax-planning field. Although it is perfectly legal to use lower tax rates offered by offshore headquarters to the company's advantage, it borderlines tax evasion based on interpretation and depending on how well a company handles their tax filing. Plenty of empirical evidence was found to prove that taxation influences the investment decision of MNEs. Hines and Rice (1994) found that the profitability level of subsidiaries in a tax heaven is higher than that of other affiliates based on the study of American MNEs. This is supported by Schwarz (2009), who reports that subsidiaries located in countries with tax rates lower than 10 % are more likely to have higher profits. Furthermore, Grubert and Mutti (2000) state that a country with a low effective tax rates is more attractive to foreign enterprises when choosing the investment location. The current corporate tax in the United States is 35 %, the highest of any developed country. Grubert and Mutti (2000) also claim that its study is valuable because that they identifies the relationship between the genuine new investment and tax rate, while other research focus on the amount of FDI, which includes repatriation behavior. Moreover, Hebous et al. (2011) divide FDI into two categories, namely, Merger and Acquisitions and Greenfield investment (new ventures). They observe the investment behavior of 3600 German's FDI investors and reveal that Greenfield investments are more sensitive to tax rate.

Preferential tax treatment is another factor that has changed dramatically since 2008. Liou (2012) studies the development of inventive policies in China and critically examines its effects on the economic development. It is found that China starts its implementation of the tax incentives from the SEZ in the coastal region and gradually broadens to the interior area towards the west. Furthermore, Halkyard and Linghui (2010) summarized the change of tax incentives for FIEs in China from the early 1980s to 2008 and concludes that tax incentives for FIEs are extended from FDI-specific to domestic companies because of new EIT law, but the scope of tax incentives is reduced and changed substantially. Moreover, they comment that tax incentives in new EIT laws are designed to shape the FDI, not increase its quantity. This idea is supported by Cheng and Shi (2012), who claimed that China adopts industry-dominated tax incentives to guide the investment of foreign investors.

3.3 The Choice of the Headquarter

There is great importance in a corporation choosing the correct location for their headquarters. With the location forming a very important aspect of a company's identity and stature, providing a basic component of its market position and how customers identify the company and its products. As part of the selection of the headquarters location, it is necessary for firms to try to quantify the strategic advantages of one region over another, with management convinced that the strategic and long-term interests of the company are best served in the chosen location.

Even though a certain location may be convenient at the time, it may no longer serve as a good location in the a few years as others migrate to a different region or as the economy shifts to a different trend. Companies should first identify what is important to them, such as lower costs, long-term growth, satisfying short-term needs, etc. Perhaps the more convenient location may also be the costliest. There is no perfect location, as it differs from industry to industry, firm to firm, depending on the types of needs and their capacity to actually establish their headquarters in a certain area. If a company focuses on inspecting imports and exports, it may find that establishing its office by the ports best serve its interests. On the contrary, such a location serves no purpose for an investment bank if being closer to clients in the financial district is a priority. It really depends on what the firm has established as its goals and priorities.

Considering Costs

Costs are one of the toughest issues to overcome when setting up a new headquarters. The costs associated with a new headquarter may be high however the firm must accept the set up costs as a long-term investment as it continues to grow and expand. If a firm is relocating its headquarters, it should ideally relocate from a higher cost location to a lower cost, or at least equal cost location. However, the cost savings of a new location are almost always less than the relocation costs. The bottom line to headquarters relocations is that they are almost always net-cost projects, i.e. the costs are greater than the savings. The cost drivers of setting up a new headquarters and relocating are very similar however relocating typically comes at a higher level. The major costs of headquarter set up and relocation are as follows:

- Property acquisition—real estate costs in the new location, such as the land, building, and legal fees associated with completing this process.
- Property disposition—real estate costs of disposing the old location, including demolishing properties, legal fees, and disposing useless equipment.
- Employee relocation—significant amounts of money for a significant numbers of people. This can include transportation to the new location, logistics, or costs of helping employees become situated in the new location.
- Employee retention—it is necessary to keep vital people on board during the transition period. With some many changes, a firm has to provide incentive for them to stay. Relocating may also raise the fear of layoffs, so the remaining employees need to know that their job is secured or they might end up leaving for another firm or competitor.
- Employee severance—significant numbers of people may be laid off. Depending on the location of the current operations, a company may be legally bound to providing assistance packages to those who have lost their jobs as a result of the relocation.
- Employee hiring—recruit, screen, and train a significant number of new employees in a new location. Not only does this cost money but it is also time consuming and may slow down the business operations because skilled employees are not ready yet.
- Physical relocation—often a more manageable cost than initially expected, but it requires moving equipment, inventory, or supplies from the old location to the new location.
- Interruption—can be minimized by effectively managing the relocation.

It is necessary for firms to try to quantify the strategic advantages of one location over another to attempt to put dollar values on the driving reasons for the final decision. However, even when accounting for these beneficial factors, the firm is faced with comparing soft-savings dollars with hard-cost dollars. Be prepared to make a decision to proceed in the face of a net- cost analytical result.

3.3.1 Image and Brand Positioning

This can cover a wide range of applications and along with costs is probably the most common reason for headquarters relocations and important for the overall brand when setting up in a new region. For many firms, the key driver is to reposition itself in the marketplace with a new identity, and one part of establishing that new identity is to choose the correct location that best suits the company image and goals. For example, a growing financial bank may find that it suits their image better to be in the heart of the financial district compared to remaining in a small office on the outskirts of the city.

3.3.2 Merger and Acquisition Activity

In major M&A projects, there will be two headquarters that will need to merge, eventually, into one. That is usually to one of the existing headquarters locations, since the challenges of moving to a new location would be doubled if they both relocated. A new headquarters location may be a necessary step to establishing a new identity for the now merged company. As markets change over time, a company may find its current location no longer gives it the proximity to customers that it once had. Similarly, as old operational facilities close and new ones open, perhaps in different countries, a company may find its current location no longer giving it efficient proximity to its other operations. As a result, many companies are driven to relocate headquarters to achieve better proximity to markets or operations.

3.3.3 Reducing Costs

Companies have now started to turn to their corporate headquarters operations for additional cost savings, following the cost cutting in their manufacturing, supply chain, and customer service departments. Many corporations look at the possibility of moving to a lower cost location to help reduce their overall costs of doing business. It is important to also keep the cost for the act of relocating in mind because even if the new headquarters incur lower costs in the long run, it may incur short-term costs that it does not have the capacity to handle. In addition, it is not unusual for a company to realize cost savings from a redesign of the organization, processes and workforce as well as from the lower cost location.

Unless a company is looking to relocate in a specific place or surrounding, sometimes it unnecessary to do so and it may actually be more cost efficient to reorganize the company from where it is. Perhaps the cost issues are actually internal, so relocating may not have a significant impact on reducing costs.

3.3.4 The Most Important Factors

The most important factors for a company's relocation differ from company to company. After defining the goals of the relocating, the next step is to determine a set of candidate locations to choose from that fit those needs. Those strategic drivers that are behind the project in the first place will go a long way toward defining the search region. The contiguous areas will most likely be a set of potential metropolitan areas that meet the fundamental strategic needs of the headquarters. Once these candidate metropolitan areas are defined, the actual communities, site, and buildings to be considered will be identified.

3.3.5 Available Labor Force

The availability of a qualified workforce for current and future hiring demand will be an important factor in evaluating new communities. The new headquarters will have a significant immediate need for a wide range of office, business and technical positions. As with any new company, especially in an office environment, turnover should be anticipated; as a result, the demand on the labor market will remain strong for a while after relocation. Those areas with a large amount of managerial operations and office sector employment will be attractive. The presence of universities offering business and engineering programs in the candidate area is important in ensuring there is a current and future supply of skilled workers within the labor force, as well as offering opportunities of R&D collaboration. Establishing headquarters in an appealing neighborhood may also be appealing to potential employees because of the desire to work at a certain location.

Another cost-saving incentive to establish headquarters in the Asia-Pacific is the access to cheap labor. Outsourcing has been a popular choice of cheap labor especially since the 2000s. It is a cheaper alternative for the quality of employee service for the company. It hurts the domestic labor force, but from the standpoint of an enterprise, this allows for higher profits as a result of lower labor costs. Skilled workers are paid far less in the Asia Pacific than those within the same industries in Europe or the United States. For foreign enterprises, this means that hiring local workers in the newly established location will save a lot on employee compensation because they are paying the average salaries amounts corresponding to the location. They have to keep in mind to abide by each country's labor regulations and laws on vacation days, sick days, bonuses, compensations, etc.

One last consideration is the willingness for current employees, especially the higher managers, to relocate. It is more important than the available, local work force because they are the ones who will help shape the direction of the new headquarter. Areas to consider can be quality of life, cost of living, personal interests, and language. A company should figure out how many capable employees they are able to outsource into the selected location during the beginning of the entire process to ensure a smooth transition.

3.3.6 *Quality of Life*

To many companies, maintaining or even improving the quality of life for their current employees is an important consideration. They have to provide an incentive for their employees to be willing to move to a foreign location, especially if there is a chance that the quality of life will be compromised. Companies look at factors such as the access to quality housing, low crime rates, shorter commute times, quality education at the primary, secondary and college levels, abundant quality day care, and access to high quality health care when evaluating potential new communities. These requirements must also include a wide range of choices in cultural, recreational, religious, housing, and education opportunities. There should be available sources to accommodate to an employee's current lifestyle, especially if it is a very strict and cannot be substituted with something else. A company should also make these resources available by either establishing it themselves or locating it. The character and personality of a community needs to be explored in order to be sure there is a "good fit" between the culture and values of the firm and those of the new community. These factors are especially important in the case of regional headquarters in order to attract key employees to move from the company's main headquarters.

3.3.7 *Cost of Living*

The cost of living between alternate headquarter locations such as Singapore and Shanghai can be drastic. This factor must be considered as it affects the ability to attract key employees and in planning overall salary and wage planning. There has to be a decision made on cost versus efficiency, or perhaps both can be found in one location.

Because doing business in the desired area means starting a new office or relocating, there is the cost of relocating employees to consider. The standard of living is completely different in Asia compared to other places around the world, where the currency and pricing is generally weaker.

Standard of living in US Dollars

	USA	United Kingdom (1:0.62)	France (1:0.79)	Hong Kong (1:7.76)	Shanghai (1:6.11)	Singapore (1:1.23)
Inexpensive meal	10	16.13	15.19	5.81	4.90	8.13
McDonald's Meal	6.50	8.06	10.13	3.87	4.09	5.69
Bottle of Coke	1.62	1.77	3.09	0.98	0.56	1.26
One way transportation	2.00	3.55	2.03	1.03	0.65	1.46
One bedroom apartment (downtown)	1027.09	1105.23	879.13	2104.22	965.63	2639.33
One bedroom apartment (suburbs)	773.53	936.44	700.30	1370.02	483.08	1705.89
Average monthly disposable salary	3304.60	2825.65	2547.27	2487.83	1179.86	3110.65

Source: Numbeo as of 10/28/2014

3.3.8 *Cost of Doing Business*

All companies when looking for headquarters are looking to also save on costs. These include operating cost savings, real estate, lower facility costs, lower initial salary rates, and lower taxes. Tax is a key factor to look at as it varies widely between states and can provide serious cost savings when comparing between different locations.

3.3.9 *Legal and Tax Environment*

Another important issue is having a good legal environment. For any firm it helps with ease of doing business and security within the system. It is particularly important to look into the legal environment if the desired locations have enacted tort reform and juries are known to be less extreme in their judgment. The details of income allocation for income tax considerations and the definition of assets for franchise tax calculations are important elements of the tax environment of a headquarters location.

Incentives

Incentives become mere important toward the latter stages of headquarter decision. As final decision nears incentives have a more significant impact due to the fact that at this stage the decision is more subjective between final headquarter choices, and the project are typically net-cost to the company. In addition to the traditional financial incentives (bond financing, tax incentives), some communities also offer direct financing in the form of grants to aid in offsetting employee relocation costs.

Language

The language of the location plays a huge role on whether business operations can be performed or not. If the location were to be in Shanghai for example, the official language is Mandarin Chinese. Although most business deals or partnerships can be done bilingually (typically English as), there are still a lot of smaller companies who work in their native, local language. This also applies to the local hires as well. Management should establish methods of communicating, whether it includes hiring translators or staffs who are bilingual. Business can still be done without this, but the opportunities are far less and it facilities the process in general.

3.3.10 Shanghai

The Shanghai Pilot Free Trade Zones (SFTZ) is a result of four merging existing bonded zones in the district of Pudong, covering an area of 28 km^2: Shanghai Waigaoqiao Free Trade Zone, Waigaoqiao Free Trade Logistics Park, Shanghai Pudong Airport Free Trade Area, and Yangshan Free Trade Port Area. It was first announced in 2009 as a way to divert the Chinese economy to focus on services and consumption as a means of sustainable growth. Although it is still in its experimental stage, the Shanghai Free Trade Zone stands out among several executives as the best choice for establishing a headquarter. As of June 2014, 1,240 foreign-capital companies have been registered and have generated over USD 7.3 billion. In the decision process to establish a regional headquarter, Shanghai can exploit a unique and non-replicable advantage: its location as the first FTZ in Mainland China provides companies with direct access to the largest market in the Asia-Pacific region. Generally speaking, this feature ascends as the main advantage sought while entering the Far East, and for the same reason, unsurprisingly makes Shanghai the best option.

Since its economic reforms in the 1990s, Shanghai has evolved into China's wealthiest center, largest business hub and main financial center, and it still continues to grow and develop rapidly. Its position on the East Coast and being the richest and most developed area of China are key features that has allowed it to flourish in export business activities. Accordingly, Shanghai offers optimal sourcing, manufacturing, and market access for MNEs in various industries. All these characteristics bring companies closer to Chinese and foreign customers and allow them to better understand their preferences. In terms of competition, the latter feature has become a great advantage in China's fast growing consumer goods market, where foreign brands face a fierce competition from local players in adapting to customers' preferences. Its location also gives it an advantage in accessing the distribution channels just because it is near the ports and located in Mainland China.

Challenges and potential issues from inside and outside China are the triggers of the conception of Shanghai Pilot Free Trade Zone. Primarily, China's export growth rate has slowed down and the domestic demand has also decreased due to global financial crisis, resulting in an excess production capacity. Moreover, the strength of low labor cost in China has been gradually vanishing and China needs to upgrade its industrial structure from the traditional labor intensive manufacturing industry to the technology intensive manufacturing industry and services industry. This requires more deregulations and a more mature capital market. Globally, a series of multilateral trading agreement such as the Trans-Pacific Partnership Agreement (TPP) and the Transatlantic Trade and Investment Partnership Agreement (TTIP) have put pressure on the growth of Chinese economy by changing the world economic rules, because none of them were initiated by China. Under these challenges, the SFTZ was fostered and carry on the mission of promoting Chinese economic growth. The opening of the SFTZ meant more lenient regulations, decreasing the number of sectors where foreign investors face with restrictions from 190 to 139.

The four bonded zones are chosen for good reasons. Since as early as 1980s, Pudong New District, which had a total acreage of 522 km^2, was formed as an industrial park aimed at creating a new commercial center and releasing the spatial stress. According to Wu (1999), RMB 300 million was allocated to Pudong by the Chinese central government each year during the 5-year plan for both hardware and software constructions. Pudong also had a history of attracting foreign direct investment. As Wei and Leung (2005) claimed that the establishment of Pudong in early 1990s made a significant progress in attracting FDI and absorbing foreign direct investment of US$35 billion by the end of 2001. Nine years later since that, Shanghai has established bonded zones including Shanghai Waigaoqiao Free Trade Zone, Waigaoqiao Free Trade Logistics Park, Shanghai Pudong Airport Free Trade Area, and Yangshan Free Trade Port Area.

Aside from historical reasons, the different types of those four bonded zones enable the sample completeness of the pilot program. Firstly, McCalla (1990) states that a port is the perfect place for free zone setting up, where the global commerce gathers. Yangshan, with 25 km shoreline and over 15 m water depth, is located at the hub between Yangtze river shipping and maritime shipping (Wang 2012), is gifted with the great natural conditions and geographical superiority. As the first bonded port zone of China, Yangshan has been developing rapidly and has the greatest input-output efficiency among the 14 Chinese bonded port zones with the most import and export volume of Chinese ports. Meanwhile, Waigaoqiao Bonded Zone is the largest bonded zone in China. The scale of professional merchandise trading there is still expanding and accounts for a large proportion of Chinese import commodity market. Pudong Airport Bonded Zone, at the intersection of eastern coastal economic belt and Yangtze River and is just next to Pudong International Airport that has the third biggest volume of cargo, started operating on 28th September 2010. With such geographical preponderance domestically, Pudong Bonded Zone is located on the triangle airline among Asia, Europe, and America.

In the past, even the restrictive monetary policies imposed by the central Government can negatively affect Shanghai. In fact, the limitations posed to the operations of foreign financial institutions, controls over RMB convertibility and the constrains imposed over capital transfers toward other countries lead to the ultimate decision of establishing in Shanghai manufacturing centers, R&D, marketing, and sales functions, while maintaining finance function outside the mainland China. However, what sets the Shanghai FTZ apart is its full convertibility of the Chinese Yuan. The State Administration of Foreign Exchange (SAFE) Shanghai Branch announced in early 2014 that they will permit the Chinese Yuan convertibility and unrestricted foreign currency exchange, which accelerates and eases the process of entering into the global market. This also allows Chinese banks to conduct offshore business, competing against London and New York, and circulate the Chinese Yuan across the globe. It is important to start implementing the ability to use or exchange the Chinese Yuan as global trade becomes increasingly vital to the economy, especially in a time when China is pushing for the Chinese Yuan to become a universal currency. China is also a key player in global trade, so it is imperative to be able to use the Chinese Yuan.

Apart from a market-related perspective, a HQ in Shanghai also allows easier access to local and international talents. This trait has become increasingly important over the past years, as competition for skilled and experienced professionals has grown. According to the Shanghai Municipal Statistics Bureau, Shanghai had a population of 152,050 registered foreigner residents in 2010, a large amount due to foreign expatriates. Shanghai, with its large metropolitan and international appeal, is highly attractive today to well-educated, young workers from both China and abroad, thus making it one of the top labor markets in the Asia-Pacific. Shanghai has been established as a center for foreigners because of its large foreigner population and ease of accessibility to everyday needs, such as transportation systems or local businesses becoming more English-friendly. As large, foreign companies extend their global offices into Shanghai, workers begin to have more opportunities and incentive to come to Shanghai for a brand new experience. Overall, Shanghai appears as an increasingly appealing target location for high-skilled talents from all over the world, so it gives companies the ability to choose from a broad selection of potential employees.

By the same token, a series of drawbacks affect the Chinese standpoint compared to Hong Kong and Singapore. First, for all Chinese sites, managers in MNEs continuously face the challenge posed by the legal and regulatory environment. In general, a low perceived level of predictability and transparency in such areas turns out higher concerns about the business environment. Furthermore, despite the increased efforts of the local government, MNEs' representatives feel a greater burden of administrative and bureaucratic procedures, a competitive disadvantage compared to the local players and a restricted access to the information. Even for issues linked to obtaining a work visa for foreigners, Hong Kong and Singapore systems are stated as less complicated and time-consuming. The second point has to do with taxes. In China, both corporate and individual income taxes are set far higher than that of Hong Kong and Singapore, which leverage a better tax environment. The following are some figures to help give a picture of the current situation: while in Shanghai corporate tax for foreign enterprises is up to 30 % and upon the personal income 45 %, they are 16.5 and 17 % in Hong Kong and 17 and 20 % in Singapore, both respectively.

Final considerations arise from the living conditions of Shanghai compared to the other two cities, such as its pollution, insufficient international exposure, and low level of English proficiency. First, based on the levels of PM2.5, Shanghai's air quality can be deemed as a hazardous city to those who are not accustomed to a polluted environment. Although it is not considered as one of the world's most polluted city, people are still wary of relocating into that kind of environment. Because Singapore and Hong Kong have had a history of interaction with the rest of the world, they have had more exposure and have become more westernized in certain aspects of the city infrastructure or culture. For example, English is one of Singapore's official languages, and even that in itself is puts Singapore at a higher position in that aspect, as sufficient English literacy skills in Shanghai is not widely common. Again, this puts Shanghai at another disadvantage because it is less international than the other two. The last set of topics directly affects the personal sphere of representatives or C-level managers involved in the HQ placement decision. According to this perspective, they will be eager to establish themselves and their families in Hong Kong and Singapore, where they can have adapt much more easily.

Shanghai has been considered as Chinese economic center for the magnitude of its economic aggregate and a higher level of market liberalization. Geographically, the four components are easy to management and regulate, which also emphasizes the comprehensiveness of special economic zone types. For all the reasons, Shanghai is considered to be the most appropriate choice to deliver the free trade experiment. Instead of seeking for a short-term booming economy, the Shanghai Pilot Program aims to stimulate the Chinese economy by reforming and gaining a sustainable growth of national power. Moreover, the Pilot Program is seeking for universal administrative methods that can be adopted cross the country. It is the ultimate purpose that differs Shanghai FTZ to other successful FTZs in Asia.

Shanghai intends to transfer itself into a new finance center of Asia and therefore lower the non-tariff enters barriers. In other words, releasing the domestic capital market from tight administrative control and letting the market automatically deploys resources would fundamentally lifting market liberalization. Referring to the Singapore free trading history, opening the capital market for free trade is an attractive trend and a path to the sustainable growth of Chinese economy.

3.3.11 Incorporating a Company in the Shanghai Pilot Free Trade Zone

The following are steps to establishing a company in the Shanghai FTZ. They are meant to serve as a guideline and only used as a reference, as the actual process may differ from company to company:

1. Company name approval; submit a Chinese and English name.
2. Approval of Commerce Committee; obtain the Certificate of Approval and the approval documents of the People's Government.
3. Pre-approval; obtain necessary business licensing or certifications, such as medical license or whole sale and distribution license.
4. Industrial and Commercial Administrative Bureau registration; get the business license (original and transcript) and begin business operations.
5. Apply for Enterprise Code Certificate and IC card. Its purpose facilitates applications of later period's personnel, bank account opening and employment visas.
6. Obtain the Tax Certificate (original and transcript).
7. Foreign exchange registration; it regulates future foreign debt registration, bank loans, and international payments of income and expenses.

8. Opening a bank account for foreign currency settlement account, capitals account, RMB basic account, and tax deduction account.
9. Statistic Certificate registration.
10. Financial Certificate application.
11. Inject register capital into capital account, issue capital verification report.
12. Change business license in accordance with paid-up capital.
13. Customs consignee and consignor registration, inspection and quarantine registration (applicable for import and export companies). The e-port system registration is recommended after actually conducting custom clearance businesses.

The following steps are tax and accounting post-incorporation phases:

1. Tax type verification, basic settings of bookkeeping.
2. Apply for general taxpayer; this is applicable for trading companies and for manufacturing companies, while service companies may skip this phase to a simplified approval.
3. Obtain the general taxpayer qualification, purchasing, installation, and training of anti-counterfeiting tax control invoice-issuing system. Get the tax control operator qualification certificate.
4. Application and training of accounting electronic declaration system.
5. Appoint tax management staff to do the tax system training.
6. Tax type verification; tax officer check working office.
7. Apply for invoices and step to normal operating period.

3.3.12 Hong Kong

Hong Kong has always been an area of interest when it comes to trading because of its liberal regulations and high trading activity. Despite having a population of just over seven million people, its Stock Exchange ranks as the second largest in Asia behind Tokyo and as one of the top worldwide, with a market capitalization of USD 2.192 trillion. It is conveniently located within 2 h by train or car from the major cities of the Pearl River Delta, which includes Guangzhou, Macau, and Shenzhen.

China has the second most foreign direct investment in the world, with two-thirds flowing into Hong Kong. Companies are able to raise a lot of cash as a result of investors who want to take advantage of the booming activity and liberal regulations. Hong Kong's share of China's GDP has been declining in the past two decades as a result of Chinese economic reforms, but even so, it remains a popular trading hub because of its laws and independent judiciary. Companies trust the Hong Kong judicial system to resolve disputes fairly, whereas they are more wary of the China's law system. Similar to Shanghai's efforts, Hong Kong also actively promotes the usage of the Chinese Yuan as a global currency. Because of the close proximity between Hong Kong and Mainland China, the usage of either currency is very convenient.

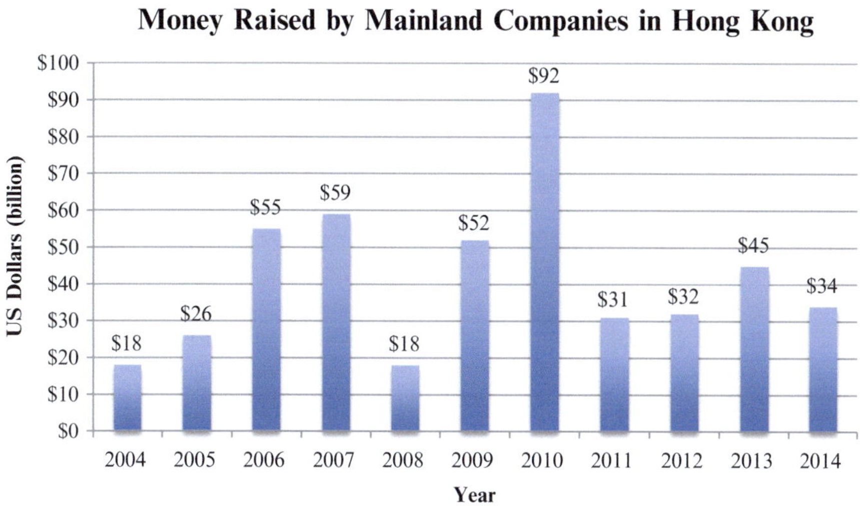

Money raised by companies in Hong Kong (Source: Dealogic)

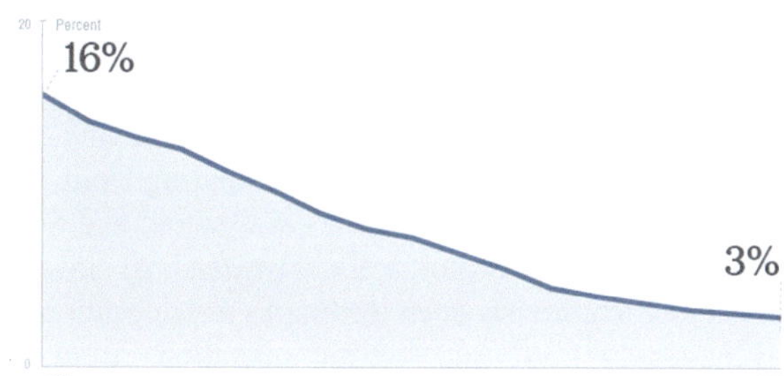

Hong Kong's share of China GDP (Source: IMF)

Hong Kong is a preferred location for MNEs' regional HQ for different reasons. First for its position, as it is at the same time close to Mainland China and a gateway to the Asia-Pacific region. Second it has been recognized over time as an established financial and business centre. According to Hong Kong Government's estimations, some 3688 regional HQs were located by 2010. Overall accounting for the measures enacted in Hong Kong to preserve an open and free economy with high regulatory transparency and a government that strongly encourages foreign investment, it is not surprising how many managers decided to establish here a regional HQ.

They particularly appreciate the favorable legal and regulatory environment, a stable and mature financial market, and the extremely competitive corporate income tax structure (resulting in the best overall tax treatment). Under the "one country, two systems" policy, Hong Kong will continue to regulate their own financial policies until at least 2047. Compared to Shanghai, seen as burdensome for its processes being highly regulated, Hong Kong is regarded as "very straightforward" when it comes to regulatory, administrative, and financial procedures. The comparative tax advantages are also regarded as a key factor in favoring Hong Kong as a preferred location for regional HQs and offices. One simple example of the highly convenient administrative process can be drawn from the fast and uncomplicated handling of visa work permits for foreigners.

The predominance of Hong Kong lies on its long-standing establishment as a strong international financial center. In fact it is home to one of the world's largest stock exchanges by market capitalization and most-developed financial services sectors. Whereas Shanghai is working on becoming a major financial hub, Hong Kong is still clearly the preferred location when it comes to financial services, as many MNEs' managers demonstrate. They appreciate the "mature and comparatively stable market", its "highly differentiated products and services offering", as well as the absence of complex regulations. While raising capital remains a major issue is Shanghai's financial market, Hong Kong is a key capital–raising centre for operations in Asia-Pacific region, both for MNEs and Chinese companies. This makes it a key source of offshore financing for Chinese enterprises today.

According to the above perspective, the future challenge for Hong Kong is to preserve its competitive position as a developed market while simultaneously leveraging the proximity to China. While Hong Kong can take advantage on its position over Singapore, this does not hold in turn when comparing Hong Kong with other emerging Chinese location such as Shenzhen, Guangzhou, and Shanghai most of all. All the latter cases can in fact exploit a direct (instead of) close access to mainland China, and this key feature has been leading to the relocation of many manufacturing and increasingly trade and logistic operations from Hong Kong to mainland.

Other potential challenges threatening the advantage positioning of Hong Kong arise from the increase in operating costs and the shortage of skilled talents. First, as many managers point out, companies are facing higher labor costs along with increased overhaul expenses to carry out their business. This trend acts as trigger for MNEs to seek elsewhere new low-cost opportunities to stay competitive. Second Hong Kong cannot rely on a big labor market when compared to mainland, and this on turn means the shortage of Human Resources and Competences required within the branch. Other issues embrace the life style conditions: although living here sounds very attractive for many employees for the city's proficiency in English, the Western style and the entertainment, increasing cost of living and environmental matter could discourage manager to establish themselves in Hong Kong for long time.

Overall Hong Kong is still regarded as a preferred choice for MNEs to coordinate operations in Mainland China mainly for its favorable environment combined with the proximity to the Chinese market. However, at the same time, it is facing several challenges coming from China. In order to avoid of remaining stuck in the middle, a set of measure should be undertaken aimed at promoting and enhancing closer ties with mainland. In this sense CEPA (the Hong Kong-China "Closer Economic Partnership Arrangement") is a direct signal of how both sides eager to facilitate mutual exchanges and trade. Furthermore the express train project Hong Kong-Shenzhen-Guangzhou (planned for 2015) is endorsed to address the issue of better infrastructure link to the mainland.

On November 17, 2014, the Shanghai-Hong Kong Stock Connect was launched, which allows for investors to buy select Shanghai stocks through the Hong Kong Stock Exchange, and vice versa. International investors have already participated in buying Chinese stocks, however, the program was not as well received because Chinese stocks listed in Hong Kong had already been available in Shanghai (and thus Chinese investors), so there hasn't really been as been much of a change. Chinese investors also have other methods of buying foreign stocks, so there isn't a big demand or need and it might even be cheaper to buy certain stocks in Shanghai than in Hong Kong. While there are certain values and small changes, overall investors have yet to see the program's full appeal. Either way, it is a start to opening China's financial market.

3.3.13 Singapore

Established as a top location for regional HQs for the Asian-Pacific area, Singapore is one of the world's leading business centers, trading hubs, and home of a major port in the Asia-Pacific region. For decades, it has been a preferred destination of foreign investments and a top location for coordinating operations across the surrounding area, as it is located right in the heart of Southeast Asia. In the recent years, Singapore has managed to maintain its attractiveness, partly due to the resilience of its economy in the challenging global economic environment following the financial crisis. Furthermore, the Singaporean government's relentless and systematic efforts to increase the competitiveness of its key industries were also instrumental. Corporate and individual taxes have been lowered (income tax rates have been reduced from 26 % in 1997 to 17 % in 2010, refer to Table 3.1 for more details) following the same trend of cost of infrastructure services and other factor of production. The financial services have been further liberalized and barriers to foreign banks have been gradually lowered. At the same time, Singapore has invested in increasing the skills and knowledge of its multicultural workforce, focusing on creativity and innovation, and a mix of hard and soft skills. The aforementioned measures have been aimed at empowering new generations to compete in the new globalized world.

Table 3.1 Corporate tax rates over the Years

1997–2000	2001	2002	2003–2004	2005–2006	2007–2009	2010–2014
26 %	25.5 %	24.5 %	22 %	20 %	18 %	17 %

Singapore also offers tax exemptions that are applied to the company's taxable income and allows for the effective income tax rate for smaller businesses to be smaller.

0 % Tax Rate on S$100 K Taxable Income
The corporate income tax rate is 0 % for the first S$100,000 taxable income for the first 3 years of a new company that meets the following conditions:

- The company is incorporated in Singapore.
- The company is a tax resident in Singapore.
- Has a maximum of 20 shareholders, where one individual holds at least 10 % of the shares.

8.5 % Tax Rate on up to S$300 k Taxable Income
After the first S$100,000 has been exempt, from S$100,001 to S$300,000, taxable income is taxed at a rate of 8.5 %. Anything above S$300,000 will be taxed at the normal corporate tax rate of 17 %. For a company that has been established for over 3 years, after the tax exemption is no longer in place, the first S$300,000 taxable income is taxed at a reduced rate of 8.5 %.

17 % Tax Rate on Taxable Income Above S$300 k
The first S$300,000 is taxed at a rate of 0 % or 8.5 %, depending on the circumstances of the company. Anything above that is taxed at a flat rate of 17 %, without any limit.

As for personal income, Singapore is also known for its low tax rates.

Most Singapore companies, whether it's new or a relocation, are registered as private limited liability companies (also known as private limited companies). A private limited company in Singapore is a separate legal entity and shareholders are not liable for the company's debts beyond the amount of share capital they have contributed (hence the term limited liability).

Singapore is considered a free port and open economy as most imports are duty-free and procedures are generally hassle-free. It currently has seven Free Trade Zones used to store and re-export dutiable and controlled goods. Until they are available in the market, goods may be stored within the zones without having to go through customs or providing documentation. Goods can be processed and re-exported without any complicated procedures.

Amid all considered features, Singapore can deploy and provide an overall better positioning over other locations because of its extremely stable and transparent political and regulatory environment and the strong enforcement of its legal system. In particular, these represent the major points of discontinuity with regard to Shanghai, endowing Singapore with a more favorable business environment. Another major point is undoubtedly the tax regime both under an individual and corporate perspective. Although Singapore does not offer the lowest tax rates, the implementation of measures ranging from the total exemption for startups to the adoption of Double Tax Treaties, Singaporean Government provides several incentives for MNEs to establish here their regional HQ. Very high living conditions, the

Table 3.2 Shanghai, Hong Kong, Singapore: a brief environmental comparison

Investment Center	Shanghai	Hong Kong	Singapore
Corporate Tax	25 %	16,5 %	17 %
Individual Tax	45 %	17 %	20 %
Market Cap 2013 (USD bn)	2,497	3,101	965
Rule of Law Index (0–1)	0,46	0,75	0.79
Rule of Law Rank	76	16	10

Source: data.worldjusticeproject.org, Asia-Pacific Headquarters Study, WFE Markets Highlights

well-established education and healthcare systems and a very international environment, make Singapore appealing to managers from all over the world.

However in Singapore the question related to the proximity to the mainland comes much higher than in Hong Kong, turning it into the most important issue. Most managers perceive concrete market entry opportunities and link to the Chinese market as more difficult to be pursued from the relative distance of the regional HQ in Singapore. Despite the shared availability of Mandarin-speaking talents and the relative proximity to Mainland China, this disadvantage in many cases far outweighs other key drivers of choice, in the HQ decision-making. Moreover, the high cost of labor and manufacturing operations are pushing out low value added industries.

All the facts considered lead toward a unique conclusion, that is: Singapore over the years has set up a favorable environment for MNEs, and probably will preserve this edge over other comparable locations in a near future. In order to achieve this goal, due to the proximity issue and the high level of cost, it will have to succeed in managing the shift toward high-tech and value-added industries such as telecommunication (Table 3.2).

Tax heavens are typically associated with money laundering and illegal financial activities. Singapore offers a legitimate offshore financial center that provides financial services in the entire region.

On average, it only takes two and a half days to get a business permit in Singapore. Research shows that on average, business owners spend 82 h annually resolving tax-related issues, compared to 172 h in the United States. The Singaporean government provides assistance throughout the process.

Visa/Immigration Information

An Employment Pass (EP) is a type of work visa issued to foreign owners or skilled workers in Singapore. EPs are valid for 1–2 years and can be renewed as long as the person continues to work for the company. After it has been granted, employees are free to travel in and out of the country without applying for additional entry visas. There is also no quota on the amount of EPs a company is allowed to have. During the application process, the following are requirements/points of consideration:

- Fixed monthly salary of *at least* S$3300
- Education (preferably a tertiary degree) and work experience

The Entrepreneur Pass (EntrePass) is a type of Employment Pass. It is the primary type of work pass for owners of newly incorporated (or to be incorporated) Singapore companies who wish to relocate to Singapore to operate their new business. EntrePasses are valid for 1 year and are renewable as long as the business continues to run. Just as the case for EPs, there is no official quota on the number of EntrePasses granted. To be eligible, business owners must have plans to incorporate a new company or incorporated a company that is less than 6 months old. The business must satisfy one of the "innovativeness" requirements that were introduced in September 2013.

Other work visa types include:

Personalized Employment Pass: valid for 3 years and allows for an employee to switch companies without reapplying for a work visa. However, they are cannot be a business owner themselves.

S Pass: valid for 1–2 years and requires a technical diploma.

Registering a company in Singapore is faster than in other jurisdictions. Here below a list of key information for the establishment of a company in Singapore.

Management must provide the following information:

- *Company name*: This must be preapproved before a company can be incorporated.
- *Directors*: There must be at least one director who is either a Singapore Citizen, Singapore Permanent Resident, or have been issued an Entrepass, Employment Pass, or Dependent Pass. There can be an unlimited number of additional directors (regardless of their nationality) as long as they are at least 18 years of age and not bankrupt or convicted for crimes in the past. They do not have to be shareholders.
- *Shareholders*: The firm can have 1–50 shareholders if it is registered as a Singapore private limited company. A shareholder can be either a person or another legal entity. New shares can be issued or existing shares can be transferred to another after the incorporation process.
- *Company secretary:* A qualified company secretary must be hired within 6 months of the firm's incorporation. It has to be noted that in case of a sole director/shareholder, the same person cannot act as the company secretary. The company secretary must be a resident of Singapore.
- *Paid-in capital*: The minimum paid-in capital for registration of a Singapore company is S$1 and it can be increased anytime after the company has been incorporated.
- *Registered address*: The registered address of the company must be a local address of Singapore. It can be either residential or commercial.

3.3.14 Required Documents

The following information is required to register a company:

- Company name
- Description of business activities
- Shareholders, directors, and company secretary particulars
- Registered address
- Memorandum and Articles of Association (MAA) provided by Singapore Company Registrar

The following documents should be prepared beforehand. If they are in a different language, it must be endorsed and translated:

- For non-residents: copy of passport, proof of address, and Know-Your-Client information such as a bank reference letter.
- For Singapore residents: copy of Singapore identity card
- For corporate entities: copy of registration documents such as Certificate of Incorporation and Memorandum & Articles of Association

Notes for foreigners:

- A professional firm must register the company because foreigners cannot self-register.
- There must be a local resident director. The person establishing the company doesn't need to be in Singapore at all times. They can come on a visitor visa for short business trips instead of relocating.
- Those who have relocated and obtained a work permit can act as the local resident director
- All incorporation procedures can be done without being physically in Singapore, except opening a bank account, depending on the bank.

There are two main procedures to incorporating a Singapore company: Company Name Approval and Company Registration. It can typically be done on the same day.

Company Name Registration
The proposed company name must be approved after filing an application with the Singapore Company Registrar. This process generally takes less than an hour unless it contains certain words (i.e. bank, law, media, etc.) that need further review by a corresponding external government authority. This may delay the process by a few days or weeks. It is best to have an original, distinct name that does not infringe any trademarks. Once it has been approved, the name will be reserved for 60 days from the date of application. Submitting a request before the expiry date can extend this.

Company Registration
After the company name has been approved, the application for company registration can be submitted. This is the process that requires all necessary documents to

be prepared, including any signatures by directors or shareholders. The nationality of shareholders or directors may delay the incorporation procedures, but this rarely happens. In the case that it does, additional information will be requested. There is a registration fee of S$300 payable to the Singapore Registrar of Companies when incorporating a private limited liability company.

Post-Registration
The certificate of incorporation and company business profile will be provided after the company has been officially approved. They can be used for all legal and contractual purposes, such as signing an office lease or opening corporate bank accounts.

Certificate of Incorporation
After the process has been completed and approved, the Company Registrar will send an email confirming of the incorporation of the company, including the company registration number. This serves as the official certificate of the incorporation. A hard copy is not needed, but can be requested for approximately S$50.

Company Business Profile
A company business profile can be obtained by submitting an application to the Company Registrar. A document containing the following information will be provided:

- Company name and registration number
- Previous company name, if applicable
- Date of incorporation
- Business activities
- Paid-up capital
- Registered Address
- Shareholder, director, and secretary details

References

Cheng S, Shi S (2012) The impact of new income tax law on foreign invested enterprises in China. Int Tax J 38:17–48

Grubert H, Mutti J (2000) Do taxes influence where U.S. corporations invest? Natl Tax J 56:487–502

Halkyard A, Linghui R (2010) China's tax incentive regime for foreign direct investment: an eassonian analysis. University of Toronto Press, Toronto

Hebous S, Ruf M, Weichenrieder AJ (2011) The effects of taxation on the location decision of multinational firms: M&A versus greenfield investments. Natl Tax J 64:817–838

Hines JR, Rice EM (1994) Fiscal paradise: foreign tax havens and American business. Q J Econ 109:149–182

Liou K (2012) Incentive policies and China's economic development: change and challenge. J Public Budg Account Financ Manage 22:407–431

Mccalla R (1990) The geographical spread of free zones associated with ports. Geoforum 21(1):121–134

Organisation for Economic Cooperation and Development (2009) Countering offshore tax evasion: some questions and answers on the project. OECD Publishing, Paris

Schwarz P (2009) Tax-avoidance strategies of American multinationals: an empirical analysis. Manag Decis Econ 30:539–549

Wang C (2012) New port development and global city making: emergence of the Shanghai-Yangshan multilayered gateway hub. J Transp Geogr 25:58–69

Wei Y, Leung C (2005) Development zones, foreign investment, and global city formation in Shanghai. Growth Change 36(1):16–40

Wu W (1999) City profile: Shanghai. Elsevier Sci 16(3):207–216

Chapter 4
Singapore vs Shanghai

One of the main questions that affects companies planning to do business in the Far East, regardless of their type of industry, is the search for the ideal location for their Asian head office. When it comes to making decisions, Shanghai and Singapore are often among the final candidates.

There are many parameters for comparing these two cities. Recent political and economic developments and historical aspects could be two way to find differences. Proximity to production bases, business partners, or markets are, of course, other highly important factors. But in order to get an idea of the distinctions that have an impact on day-to-day operations, it makes sense to take a closer look at the ease of conducting business in each city and examine some of the main areas that will have an impact on foreign companies' choice of Asia headquarters.

Choosing the optimal jurisdiction for a business is an important decision as it determines the future and success of that business. Factors such as political and economic stability, financial and physical infrastructure, company and labor laws, taxation system, legal environment, intellectual property protection, availability of human resources, cultural fabric, and language play a vital role in choosing a country for business incorporation.

Comparing jurisdictions on the basis of the above-mentioned factors is an effective mean of assessing the compatibility of a country to company's business goals. A comparative analysis of Singapore's and China's performance in various economic and business surveys shows that Singapore is highly ranked as a business jurisdiction as compared to the mainland. The analysis reveals some differences between the two jurisdictions. For example, according to the World Bank's Doing Business 2009 study, Singapore appears to be the most attractive city in which to establish an office and the easiest country in which to do business. Singapore has excellent telecommunication, financial and transport infrastructures, and its strategic location at the crossroads of maritime routes and proximity to the big markets is an advantage. The country offers tax concessions and easy loan conditions as part of investment incentives.

L. Riccardi, *Investing in China through Free Trade Zones*,
DOI 10.1007/978-3-662-47354-2_4

Singapore is open to foreign investment and offers tax incentives to companies after they register with *Economic Development Board*. However, the country continues to maintain monopolies in certain sectors such as financial services, professional services, media, and telecommunications. Government linked corporations play a dominant role in the domestic economy and, to a large extent, on investment. Singapore has signed investment promotion and protection agreements with a wide range of countries. These agreements mutually protect nationals or companies of either country against war and non-commercial risks of expropriation and nationalization for an initial period of 15 years and continue thereafter unless otherwise terminated.

Still, Singapore is ranked as the 1st place in the world for simplification of doing business in the World Bank's "Doing Business 2011" report. In comparison, China's 79th position indicates that its regulatory environment is less favorable to business. There was remarkable difference in the areas of starting a business (rank n. 151 vs n. 4), paying taxes (rank n. 114 vs n. 4), protecting investors (rank n. 93 vs n. 2), getting credit (rank n. 65 vs n. 6), and trading across borders (rank n.50 vs n.1). An analysis of company set up in Singapore vs China shows that Singapore company registration takes only two procedures and one-day's time while China incorporation can take up to 2–3 months due to the complex procedures involved.

Singapore is the 2nd freest economy in the world according to Heritage Foundation's "2010 Index of Economic Freedom." An efficient regulatory environment, competitive tax regime, lack of corruption, transparency and efficiency of services, highly flexible labor market, equal treatment of foreign and domestic investors, and a highly effective legal system were factors that boosted Singapore's economic freedom score. China ranked n.140 in the Index due to the lack of business freedom, lack of legal and regulatory transparency, high income tax rates, restrictions on foreign investment, tightly controlled financial system, wide-spread corruption, and restrictive labor regulations. Singapore's economy is the most open to trade in the world reaffirms WEF's "2010 Global Enabling Trade Index" while China's position was n.48. According to the report, China's transport infrastructure presents major shortcomings. The time required to complete customs procedures ranges from 21 to 24 days, far longer than Singapore's 3 to 5 days. Border administration remains subject to irregular payments and corruption in China. Moreover, China imposes high import tariffs and restrictions on international capital flows. By contrast, Singapore's border administration was described as "top-notch" in every respect. It aced the customs services index. Border clearance of goods is fast and efficient. Finally, the quality and availability of its transport infrastructure is excellent.

To sum up, Singapore has based its economic development on a proactive strategy of attracting FDI and trade openness. According to the World Bank, Singapore tops the ranking on Ease of Doing Business. Favorable lending to foreign investors, simple regulatory system, tax incentives, high-quality industrial real estate park, political stability, and absence of corruption make Singapore an attractive destination for investment.

Country comparison for the protection of investors

	Singapore	East Asia & Pacific	United States	Germany
Index of transaction transparency	10.0	5.0	7.0	5.0
Index of manager's responsibility	9.0	5.0	9.0	5.0
Index of shareholders' power	9.0	6.0	9.0	5.0
Index of investor protection	9.3	5.4	8.3	5.0

Source: Doing business – Last available data

A glance at country rankings: Singapore vs China

Year	Category	Singapore's rank	China's rank	Source
2010	Ease of doing business	1	79	World bank, 2011 ease of doing business report
2009	Country with lowest tax misery	11	64	Forbes tax misery and reform index
2010	World's most competitive economy	3	27	World economic forum, global competitiveness report
2010	Country most open to trade	1	48	World economic forum, global enabling trade report
2010	World's most competitive economy	1	18	IMD, world competitiveness yearbook
2010	Ease of paying taxes	4	114	PWC, IFC, World bank's 2011 paying taxes survey
2010	World's freest economy	2	140	Heritage foundation's index of economic freedom
2010	World's best country for life experience	12	21	HSBC's 2010 expat experience report
2010	World's best labor force	1	–	BERI's labor force evaluation measure
2010	Country with least corruption perception	1	78	Transparency international's corruption perceptions index
2010	World's best country for business	5	90	Forbes' best countries for business index
2010	Most efficient bureaucracy in Asia	1	7	Political and economic risk consultancy survey 2010
2010	Best place for Asians to live	1	12	ECA international's 2010 location ratings system
2010	World's lowest risk city for employers	3	52	Aon consulting's people risk index

Source: www.guidemesingapore.com

Singapore is a small nation covering only about 700 square km, but it has five Free Trade Zones. It could almost be said that Singapore itself is a free trade zone. Now, the point is: Which lesson can Shanghai draw from Singapore? Singapore's status as a trading hub dated back to its colonial days. But today Singapore has a highly developed trade-oriented market economy and has been ranked as the most open in the world, least corrupts, most pro-business, and one of the highest per-capita GDP among all the developed countries.

How to replicate Singapore's success in embracing free trade? Will Shanghai pose a serious threat to Singapore? China (Shanghai) Pilot Free Trade Zone, a "laboratory" for extensive financial reforms, providing a blueprint for the marketization of China's financial sector, aims to create a more investor-friendly regulatory environment for business operations in China and aims to promote RMB internationalization. Moreover, the main goal of SH PFTZ is to close the gap with Singapore which attracts a great deal of foreign investments each year.

For a long time, Shanghai has been trailing behind regional financial centers like Hong Kong and Singapore in cross-border banking services due to strict regulatory control over capital flows imposed by mainland authorities. As a result, only a select group of domestic banks was allowed to be engaged in offshore banking business while foreign lenders faced quite a few limits in terms of offering international banking services on the mainland.

However, the industry landscape will likely be changed after the Chinese central government gives the green light to Shanghai, the country's financial capital, to start a new wave of reforms in a pilot free trade zone (September 2013). The new zone allows free yuan convertibility under the capital account, interest rate liberalization, and cross-border yuan usage. Apart from establishing new outlets, foreign banks are also allowed to form joint venture banks with private capital in the zone. As for private banking and wealth management, the new Shanghai FTZ brings investment opportunities for foreign investors, due to further opening of business scope. For example, in order to achieve full convertibility of the yuan and build Shanghai into an international financial center, China may speed up the liberalization of its capital account within the FTZ.

Based on the general guidelines, foreign individuals employed in the zone are allowed to set up non-resident individual accounts with securities firms to carry out investment in domestic securities market, while individuals employed in the zone can also invest in foreign securities market. This will generate new business for foreign banks and asset management companies in the area of wealth management.

However, Singapore is still a prevailing destination of the special purpose vehicle (SPV) for Multinational Enterprises (MNEs) to invest in China and is one of the tax havens whose fame rest on its tax benefit. This country is favored by MNEs because they can take advantages of the low-tax-rate, or even nil-tax-rate to reduce their tax liability considerably. The most popular way is to establish holding company or SPV, which works as an intermediary in the outbound investment of the multinational enterprises (MNEs). What gives Singapore dominate advantage is the Double Tax Treaties (DTT) that it signed with considerable countries, for instance, India and China: this is because that DTT can reduce the withholding tax imposed on dividends, royalties, and interest when investing into China and avoids double taxation.

4.1 Effect of Double Tax Treaty

Tax Treaties can reduce double taxation, which is one of the most essential hinder to FDI. DTT can increase the tax certainty and mitigate the adverse impact of tax heaven on international tax competition. In this logic, DTT should exert positive effect on FDI.

However, empirically, plenty of scholars do not find the evidence to support the positive effect. Egger et al. (2006) even finds that DTT reduce the FDI. Davies et al. (2009) summarize the explanation for this phenomenon. They suggest that this might be caused by negative impact of information change and transfer pricing regulations embedded in DTT.

In attempt to find evidence for the positive relation between DTT and FDI, some scholars did further researches in recent years. Neumayer (2007) claims he is the pioneer to prove this point by finding that a country which does not sign DTT with U.S. receive less FDI from U.S.; in addition, Barthel et al. (2010) also find the positive relationship between DTT and FDI by utilizing a huge unpublished database. Moreover, Hossain et al. (2012) find that DTT positively influence FDI and can mitigate the adverse effects of perceived corruption.

From a firm-perspective, MNEs is the major beneficiary of the DTT. Blonigen and Davies (2004) suggest that MNEs can enjoy lower withholding tax and higher tax certainty thanks to the DTT. Davies et al. (2009) provide empirical evidence on the effect of DTT on MNEs by analyzing the firm-level data for the first time. They find that valid DTT increases the possibility of investment in one country for MNEs.

4.2 Effect of New EIT Law

Considerable number of paper focus on the effect of the new EIT law. One leading topic is whether new EIT will affect the FDI in China. Halkyard and Linghui (2010) predicted with confidence that FDI will not be influenced by new EIT law. Halkyard and Linghui (2010) state that 25 % is still a relatively low rate compared with the average worldwide corporate income tax rate, although it is 10 % higher than the preferential rate in former Foreign Enterprise Income Tax law. Furthermore, they also claim that tax is only one of the massive numbers of factors for FDI, and the other factors in China besides tax remains attractive to foreign investors.

Zollo et al. (2007) examine the effect of new EIT law for MNEs together with other tax including VAT and customs. They analyze the effect on five prevailing commercial models adopted by MNEs to invest in China. They advise MNEs to revise the corporate structure of MNEs to minimize its tax burden in China considering the fact that new EIT law makes fundamental changes of tax treatment for foreign enterprises. Cheng and Shi (2012) make the same suggestion after their thorough comparison of former Foreign Enterprise Income Tax law and new EIT law. In the paper of Zollo et al. (2007), Singapore is suggested to be a good location of intermediate holding company for several commercial models.

Ng (2013) studies the effect of new EIT laws on both FDI inbound and outbound to China. She stresses the impact of anti-tax avoidance rules and regulations and propounds suggestions that changing holding structure can help to minimize world-wide tax burden of MNEs.

4.3 Data Analysis

When presenting the tax benefit in Singapore and effect of new EIT law, "compare and contrast" is used to analyze the change in tax policies after 2008. This method can help MNEs to understand the difference tax policy before and after 2008 and can adjust their strategy to the newest situation. Furthermore, there are always qualifying conditions to enjoy certain tax benefit and some requirements are overlapped. Hence, compare and contrast these requirements can help MNEs to know better what benefits they can enjoy based on their status.

Singapore's Total Direct Investment in China
From Fig. 4.1, it is evident that Singapore's direct investment in China staged a steady increase of approximate $ 64 billion in investment value from 2005 to 2012. While its investment in China as a percentage of total direct investment abroad experienced some fluctuations despite its overall upward trend.

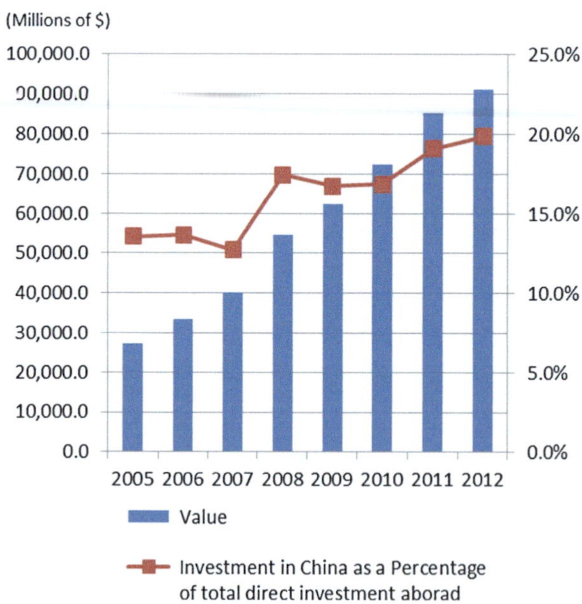

Fig. 4.1 Singapore's direct investment in China, 2005–2012

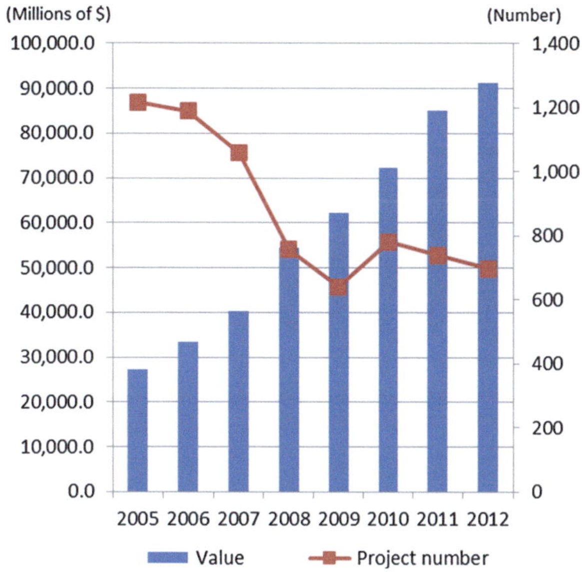

Fig. 4.2 Singapore's direct investment in China, 2005–2012

Figure 4.2, instead, illustrates that the value of investment increased inversely related to the number of new investment project implemented in China. Furthermore, it is also noticeable that 2008 witnessed a remarkable decline of 25 % in number of new project. This indicates that Singapore's investors keep increasing the investment value in existing project, but it is more cautious about the choice of new project.

4.4 Tax Benefits in Singapore

In Singapore, company's taxable income contains two parts. One is the income derived from Singapore, and the other is the income received in Singapore from abroad, as stated by Inland Revenue Authority of Singapore (IRAS – Inland Revenue Authority of Singapore – 2010).

The headline tax rates of corporate income are shown in the table below, where it is evident that the headline tax rates are decreasing constantly in recent years. This indicates the intention of establish business-friendly environment by relaxing taxation policy.

Corporate income tax rate in Singapore

Year of assessment	2005–2007	2008–2009	From 2010
Tax rate	20 %	18 %	17 %

Tax Exemption Schemes

There are several tax exemption schemes in Singapore, which will effectively reduce the tax burden for companies by granting certain amount of income exempted from corporate income tax. The following schemes addressed in this paper are those schemes which remain effective after 2013.

Tax Exemption for New Start-up Companies

Tax exemption is given to qualified new start-up companies for each of its first successive three YAs. To be specific, for its first $100,000 income, company can claim full exemption on tax payment. Regarding to next $200,000, half of the amount can be exempted from taxation. Therefore, new start-up companies can enjoy the benefit of maximum $200,000 tax exemption in each of the first three YAs, which is $100,000 more than that of each year before YA 2008.

Exempt amount for new start-up companies since YA2008

First $100,000	@ 100 %	= $100,000
Next $200,000	@ 50 %	= $100,000
Total $300,000		$200,000

Source: IRAS (2014a) *Tax rates & tax exemption schemes.* Singapore: Inland Revenue Authority of Singapore

4.4.1 *Partial Tax Exemption*

The "partial tax exemption" policy implemented now is effective from YA2008 in Singapore. For YA 2005–2007, the upper limit of partial tax exemption is $52,500. As following table shows, the maximum exempt amount increase to $152,500 since YA2008. Furthermore, this "partial tax exemption" policy will save companies tax payment of $25,925, if applying the current headline tax rates, 17 %.

Exempt amount for companies under "partial tax exemption"

First $10,000	@ 75 %	=$7,500
Next $290,000	@ 50 %	=$145,000
Total $300,000		$152,500

Source: IRAS (2014a) *Tax rates & tax exemption schemes.* Singapore: Inland Revenue Authority of Singapore, [Online]

4.5 Tax Benefit Related to Foreign Sourced Income

Income received in Singapore from abroad is obligated to tax. However, there are some schemes that company can apply to reduce its tax burden on foreign sourced income. Generally, there are two ways to achieve this, seeking exemption or claiming credit.

Foreign Sourced Income Exemption (FSIE) Scheme
This scheme grants tax exemption on three kinds of foreign income to Singapore tax resident company, namely, foreign-sourced dividend, foreign branch profits, and foreign-sourced service income.

Several conditions need to be fulfilled to claim this tax exemption:

1. The headline tax rate of the foreign income is not below 15 % when the foreign income is repatriated to Singapore.
2. The foreign country had charged tax on the foreign income at headline tax rate or different rate for some appropriate reason.
3. The comptroller is pleased with the fact that Singapore resident person will benefit from this scheme.

Claim Foreign Tax Credit (FTC)
Foreign Tax Credit is the approved credit granted by Singapore tax authority to offset the tax payable in Singapore because the same income has already been taxed in another country. It can be double tax relief or unilateral tax credit.

Double Tax Relief (DTR)
A DTR is the credit relief provided for under an Avoidance of Double Taxation Agreement (DTA) to reduce this double taxation. A DTR is granted by allowing the Singapore tax residents to claim a credit for the amount of tax paid in the foreign country against the Singapore tax that is payable on the same income. A company is a tax resident of Singapore if the control and management of its business is exercised in Singapore.

Unilateral Tax Credit (UTC)
For countries with which Singapore does not have a DTA, UTC may be allowed for foreign tax paid by Singapore tax residents on the following types of income derived from foreign country if such income is repatriated to Singapore.

Qualifying Conditions for Claiming FTC (IRAS 2014b)

1. Only Singapore resident company can claim for FTC, and the recognition of residence status will be addressed in the "interpretation of DTT between Singapore and china."
2. The foreign country has charged or will charge tax on the same income.
3. The income is taxable in Singapore.

New FTC Pooling System
FTC pooling system is the enhanced version of former FTC system, which was introduced in Budget 2011 (Iras 2013). Under former FTC system, the credit is calculated on "source-by-source and country-by-country" basis. This means that credit given on one certain income type can only be used to offset the tax payable on the same kind of income. Likewise, tax credit granted on income from Country A cannot be used to reduce the tax payable on the income derived from Country B (Iras 2013). Under the new FTC pooling system, all tax paid on foreign-sourced

income is aggregated, no matter type or country-sourced, and then is used against any tax payable in Singapore derived from foreign income (Iras 2013). This new pooling system makes sure that all of the tax paid in foreign country can be reduced from tax payable in Singapore as long as the tax credit is not higher than total tax payable. To enjoy this benefit, certain extra conditions are required (Iras 2013):

1. Foreign country must have charged tax on the income.
2. The headline tax rate of the foreign income is not below 15 % when the foreign income is repatriated to Singapore.

One important reminder is that company must elect for claiming FTC under the FTC pooling system if they want to enjoy this benefit. Otherwise, FTC will still be calculated on 'source-by-source and country-by-country' basis (Iras 2013).

4.6 Productivity and Innovation Credit (PIC)

PIC scheme is the tax incentive given by Singapore tax authority to encourage company to invest in innovation and productivity. Company can reduce its tax payment by extra tax deductions or cash payout. For YA 2013 to 2015, company can further enjoy PIC Bonus (IRAS 2014d).

There are six kinds of activities which can qualify company for claiming PIC:

1. Acquire or lease IT and automation equipment
2. Register the patents, designs, trademarks, and plant varieties
3. Acquire or in-license Intellectual Property Rights
4. Design projects which are approved by
5. Train employees
6. Do research and development activities.

If company does any of those activities, company can deduct the qualifying cost fourfold capped at $400,000 for each of the activities, when calculating the tax payable. In Budget 2014, IRAS increase the upper limit to $600,000 for each year of YAs 2015–2018 (IRAS 2014e). Alternatively, it can elect to change its cost into a cash payout at 60 % which is not taxable, and the cap is $100,000 for all six activities each YA. This alternative will benefit the company if it is constrained in cash (IRAS 2014e).

PIC Bonus is that tax authority will give a dollar-for-dollar bonus to the money spent on those qualifying activities. The upper limit is $15,000 for three YAs from 2013 to 2015. However, following conditions needs to fulfill to claim this benefit (IRAS 2014d).

1. The qualifying cost incurred in the year of application is no less than $5,000.
2. There are at least 3 local employees.
3. Business operations of the company are active in Singapore.

The table gives a clear summary of the upper limit of these benefits:

Upper limit of PIC scheme benefits

	Upper limit ($)	Each/All activities	Each YA/Several YAs
400 % tax allowance	400,000	Each	Each
	600,000	Each	Each (YAs 2015 to 2018)
Cash payout option @ 60 %	100,000	All	Each
PIC bonus	15,000	All	YAs 2013 to 2015

4.7 Interpretation of Double Tax Treaty Between China and Singapore

Double tax treaty between China and Singapore can influence Singapore invested company for mainly three reasons:

1. It offers preferential withholding tax rate on passive income received in China for some companies. Therefore, it's beneficial for company to the qualifying condition to claim this treaty benefit.
2. It specifies the condition under which China has the right to tax the capital gains of Singapore's company.
3. The article 22, elimination of double taxation, helps to save tax expense for Singapore Company by avoiding double taxation on the same income. It's important for company to know how much credit they can get to set off the tax charged in Singapore.

If the company in Singapore wants to claim the benefit of double tax treaty, it must be the tax resident company in Singapore, which indicates that its control or managerial activity of the company occurs in Singapore. This can be proved by Certificate of Residence (COR) issued by IRAS. IRAS usually recognize the company as tax resident company if the board of director's meeting was held in Singapore (Iras 2014a, b, c, d, e, f, g).

4.7.1 Withholding Tax Rate of China-Sourced Passive Income

Passive income consists of dividends, interest, and royalties. Different withholding rate are shown in the following table which is generated based on double tax treaty between China and Singapore.

Withholding tax rates under double tax treaties between China and Singapore

Income	Dividends	Interest	Royalties
Withholding rate (%)	5/10	7/10	6/10

Different number of one item is means that there will be preferential treatment under some circumstances.

4.7.2 *Beneficial Owner*

"Beneficial owner" is the threshold to enjoy some significant treaty benefits, for instance lower withholding tax rates charged on passive income. State Administration of Taxation (SAT) issued several documents to guide the recognition of "beneficial owner." For instance, the first relevant official notice is the Circular 601 released in 2009; and the second one is the Public Note 30. The basic principle of determining whether one applicant is "beneficial owner" is "substance over form," which indicates that the recognition of "beneficial owner" mainly depends on whether the applicant has the ownership and right to use and dispose the received passive income derived from China (SAT 2012b). The table below shows seven requirements that applicants need to meet to be identified as "beneficial owner" and supporting documents needed (SAT 2009a, 2012a, 2013).

Requirements of "beneficial owner" and supporting documents

Requirement (Circular 601)	Evidence (Public Notice30 & Opinion165)
1. Applicant has no obligation to distribute all or the majority (e.g. more than 60 %) of its received passive income to a resident in a third country or region within a stipulated time period (e.g. 12 months).	Valid articles of association
	Contracts, pacts, or resolutions agreed by applicant and related holding company
2. Applicant must have other substantial business activities besides receiving the passive income.	
3. If the applicant is a company, the equity value, scale and allocation of personnel should be congruent with its received passive income.	Financial statement
	Documents on resources of capital and investment risk bearing
	Expense records concerning personnel
	Materials stating responsibility of staff and essence of their job
4. Received passive income and property from which the income is generated are controlled by the applicant. Further, applicant bears the risk of utilizing them.	Legal documents about the right to "control"
	Records of past events related to reinvesting or redistributing the received income
	Materials proving that above disposals were made on applicant's own decision (e.g. Minutes and resolutions of the board of directors meeting)
5. Applicant is better not resident in a country which levies no or extremely low tax on received passive income generated from China.	
6. There are no back-to-back loans with similar value and assignment date.	Loan contracts
7. There are no back-to-back arrangements on the contract concerning royalties.	License agreements

4.7.3 Tax on Capital Gains Derived from Alienation of Shares

Singapore does not impose tax on capital gains. Therefore it is only necessary to understand under what circumstances a company will be subjected to tax in China. The first criterion is that more than 50 % of the alienated shares are directly or indirectly sourced from immovable property in China. If this criterion is satisfied, Singapore resident company will be taxed no matter how many percentage shares it holds in the investee company (SAT 2010). The other criterion is that the company has to hold directly or indirectly at least 25 % of the capital of the investee company.

4.7.4 Elimination of Double Taxation

The article 22 in DTT stipulates that when company of Singapore receives income from China and was subject to tax in China, Singapore tax authority will grant credit to offset the tax payable in Singapore no matter the tax is directly paid by company or is deduced from the income.

When one company of Singapore directly or indirectly owns no less than 10 % of capital of the investee company, the Foreign Tax Credit given on China-sourced dividends should also take into account tax charged on the profit from which the dividend was distributed.

The amount of FTC granted on china-sourced income is calculated based on the assumption that China government has not grant any exemption, reduction, or refund.

4.8 New Enterprise Income Tax Law

New Enterprise Income Tax (EIT) law came into effect since January 1, 2008, which unifies tax treatment for *foreign invested enterprises* (FIEs) and *domestic enterprises* (DEs). This exerts great impact on FIEs from several following aspects.

4.8.1 Tax Resident Enterprise (TRE)

Under Foreign Enterprise Income Tax law (FEIT) law, foreign enterprises are only subject to tax on income sourced from China. However, under new EIT law, company registered in foreign country but with substantial management in China is identified as TRE whose worldwide income is subject to EIT.

4.8.2 Corporate Tax Rate and Dividend Withholding Tax

The headline corporate tax rate for FIEs increased from 15 to 25 % since 2008. Furthermore, there is no withholding tax on dividend payment to FIEs according to former FEIT law. The new EIT law states 20 % withholding tax is imposed on the China-sourced passive income (e.g. dividend). The rate was revised to 10 % for FIEs in the following Implementation Rules of EIT law.

Therefore, the overall tax rate of the FIE in China increases from 15 to 32.5 % because of the new EIT law, as shown in the following table.

	Under FEIT Law		Under EIT Law	
	Tax rate	Income statement	Tax rate	Income statement
FIE level				
FIE profits before tax		100		100
Underlying tax liability	15 %	(15)	25 %	(25)
FIE profits after tax		85		75
Foreign investor level				
Withholding tax	**0 %**	(0)	10 %	(7.5)
Net repatriation		85		67.5
Overall tax rate		**15 %**		**32.5 %**

Note: *FEIT* foreign enterprise income tax, *FIE* foreign-invested enterprise, *EIT* Enterprise income tax

However, the most visible change of the new EIT law is the additional chapter of "special tax adjustment." The aim of this new chapter is to provide guidelines for anti-tax avoidance. In order to reduce tax avoidance behavior, EIT law develops a new measure to punish the tax avoidance. If there is adjustment of the tax payable for one company, tax authority will charge interest on the unpaid amount at certain interest rate for every day in arrears. The interest rate adopted is 5 % higher than the normal interest rate. Furthermore, this penalty expense cannot be deducted from taxable income.

General Anti-avoidance Rules

Article 47 in EIT law empowers tax authority to make adjustment to the taxable income, if there is improper business arrangement intended to reduce, avoid, or defer the tax payment. Circular 2 specifies four certain suspicious arrangements, namely, abuse of tax treaties, preferential tax treatments, corporate structure, and tax heavens. SAT issued several papers to preclude "tax avoidance." For instance, Circular 601 was released to prevent abuse of tax treaties, and Guoshuihan [2009] No. 698 (circular 698) was issued to preclude the abuse of corporate structure (SAT 2009b).

Tax Incentives

New EIT law changed the original tax incentive system offered to FIEs. Under FEIT laws, dominant preferential treatment is that productive FIEs in Special Economic Zones and Economic and Technological Development Zone (ETDZ) are taxed at 15 % on its taxable corporate income. Another remarkable treatment is the tax return on reinvestment. Both advantages were removed by new EIT laws and replaced by predominantly industry-oriented tax incentive policy.

Tax incentives in new enterprise income tax laws

	Preferential treatment		Method
Technology related			
High/ New Tech Enterprises (HNTEs)	Concessionary corporate tax rate of 15 %		Preferential tax rate
Qualified income generated from transfer of technology	First 5 million Yuan income each YA	Exempt	Tax deduction or exemption
Equity investment of Venture Capital Enterprise (VCE) in a non-listed small/medium sized HNTEs	70 % of its investment is allowed be deducted from its income tax payable of the third year since investment	Reduce tax payables by 50 %	Extra tax allowance
	Any excess amount can be carried forward to against its taxable income in the following years		Extra tax allowance
R&D cost incurred during developing new technology or product	Expenses are deducted at 150 %		
	Intangible asset are amortized on the 150 % of the cost		
Environment related			
Qualified environment-protecting and energy conserving project	"3 + 3" tax holiday		Tax holiday
Acquisition of environment-protecting and energy-conserving equipment	10 % of its investment value is allowed be deducted from its income tax payable for the corresponding year		Extra tax allowance
	Any excess amount can be carried forward to against its taxable income in the following 5 tax years		
Non-resident company related			
Dividend income distributed by a resident company in China received by non-resident company who had set up institutions in China to which the dividend income is substantially related	Exempt		Exempt income
Passive income sourced from China received by non-resident enterprise who has not established institutions in China	Concessionary tax rate of 10 %		Preferential tax rate
Other important item			
The public infrastructure project encouraged by government	"3 + 3" tax holiday		Tax holiday
Agricultural, forestry, animal husbandry, and fishery	Total or half exemption		Tax deduction
Small enterprises earning low profits	Concessionary tax rate of 20 %		Preferential tax rate

The above table shows the major tax incentives in EIT laws and its implementation rules.

4.9 Analysis and Conclusion

Based on above information, it is evident that tax environment has experienced considerable change in both China and Singapore since 2008.

Basically, China tightens its regulations regarding to "tax-avoidance" since 2008 and eliminates most preferential treatments which are only enjoyed by foreign enterprises before 2008. By contrast, Singapore broadens the tax benefit offered to MNEs from many perspectives after 2008. Therefore, with an attempt to reduce its worldwide tax burden, it is wise for MNEs to invest in China through holding company in Singapore and exploit the existing tax benefit in both countries extensively.

4.9.1 Recommendations for Multinational Enterprises

1. It is recommended for MNEs to set up its regional headquarter, conduct managerial activity, holding board of directors meeting in Singapore. After that, MNEs can invest in China through holding company in Singapore.

   There are several benefits of this strategy:

   - MNEs can enjoy corporate tax rate of 17 % for its income received in Singapore. Moreover, if it meets the requirement of HQ Programme, lower rate will be granted.
   - With its managerial activity conduct in Singapore, MNEs in Singapore will be qualified for Certificate of Resident. This will allow MNEs to enjoy all tax exemption schemes mentioned above in Singapore, e.g. FSIE scheme.
   - Managerial activity is deemed to be substantial activity and is helpful when applying for "Beneficial Owner" to enjoy the DTT benefit between Singapore and China, e.g. 5 % dividend withholding tax rate.
   - Dividends received in Singapore are exempt from tax and Singapore does not levy withholding tax on dividends paid. Therefore, there is no extra tax cost setting up holding company in Singapore for MNEs.
   - If MNEs set up subsidiaries in China directly and the effective management is also conducted in China, it is likely that this subsidiary will be treated as resident company and be taxed on its worldwide income. Above strategy will solve this problem.

2. MNEs should pay attention to HNTE incentives in China and try to meet the qualifying conditions if possible.

3. MNEs are suggested to do research and development in Singapore considering that PIC scheme can considerably reduce the tax burden. Furthermore, the corporate income tax rate of 17 % is much lower than that of China. Therefore when there are profits generated from intellectual property (IP), the tax burden incurred is smaller if IP is owned in Singapore.
4. MNEs should take advantage of environment related tax preferential treatment. This not only can reduce the tax payable, but also helps MNEs to achieve their social responsibility and enhance their reputation.
5. MNEs may need to revise the capital structure of its subsidiary in China because of thin capitalization rule.
6. MNEs are recommended to keep extensive documents regarding to related party transactions in case of investigation.
7. It is suggested that MNEs invest some projects or establish branches in western area in China.

In conclusion, China has been ranking in the top choices of the location for foreign direct investment (FDI), and Singapore is a prevailing destination of the SPV for Multinational Enterprises (MNEs) to invest in China.

However, the investment environment in China experienced several changes regarding to taxation policy since 2008. There are still critical views of whether tax heaven benefits MNEs. Turning to effect of DTT, some analyst believe DTT can have a positive effect on FDI theoretically. However, most empirical researches do not have supported this opinion until recent years. Regarding to the study of effect of new EIT law, most scholars perceive that new EIT laws would not negatively affect FDI into China and this is proved to be right thanks to empirical data.

References

Barthel F, Busse M, Neumayer E (2010) The impact of double taxation treaties on foreign direct investment: evidence from large dyadic panel data. Contemp Econ Policy 28:366–377

Blonigen BA, Davies RB (2004) The effects of bilateral tax treaties on US FDI activity. Int Tax Public Finance 11:601–622

Cheng S, Shi S (2012) The impact of new income tax law on foreign invested enterprises in China. Int Tax J 2:215–228

Chinese State Administration of Taxation (2009a) Guoshuifa [2009] no.2. State Administration of Taxation, Shanghai, China

Chinese State Administration of Taxation (2009b) Guoshuihan [2009] no. 698. State Administration of Taxation, Shanghai, China

Chinese State Administration of Taxation (2010) Guoshuifa [2010] no.75. State Administration of Taxation, Shanghai, China

Chinese State Administration of Taxation (2012a) SAT public notice [2012] no.30. State Administration of Taxation, Shanghai, China

Chinese State Administration of Taxation (2012b) Interpretation of SAT public notice [2012] no.30. State Administration of Taxation, Shanghai, China

Chinese State Administration of Taxation (2013) Shuizonghan [2013] no.165. State Administration of Taxation, Shanghai, China

Davies R, Norbäck P, Tekin-Koru A (2009) The effect of tax treaties on multinational firms: new evidence from microdata. World Econ 32:77–110
Egger P, Larch M, Pfaffermayr M, Winner H (2006) The impact of endogenous tax treaties on foreign direct investment: theory and evidence. Can J Econ/Revue Canadienne D'économique 4(3):8–13
Halkyard A, Linghui R (2010) China's tax incentive regime for foreign direct investment: an eassonian analysis. University of Toronto Press, Toronto
Hossain T, Keep W, Peters S (2012) Corruption and foreign direct investment: the moderating effect of bilateral tax treaties. Int J Bus Insight Transf 39(3):901–931
Iras (2010) Taxable income. Inland Revenue Authority of Singapore, Singapore
Iras (2013) Iras e-tax guide-income tax: foreign tax credit pooling. Inland Revenue Authority of Singapore, Singapore
Iras (2014a) Tax rates & tax exemption schemes. Inland Revenue Authority of Singapore, Singapore
Iras (2014b) Claiming foreign tax credit. Inland Revenue Authority of Singapore, Singapore
Iras (2014c) Productivity and innovation credit. Inland Revenue Authority of Singapore, Singapore
Iras (2014d) PIC bonus. Inland Revenue Authority of Singapore, Singapore
Iras (2014e) How PIC benefits you. Inland Revenue Authority of Singapore, Singapore
Iras (2014f) What is taxable income. Inland Revenue Authority of Singapore, Singapore
Iras (2014g) Applying for certificate of residence (COR). Inland Revenue Authority of Singapore, Singapore
Neumayer E (2007) Do double taxation treaties increase foreign direct investment to developing countries? J Dev Stud 43(8):1501–1519
Ng C (2013) International tax planning considerations and strategies-investing into and out of China. Int Tax J 39(2):73
Zollo T, Kvalseth J, Zuvich D, Tao A (2007) Chinese procurement under the new enterprise income tax law. Int Tax J 33(5):39

Chapter 5
The New Concept of China (Shanghai) Pilot Free Trade Zone

The establishment of China (Shanghai) Pilot Free Trade Zone is a strategic decision by the Central Government, and is a significant measure to boost China's reform and opening up under the new circumstances. The China (Shanghai) Pilot Free Trade Zone is critically meaningful and aims to expedite the functional transformation of the government, explore administrative innovation, stimulate trading and investment facilitation, and accumulate experience on achieving a more open China economy. (The State Council)

5.1 The New China (Shanghai) Pilot Free Trade Zone: An Overview

The new China (Shanghai) Pilot Free Trade Zone was established by the Chinese government on September 27, 2013. It covers an area of around 29 km^2, including four previous free trade zones (Waigaoqiao Free Trade Zone, Waigaoqiao Bonded Logistics Park, Yangshan Bonded Port, and Pudong Airport Bonded Logistic Center).

Shanghai free trade pilot zone is created on the basis of four former bonded zones, but not on a simple aggregation of the four zones' functions. It has been created with the purpose of opening the way to adopt modern reforms replicable to other Chinese cities, just as the word "pilot" indicates. Compared with other successful FTZs, Shanghai Pilot Free Trade Zone concentrate mainly about reforming and innovating a system still not completely accessible from foreign players and makes a great revolution on service industries within the zone. According to the collectivity scheme (2013), government function transformation, foreign investment management reform, and the formation of a new type of commercial trading and capital market environment would have all been achieved in the next 2–3 years. Briefly, China (Shanghai) Pilot Free Trade Zone is set up for experimenting the attempt to expand and deepen the reform of China rather than simply speeding up the economic growth in a short period of time. Multiple types of zones are therefore chosen to enlarge the sample in order to introduce directly the new policies in other generalized special economic zones associated with ports, airports, industry parks, or logistics parks.

Certainly, converting a bonded zone into a free trade zone requests many requirements. By the end of year 2012, Shanghai's GDP amounted to 2,010.133 billion RMB with Pudong New District contributing roughly 29.5 % (592.991 billion

L. Riccardi, *Investing in China through Free Trade Zones*,
DOI 10.1007/978-3-662-47354-2_5

RMB) to the total number. Fiscal revenue of Shanghai local government achieved 374.371 billion RMB, with year-on-year growth of 9.2 % and residential population increased up to 23.8 million. Being the economic center of China, Shanghai has been requested for going further into the global market to reach the main stage. Ever since the reform and opening started 30 years ago, over 200 billion RMB have been allocated to Shanghai Pudong New District (Lee et al. 2013). Together with hundreds of great infrastructure projects in the district, Shanghai deployed several advanced functional transportation conjunctions, such as Yangshan deep water port and Pudong international airport, and made them the landmarks of Shanghai Pudong New District. As a result of long-time fiscal support from the central government, Shanghai has a well-developed city infrastructure to support the building of international trading and financial center. Another highlight would be the transportation network including subsea tunnel, cross-sea bridge, maglev train, and subway which leads to a seamless connection between Pudong New District and the downtown, and the affluent neighboring provinces that are actually the supportive hinterland of Shanghai port.

Chinese central government stated three main aspects in "China (Shanghai) Free Trade Zone collectivity scheme" (collectivity scheme), concerning the general objectives, the principal missions, and regulatory and taxation environment. The general objectives are the backbone of the pilot project, claiming that Chinese economy is entering a new phase that desires a government function transformation from proactive explorations into innovative management methods. The essence of Shanghai FTZ project is therefore identified as an experiment to verify universal economic policies for Mainland China, aiming to a long-term progress rather than a mere collection of political incentives.

Together with a lot of amendments, the principal mission is well defined in the framework released by the Chinese State Council as well as a sketch of how businesses would be conducted in the China (Shanghai) Free Trade Zone, in particular in the services sector. For investments not related to the banking and telecommunication sectors, restrictions on requirements for registering enterprises, percentage of ownership, and scope within licenses would be suspended or removed. Meanwhile, the Shanghai local government is attempting to use the *negative list approach* to simplify the accession of foreign investments in the zone, integrated with a series of new administrable regulations such as replacing approval systems with the file systems, assorted with the concept of deregulation on the entry but reinforcement of the supervision on the processes and outcome of foreign businesses. Fundamentally, local authorities would be endeavoring to supervise enterprises after their registrations to reduce entry barriers at the first stage.

The State Council will lead and coordinate promotion of the China (Shanghai) Pilot Free Trade Zone. The Shanghai Municipal People's Government is responsible for organizing implementation, improving the working mechanism, and allocating detail responsibilities. Based on the targets which were clearly set out in the framework plan and pilot tasks, in accordance with the principle of "go ahead with the matured ones and follow by perfection," the Shanghai Municipal People's Government can create a practical implementation plan and enforce without delay.

During the implementing, the Shanghai Municipal People's Government studied new cases, resolved new problems and reported rapidly to the State Council significant issues. All relevant departments need to support actively, provide cooperation, guidance and evaluation feedback, work together to promote the innovation on relevant system, mechanism, and policy, and construct and well-manage the China (Shanghai) Pilot Free Trade Zone.

The following table summarizes the key objectives the State Council wishes to achieve by implementing China's (Shanghai) Pilot Free Trade Zone:

Shanghai FTZ key objectives for 2013 onward
1. Promoting China as a service-oriented economy
2. RMB Internationalization
3. Establishing more competitive and sophisticated tax rates
4. Reducing the complexity for establishment and approval for foreign investors
5. Simplifying and securing cross-border capital flows
6. Promoting Shanghai as a center for International trade, finance, shipping, and logistics

Source: Official website of the China (Shanghai) Pilot Free Trade Zone

5.2 The Areas Comprised in the Shanghai Free Trade Zone

The four bonded zones were not chosen casually. Since 1980s, Pudong New District, which had a total acreage of 522 km^2, has been formed as an industrial park aimed at developing a new commercial center. Wu (1999) stated that 0.3 billion Yuan was allocated to Pudong by the Chinese central government each year during the eighth 5-year plan, for both hardware and software constructions. Pudong is also well known for attracting foreign direct investments. As Wei and Leung (2005) claimed in one of their works, the establishment of Pudong in early 1990s made a significant step in attracting foreign direct investments. The amount of foreign direct investment was of 35 billion USD by the end of the year 2001. Nine years later, Shanghai synthesized bonded zone including Yangshan bonded port zone, Waigaoqiao bonded zone, and Pudong airport bonded zone. Except for historical reasons, the different types of those four bonded zones enabled the sample completeness of the pilot program. Firstly, a port is the perfect place for free zone setting up, where the global commerce gather. Yangshan, with 25 km shoreline and over 15 m water depth, is located at the hub between Yangtze river shipping and maritime shipping and is gifted with the great natural conditions and geographical superiority. As the first bonded port zone of China, Yangshan has developed rapidly and has the greatest input-output efficiency among the 14 Chinese bonded port zones with the most import and export volume of Chinese ports. Meanwhile, Waigaoqiao bonded zone is the largest bonded zone in China. The scale of professional merchandise trading here is still expanding and accounts for a large proportion of Chinese import commodity market. Pudong airport bonded zone, at the intersection of eastern coastal economic belt and Yangtze River and just next to Pudong International Airport that has the third biggest volume of cargos, started operating on September 28, 2010. With such geographical preponderance domestically, Pudong bonded zone is located on the triangle airline among Asia, Europe, and America.

The China (Shanghai) Pilot Free Trade Zone will count on the Waigaoqiao Port, Yangshan Deep-Water Port, and Pudong International Airport to create a shipping development system and operation model that will bring to get relevant global competitive advantages. Shipping related services such as shipping financing, international ship transportation, international ship management, and international ship brokerage will be proactively promoted. Moreover, the creation of freight index derivatives will be accelerated. Foreign ships owned or indirectly owned by Chinese invested companies are permitted to pilot the coastal shipping between domestic coastal ports and Shanghai port. Pudong International Airport has increased the number of flights for cargo transportation. With the geographic advantages offered by Shanghai and the preferential taxation on Chinese "flag of convenience" ships, authorities is willing to encourage qualified ships to register in Shanghai. Maybe the China (Shanghai) Pilot Free Trade Zone will adopt the international ship registration policy already experimented in Tianjin. With the new regulation, the main task was the simplification of the application process on permitting international shipping, creating a more efficient ship registration system. Enterprises within the Pilot Free

Trade Zone may take "China Yangshan Port" as their registration port and engage in international shipping business.

The China (Shanghai) Pilot Free Trade Zone is founded on the Waigaoqiao Port, Yangshan Deep-Water Port, and Pudong International Airport with the duty to improve transport connections with industrial areas outside the Pilot Free Trade Zone.

The location of China (Shanghai) Pilot Free Trade Zone

Waigaoqiao Free Trade Zone, China's first bonded area, is located in the Yangtze River estuary, where a "golden waterway" and a "golden coastline" converge. Adjacent to the Port of Waigaoqiao, the zone will cover 10 km^2 when fully completed. Thus far, 8.9 km^2 has been put into operation. The zone is the biggest and the most profitable of all areas under the special administration of the General Administration of Customs.
Waigaoqiao Free Trade Logistics Park, located next to the port, covers 1.03 km^2 and is the first site in China to integrate the function of functions of a bonded area and a port that allows companies to benefit from policies in both.
Yangshan Free Trade Port Area comprises the land portion of Shanghai Luchao port, the Donghai Bridge, and the Little Yangshan port in Shengsi in Zhejiang Province. When fully developed, it will cover 14.16 km^2. The zone was created under a joint cooperative effort of the Shanghai and Zhejiang governments.
Pudong Airport Free Trade Zone is located to the west of the third runway at Pudong International Airport. It connects with the Waigaoiqao Free Trade Zone in the north and with the Yangshan Free Trade Port Area in the south. With an operational area of 3.59 km^2, the zone sits at the center point of the coastline of the Pudong New Area.

Source: Official website of the China (Shanghai) Pilot Free Trade Zone

5.3 The Fields of Intervention

"The Pilot Free Trade Zone shall proactively expand the opening up of the service sector and promote the reform of the investment administrative system; accelerate the transformation and upgrading of trade; intensify the opening up of the financial sector; innovate supervision service model; explore and create an administrative system in line with international investment and trade rules, and cultivate an internationalized business environment so as to play a proactive demonstration role in leading and serving nationwide." The Shanghai Municipal People's Government, decree n°7, art. 3, September 29, 2013.

In the Master Plan for the China (Shanghai) Pilot Free Trade Zone, released by the State Council, it is clear in which sectors the government intends to initiate reforms to the current system.

- Financial reform
- Trade liberalization
- Simplification of administrative systems
- Investment liberalization

There is obviously a strong dependence relationship between them.

Chinese government focuses in promoting Shanghai as a center for international trade, shipping, and logistics. Simplification and reduction of approval requirements for foreign investors, the creation of an easy-going tax regime, upgrading and reinforcement of the zone as a financial center, and the consequently adjustment of the rules with the scopes of the zone are the operative paths that policy makers are following to create the requested market environment.

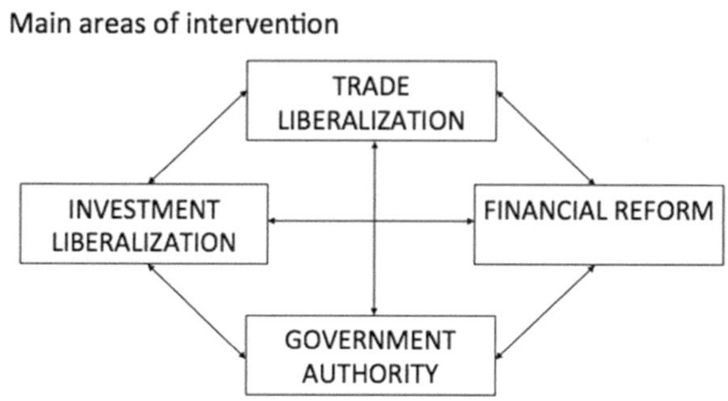

The financial reform is without any doubt the most attractive one as we can see from the great amount of attention paid by the media and the global investors. In this area, innovations are mainly promoted in two sections. First, banking sector in Shanghai Pilot Free Trade Zone tends to absorb more foreign and private capital injections every year, as the prohibitions on foreign banks' entries have already been removed in the fifth year after World Trade Organization accession. Second, innovations in the financial sector are encouraged on four aspects considered as a must for bracing Shanghai becoming the new global financial center, which are RMB cross-border payment, market-based reforms of interest rates, the convertibility of RMB capital account, and foreign exchange management. These four factors are all required for the liberalization of the financial market. For instance, direct foreign capital injections require a free floating of interest rates to avoid arbitrage and other speculating activities. To serve the free trading needs of the China (Shanghai) Pilot Free Trade Zone, Chinese government would further raise the upper limit of deposit rate. Another highlight point confirming Chinese central government's determination is the permission for foreign enterprises to participate in the trading of commodities futures.

The China (Shanghai) Pilot Free Trade Zone is intended to create advantages for both foreign and domestic companies.

Foreign companies will have gradually a direct and cheaper way to access Chinese customers; there will be the possibility to take advantage of the opportunities offered by the Chinese market with better business conditions in the economic environment; currently rigorous regulations will be substituted by business-friendly and market-driven rules; taxes must be paid only when goods leave the free trade zone according to the pro-rata method.

On the other side, local companies can access directly imported goods; there is always an import tax, but now it is calculated on the cost price rather than on the purchase price; their customers have to pay the taxes only when goods are moved over the free trade zone.

Regarding about the sectors that will benefit from FTZ these are mainly:

- Financial Services
- Processing and Manufacturing
- Transportation and Logistic Services
- Healthcare and Medical Institutions
- E-Commerce

As we can see from the list above, China is mainly opening up the service industry because its sectors can take more advantages from collaborations with foreign partners bringing new clients and technologies.

These are words of the State Council in the framework for China (Shanghai) Pilot Free Trade Zone: "The financial services, transportation services, commerce and trade services, professional services, cultural services, and public services sectors are selected to be enlarged and opened, and market access restrictions such us requirements concerning the qualification of investors, limitations on foreign participation, restrictions concerning business scope, etc.…(except in respect of banks, information and communication services) will be suspended or cancelled, in order to create an environment of equal market access for the benefit of all investors."

5.4 Simplifications and Reforms in the Administrative System

To create a regulatory environment in line with the international practice, the Pilot Free Trade Zone will establish an administration and service model with high efficiency to facilitate investment and trade. Shanghai Municipal People's Government, decree n° 7, art. 26, 29th September 2013.

Generally China is known by foreign investors for its complex administrative system with a number of registration forms and authorizations required. The Shanghai Pilot Free Trade Zone is a first attempt to switch to a simplified version of the current system and you will surely notice in the following paragraphs (regarding the financial reform, investment sectors, customs, etc.…) that many innovations simply consist in a reduction of red tape steps. This is the reason because we begin from analyzing changes in the administrative system.

As required for implementing changes in the administrative system, authorities started with streamlining administration and delegating powers to the lower levels, coordinating the delegation and supervision, promoting the notification-promise system and others, and establishing an administrative management system in the new China (Shanghai) Pilot Free Trade Zone with a logic allocation of powers and efficient, unified management and open, transparent operation. To get these results, the Shanghai's Municipal Government established the Administration Committee of the China (Shanghai) Free Trade Pilot Zone, combining the previous Administration Committees of Shanghai Waigaoqiao bonded zone, Yangshan bonded zone, and

Shanghai comprehensive bonded zone. The Administration Committee is responsible for suggesting, developing, and promoting reform opportunities in the Pilot Free Trade Zone and managing and coordinating the administrative issues of the Pilot Free Trade Zone. Relevant departments of the Shanghai Municipal People's Government as well as the People's government of Pudong New Area and the other local government entities at the district and county levels cooperate and work with the Administration Committee on various assignments.

After the establishment of the Administration Committee, branch offices of Customs, inspection and quarantine, marine, industry and commerce, quality supervision, taxation, public security, and other government administrative authorities were obviously set up in the Shanghai Pilot Free Trade Zone fitting with the current laws to perform supervision and administrative duties in the zone.

The Administration Committee has the duty to divulgate periodically all the policies, regulations, procedures, and rules formulated or obtained as well as all the relevant authorities. Their amendments and reports have to be publicly disclosed, transparent, and easily accessed by enterprises.

The China Shanghai Pilot Free Trade Zone is bringing the functional transformation of government and governmental administrative management innovation. An administrative management system suitable with international trade and investment standards is being slowly adopted. The base consists in shifting administrative management procedures from prior approval to mid-event control and subsequent supervision. Services will be organized to materialize one-off acceptance, integrated examination, and share information amongst different supervising units. A modern and flexible mechanism of industry information recording, supervision, and collection will be established to improve the tracking, management, and supervision of activities operated outside the zone but conducted by entities registered in the China (Shanghai) Pilot Free Trade Zone. A comprehensive control and enforcement system will be established to cover the areas of quality and technical supervision, food and drug supervision, intellectual property, industry and commercial administration, and tax administration to reach congruous efficiency. Moreover, an intellectual property related dispute resolution and assistance system will be defined.

In addition to the introduction of new management system, transparency of administration entities is another big task that authorities want to promote in the new China (Shanghai) Pilot Free Trade Zone. An information disclosure mechanism that reflects the participation of investors and is in line with international standards will be established. To defend the interest of investors, various administration reforms are being studied to enhance fair competition and to allow qualified foreign investors to remit investment gains at their discretion.

Simplified procedures have been elaborated not only in the administrative sector, but also in law and regulation codes, for instance in defining which kind of investments can be done by foreign entities. The overall scope is the construction of an environment where foreign investors will receive the same treatment reserved to their domestic counterparts. For example, foreign companies will find less entry barriers with less administrative requirements: apart for the investment areas linked with the "negative list" (that we will talk about further), the usual approval requirements are substituted by a record filing system in order to not slow down the activity of the interested company. Then authorities can eventually check furthermore the presence of lacks as it happens with local companies. On the other side, the Shanghai Free Trade Zone has been created to encourage domestic enterprises to invest abroad. Instead of having to follow the time-consuming process of seeking approval from relevant government authorities, local companies located in the Shanghai Free Trade Zone are only required to file a record for general outbound investment projects.

There are many other types of administrative simplifications with the creation of the Shanghai Pilot Free Trade Zone but we prefer to analyze them during the presentation of the reforms concerning finance, customs, and access to the different sectors for foreign entities. The main remark that we can premise is the change from approval systems to simple registration systems adopted by Chinese authorities in the China (Shanghai) Free Trade Zone to give the opportunity to move faster in the Chinese market.

Finally, simplification doesn't mean less controlling. Under the principle of protecting national security and fair competition in the market, coordination and information exchange will be enforced between the relevant departments and the Shanghai Municipal People's government. The China (Shanghai) Pilot Free Trade Zone will report and collaborate continuously with relevant departments of the State Council to strictly implement the established regulation in respect of anti-monopoly investigations. In order to streamline supervision, cooperation between various government units will be established, including that between the Customs, Inspection and Quarantine, Industry and Commerce, Taxation, Foreign Exchange, and other administrative authorities. The China (Shanghai) Pilot Free Trade Zone will establish a port supervision institution and will evaluate the possibility of creating an electronic monitoring system and setting up an effective risk management system.

In conclusion regarding the authorization for new investment projects, the industry and commerce authority in the China (Shanghai) Pilot Free Trade Zone will cooperate with administrative authorities such as tax and quality supervision as well as the Administration Committee to set up a mechanism of "one form" declaration and "one window" acceptance for foreign investment project approval (filing) and enterprise establishment (changes of registration information). In the next future, the industry and commerce authority should accept the application materials submitted by the applicants in a unified manner and deliver relevant documents to the applicants in a unified manner as well. The Administration Committee will also establish a mechanism of "one-form" declaration and "one window" acceptance for the filing of outbound investment made by companies in the Pilot Free Trade Zone to uniformly accept the application materials submitted by the applicants and uniformly deliver the relevant document to the applicants.

5.5 Financial Reform

5.5.1 Financial Entities in the Shanghai Pilot Free Trade Zone

Chinese-funded banks are invited to set up their activities in the China (Shanghai) Pilot Free Trade Zone. National Chinese-funded commercial banks, policy banks, and banks in Shanghai are encouraged to move new branches or special institution in the Shanghai Free Trade Zone. The existing bank outlets in the Shanghai Free Trade Zone are permitted to upgrade to branches or sub-branches. The creation of new free trade zone branches and upgrading existing free trade zone outlets to branches/sub-branches will not be subjected by the banks' annual branch establishment plan.

The setting up of non-banking finance companies in the China (Shanghai) Pilot Free Trade Zone is supported too. Qualified large companies groups in the Shanghai Free Trade Zone are encouraged to establish group finance enterprises; qualified investors are supported to establish auto finance companies and consumer finance companies in the Shanghai Free Trade Zone; trust companies in Shanghai are allowed to move into the Shanghai Free Trade Zone; national financial asset management companies are supported to establish branches in the Shanghai Free Trade Zone; finance leasing companies are permitted to move specialized subsidiaries in the Shanghai Free Trade Zone.

More interesting in a global point of view, also foreign-invested banks are supported to carry out business in the China (Shanghai) Pilot Free Trade Zone. Qualified foreign-invested banks are allowed to set up subsidiaries, branches, special institutions, and Sino-foreign equity joint-venture banks in the Shanghai Free Trade Zone. Sub-branches in the Shanghai Free Trade Zone of foreign-invested banks are permitted to upgrade to branches. There is also the willingness of authorities to properly shorten the statutory period for a Free Trade Zone representative office of a foreign bank to be allowed to upgrade to a branch, and the statutory period for a Free Trade Zone branch of a foreign bank to be allowed to carry out RMB business.

Finally, private capitals are allowed to enter into the banking industry in the China (Shanghai) Pilot Free Trade Zone. Qualified private investors are permitted to establish banks, finance leasing companies, consumer finance companies, and other finance institutions which can assume their own risks in the Shanghai Free Trade Zone. Qualified private investors are encouraged to take part in setting up Sino-foreign equity joint-venture banks with other Chinese or foreign financial institution investors.

Cross-border investment and financing service are encouraged in the China (Shanghai) Pilot Free Trade Zone. Banking financial institutions in the Shanghai Free Trade Zone are allowed to carry out cross-border financing business, comprehensive to commodity trade finance, whole supply chain finance, offshore vessel finance, financial support to modern service sectors, onshore loans against offshore guarantees, commercial instruments, etc. Banking financial institutions in the Shanghai Free Trade Zone are encouraged to stimulate finance services for cross-border investments, including cross-border M&A loans and project loans, guaranty for offshore loans, cross-border assets management and wealth management business, real estate investment trust, etc.

Offshore business is absolutely encouraged in the China (Shanghai) Pilot Free Trade Zone. Qualified Chinese banks are permitted to engage in offshore banking business in the Shanghai Free Trade Zone.

In line with the objectives of the establishment of a new pilot free trade zone, the administration procedure on market access will be simplified in the China (Shanghai) Pilot Free Trade Zone. Concerning banks' sub-branches (including branch offices below the sub-branch tier) in the Shanghai Free Trade Zone, a reporting requirement, instead of the existing pre-approval, is being studied by controlling authorities to be applied for items in respect of the qualifications of the branch office, senior management, and certain business permission. A "green channel" is also being developed to grant the market access for banking industry in the Shanghai Free Trade Zone to enhance the administration efficiency by setting time limits for certain items.

5.5.2 *Innovations in the Financial Sector*

"The Pilot Free Trade Zone will pilot innovations in financial sector. A mechanism will be established to associate financial reforms in the Pilot Free Trade Zone with Shanghai's development into an international financial center." Shanghai Municipal People's Government, decree n° 7, art. 19, September 29, 2013.

The financial reform is probably the most massive part of the new regulation consequently the new China (Shanghai) Pilot Free Trade Zone, with the internationalization of the RMB that is uprising the attention of the world financial market. The reform is supposed to increase investments in the area through a step by step simplification and innovation of the financial sector.

The financial reform has been elaborated with the collaboration between the People's Bank of China (PBOC, the central bank of China), the State Administration of Foreign Exchange (SAFE), and policy makers in the banking, insurance, and securities sector. SAFE is an administrative agency, which is responsible in China for regulating the foreign exchange market activities and controlling the state foreign exchange reserves. These entities elaborated guidelines and suggestions for implementing the project defined in the Master Plan. On December 2, 2013, the People's Bank of China divulgated the *Opinions on Financial Support for Building the China (Shanghai) Pilot Free Zone* (defined easily also as the *Opinions*). These opinions were not the specific regulations, but useful instruments to define the borders of the area of intervention. They can be properly defined more as principles, rather than rules.

The followings are reported by the People's Bank of China as the *general principles* that will address the financial reform in the Shanghai Pilot Free Trade Zone:

(1) Finance should always serve real economy by further facilitating trade and investment, opening up the financial sector to foreign investors, and elevating the Pilot Zone to a higher level to participate in the international competition.
(2) We should stick to the reform and innovation, dare to pilot, and in particular, promote the cross-border use of RMB, RMB's convertibility under capital account, interest rate liberalization and reforms in foreign exchange administration.
(3) We should keep the risk under control and steadily progress the reform; any reform measure should not be launched until conditions permit and pilot should be carried out in a timely and organized manner.

Rules started to be edited during February 2014 with the following *Circulars* released by the People's Bank of China and its branches:

- February 18, 2014, *Implementing Opinions of the Shanghai Head Office of PBOC on the Provision of Cross-border RMB Payment Services by Payment Institutions in the Shanghai Municipality* (the "Payments Opinions")
- February 20, 2014, *Circular Supporting the Expansion of Cross-border Use of Renminbi in the Shanghai Pilot Free Trade Zone* (the "RMB Circular")
- February 27, 2014, *Circular on Effecting Anti-money Laundering and Anti-terrorism Financing in the Shanghai Pilot Free Trade Zone* (the "AML Circular")
- February 28, 2014, *Detailed Rules Supporting Foreign Exchange Management in the Shanghai Pilot Free Trade Zone* (the "Forex Management Circular")
- March 1, 2014, *Circular of the Shanghai Head Office of PBOC Lifting the Caps on Interest Rates on Small-amount Foreign Currency Deposits within the China (Shanghai) Pilot Free Trade Zone* (the "Interest Rates Circular").

On March 25, 2014, the Shanghai Municipality Financial Services Offices published some documents reporting situations in which the new regulation had already been applied. At the same time, authorities declared that the main aim of the financial reform is accommodating trade and investment companies in the Free Trade Zone, rather than transforming the Shanghai Free Trade Zone in a more attractive financial center.

In the next paragraphs, we are going to expose the regulation defined in the "Opinions" and in the "Circulars" that is being progressively implemented. We focus on the interventions which involve actual and potential foreign investors in China, reporting also differences between the Shanghai Pilot Free Trade Zone and Mainland China.

Free Trade Accounts

"The capital account items are convertible within the Pilot Free Trade Zone. Under the premise of risk control, business and management models will be innovated with capital flows in respect of the Pilot Free Trade Zone being separately accounted for" Shanghai Municipal People's Government, decree n° 7, art. 20, September 29, 2013.

It will be possible for both Chinese and foreign companies, which operate in the China (Shanghai) Pilot Free Trade Zone, to have free trade accounts (FTAs) that are considered like bank accounts situated outside China. These can be established in RMB or also in a foreign currency. Also individuals working in the area have the opportunity to do so. The followings are the conditions after this innovation:

- The transfer of funds (A) between FTAs, (B) between FTAs and offshore accounts, and (C) between FTAs and non-resident bank accounts in China located not in the Free Trade Zone is not subjected anymore to the constraints linked with the movement of funds between China and overseas accounts.
- To balance the previous point, transfers between FTAs and onshore accounts in China will be considered cross-border movements of money and the related regulation is applied. The cross-border regulation is not applied if the FTA and the onshore account in China are of the same entity.
- Through FTAs, cross-border financing and security are allowed.
- Banks and financial entities can open separated free trade accounting units in Shanghai for companies and individuals inside the Shanghai Free Trade Zone.

When foreign individuals opening RMB bank settlement accounts, they shall present residence certificate with valid period at least 1 year issued by the Exit/Entry Administration Public Security Authority.

Outside the Shanghai Free Trade Zone individuals cannot move cross-border China more than 50,000 USD without demonstrating that they are for a legitimate and genuine transaction. For companies, the limit varies basing on many particulars and factors and also here there is the duty to show evidently that the purposes of the transaction are justified. SAFE approval has always been required for cross-border transactions, but with the latest amendments China is progressively relaxing the procedure changing from an approval system to a registered one. Moreover for some type of transactions, banks have the right to assent the transaction basing on data held in SAFE system.

On June 18, 2014, finally five banks opened the first free trade accounts for companies in Shanghai Free Trade Zone for facilitating cross-border money transfers. These banks were Industrial and Commercial Bank of China, branches of Bank of China, China Construction Bank, Pudong Development Bank, and the Bank of Shanghai; also Bank of Communications and China Merchants Bank are moving on the same path. "The free trade account offers easier yuan transfers under direct foreign investment and current accounts," these are the words of Zhang Xuhong, general manager of Bank of Shanghai's international business department, remarking the openness of banks to the latest amendments of the government. Contrarily there is still to wait for FTAs for individuals working in the Shanghai Free Trade Zone because central bank officials reported that qualifications have yet to be determined. Also insurers and brokerages are still working to set up a free trade account system for clients to handle cross-border business.

Investment and Financing: Currency Exchange

In the China (Shanghai), Pilot Free Trade Zone is much easier to bring on foreign investment projects thanks to many facilitations compared with the rest of China and are also possible cross-border investments, which are rarely permitted in Mainland China and with additional costs and troubles. In the Shanghai Pilot Free Trade Zone:

- The registration to SAFE for forex for foreign direct investment is no longer required. The forex registration can be done directly through commercial banks and probably it will be completely removed in the next future in the Shanghai Free Trade Zone.

- Chinese individuals are allowed to buy foreign securities with less restrictions.
- Foreign individuals would be permitted to buy Chinese securities through free trade accounts. Previously foreign individuals were allowed to buy Chinese "B shares", now they could buy also "A shares."
- Financial institutions and enterprises can invest in the securities and futures markets in the Shanghai area. Moreover, parent companies of entities located in the Shanghai Free Trade Zone are permitted to issue bonds in RMB in the Chinese domestic capital market. These bonds are also called "panda bonds."
- Companies are allowed to raise RMB and forex funds from overseas, but they have to prepare documentation showing the reasons how they intend to manage the debt service and risks.
- Entities will be able to buy risk-hedging instruments within the FTZ and also overseas with the demonstrations of the inexistence of speculative intents.

There is anyway a strict regulation to take in consideration in China when we regard about currency exchange, even if we are in the Shanghai Free Trade Zone.

When an enterprise in the Shanghai Pilot Free Trade Zone enters into guarantee agreement with overseas parties, it shall, according to relevant regulations, perform guarantee registration formalities and apply for pre-approvals before it fulfills the guarantee (in case the guarantee defaults its relevant contractual obligations); the enterprise shall also comply with the restrictive rules regarding the use scope of funds under guaranty.

According to its operation needs, a qualifying enterprise in the Shanghai Pilot Free Trade Zone may open an International foreign exchange funds master account. The flow of funds between the International foreign exchange funds master account and overseas is free of foreign exchange restrictions and controls. Funds may be freely transferred between the entity's Domestic foreign exchange funds master account and International foreign exchange funds master account, subject to a quota prescribed by the foreign exchange bureau.

The foreign exchange bureau shall perform off-site supervision and monitoring over foreign exchange receipt/payment in goods trade of enterprises in the Shanghai Free Trade Zone, carry out on-site inspection under any abnormal or suspicious circumstances, and conduct different administrations according to the on-site inspection results respectively. The foreign exchange bureau may take relevant temporary measures when serious unbalance arises or may arise in international receipt/payment.

It is increased the offer of diversified risk-hedging tools: based on real management needs in respect of matched-currency or maturity, Pilot Zone institutions may conduct risk hedging within the Pilot Zone or in overseas pursuant to relevant regulations. Qualified Pilot Zone enterprises may be allowed to make foreign securities and foreign derivative investments pursuant to relevant regulations. A Pilot Zone Unit's open positions arising from free currency conversion with institutions in the Pilot Zone and overseas should be closed or hedged in the Pilot Zone market or in overseas. A Pilot Zone Unit may participate in derivative trading in international financial markets to control its own risk. Subject to approvals, a Pilot Zone Unit may conduct inter-banking lending or repos in the domestic inter-bank market within approved amounts.

The China Securities Regulatory Commission agreed to the founding of the Shanghai International Energy Trading Center Co., Ltd., in the Shanghai Free Trade Zone by the Shanghai Futures Exchange. The Shanghai International Energy Trading Center is responsible for enhancing the establishment of a trading platform of international crude oil futures. Foreign investors will be fully introduced to participate in the domestic futures trading based on the platform, and the China Securities Regulatory Commission will take this opportunity to promote the opening-up in Chinese futures market. The aim of the China Securities Regulatory Commission is the encouraging qualified entities and individuals in the Shanghai Free Trade Zone to make investments in foreign and domestic securities and futures markets in accordance with relevant regulations. Financial institutions and enterprises in the Shanghai Free Trade Zone may carry out investments and trading in securities and futures exchanges of Shanghai in accordance with relevant regulations. Qualified foreign individuals who work in the Shanghai Free Trade Zone may set up special non-resident individual accounts with securities and futures institutions in the Shanghai Free Trade Zone to carry out investments in domestic securities and futures market in accordance with relevant regulations. Consequently both qualified financial institutions and enterprises located in the Shanghai Free Trade Zone and qualified individuals who are employed in the Shanghai Free Trade Zone may carry out investments in foreign securities and futures market in accordance with relevant regulations. The China Securities Regulatory Commission encourages securities and futures institutions to register and open specialized subsidiaries in the Shanghai Free Trade Zone. Currently, institutions like Haitong Futures, Hongyuan Futures, GF Futures, Shenyin and Wanguo Futures, and HuaAn Funds are setting up or preparing to set up risk management subsidiaries and assets management subsidiaries in the area. Finally the China Securities Regulatory Commission supports securities and futures institutions in the free trade zone to carry out over-the-counter ("OTC") transactions of commodities and financial derivatives for domestic clients.

On March 8, 2014, the Shanghai Stock Exchange obtained the approvals from regulators in order to establish an international trading center in the China (Shanghai) Pilot Free Trade Zone, as reported by Gui Minjie, the chairman of the bourse. This new platform should give the allowance to more foreign investors to join world's fourth-largest stock market by capitalization and permit foreign companies to issues shares on the Chinese market. Regarding Gui Minjie's opinion, significant progress were made in the recent years to list Chinese firms on overseas markets and this is the time to do something for overseas entities willing to do the same in the Chinese market. Moreover, the government confirmed continuously this year the intent to allow a trial of a fully convertible yuan capital account in the Shanghai Free Trade Zone in order to relax controls that currently stop foreign companies to raise capital through IPOs. The problem is that the process of full convertibility of RMB actually never took off, and the first disappointments about this topic are starting to arise in the public opinion. Companies are waiting for more clearance certified by real facts, not announcements.

On September 19, 2014, also the Shanghai Gold Exchange officially launched its international trading platform in the Shanghai FTZ with the aim of increasing its influence globally and setting benchmark prices for the gold in Asia. The Shanghai Futures Exchange is still planning to move in the same way for the trading of oil futures and other key commodities such as iron. But currently for foreign investors persist the problem to access this markets since the yuan is not fully convertible.

RMB: Cross-Border Use

> The cross-border RMB settlement for institutions within the Pilot Free Trade Zone will not be subject to a pre-approval requirement. Enterprises within the Pilot Free Trade Zone may carry out innovative cross-border RMB business based on their business needs to facilitate cross-border use of RMB. Shanghai Municipal People's Government, decree n° 7, art. 22, September 29, 2013.

Founding on the three principles (i.e. "Know your customer", "Know your business" and "Due diligence"), banking entities in Shanghai may directly process cross-border RMB settlement under current account or direct investment items for entities (except for those entities on a monitoring list for cross-border RMB settlement purpose) or individuals in the Pilot FTZ according to their receipt/payment instructions.

The "Opinions" reports the following statements for the use of RMB outside China:

- Financial institutions in Shanghai will be allowed to carry out cross-border RMB account and direct investment transactions as indicated by entities in the Shanghai Free Trade Zone.
- E-commerce: banking institutions in Shanghai, but outside the free trade zone, can guarantee payment services for cross-border e commerce transactions with qualified institutions within the Shanghai Free Trade Zone.
- Both domestic and foreign financed entities located in the Shanghai Free Trade Zone can now get RMB loans from overseas and provide RMB securities and loans to overseas party. RMB funds cannot be used to purchase negotiable securities, derivatives and to make entrusted loans.
- Free trade zone enterprises will be allowed to carry out two-way RMB cash pooling to provide centralized collection and payment services. Group companies have the possibility to collect money in a master account and transfer than money to those entities with debit. The advantages are a more efficient use of cash and the possibility to reduce interest rates on bank accounts.

Then the "Circulars" make some adjustments to the statements just mentioned above:

- For cross-border direct investment transactions in areas included in the *Negative List,* banks are forced to ask the transacting party to demonstrate that the transaction has been approved by the required authorities.

- There is a restricted borrowing capacity for enterprises located in the Shanghai Free Trade Zone: enterprises will be able to borrow up to 1x or 1.5x (further better defined) their paid up capital multiplied for the prudential policy parameter determined by the central bank of China. Moreover, the term of RMB loans cannot be less than 1 year and the borrowed funds must be dedicated only to operations or projects in the Shanghai Free Trade Zone or for projects outside China.
- It is specified that cash pooling accounts are allowed only if opened by the Group Company that must be established in the free trade zone. Cash flow generated by financing activities cannot be used for cash pooling. Finally Group Companies and banks have to find an agreement about the cash pooling arrangement in order to satisfy the obligations about anti-money laundering, anti-terrorism, and anti-tax avoidance.
- About e-commerce, it is noticed that Chinese consumers have limited channels for making purchases offshore via the Internet and most of them consider the available platforms not sufficiently reliable for buying products. Payments through e-commerce are only for goods and services.

RMB borrowing from overseas Financial institutions and enterprises in the China (Shanghai) Pilot Free Trade Zone may borrow RMB funds from overseas (except trade credits and intercompany operational financing) to use in the fields that are in line with national macro-control direction. These funds temporarily cannot be invested in securities (including assets management products such as wealth management products), derivatives, or used for entrust loans purpose. The balance of RMB fund borrowed from overseas by the enterprises in the Shanghai Free Trade Zone must not exceed the ceiling amount which is calculated as paid-in capital*1time*macro prudential policy parameters. The paid-in capital is determined based on the latest capital verification report and the loan term shall be more than 1 year. These companies may, according to rules under the *Administrative Measures on RMB Bank Settlement Accounts*, open dedicated deposit account in the banks in Shanghai to deposit the RMB funds borrowed from overseas only, and such funds can only be used within the free trade zone or overseas, including production and operation in the free trade zone, projects construction in the free trade zone and overseas projects constructions etc. Differently, the balance of RMB fund borrowed from overseas by the (non-banking) financial institutions in the Shanghai Free Trade Zone shall not exceed the ceiling amount which is calculated as paid-in capital*1.5times*macro prudential policy parameters. The loan term shall be more than 1 year. As for enterprises, such funds may re-deposited in the dedicated deposit accounts opened in the banks in Shanghai and can only be used within the free trade zone or overseas, including operation in the free trade zone, projects construction in the free trade zone and overseas projects constructions, etc.

Cross Border Cash Pooling

According to operation and management needs, enterprises in the Shanghai Pilot Free Trade Zone will have the possibility to launch a cross-border two-way RMB cash pooling within the group. A "group" is intended as a multinational group of companies including an enterprise (including finance company) in the free trade zone, consisting of related parties connected mainly by capital, such as parent companies, subsidiaries, companies with capital participation, etc. The cross-border two-way RMB cash pooling refers to the two-way cash pooling among the domestic and overseas affiliated enterprises within the group. It shall be regarded as an operational financing activity within the group. To undertake cross-border two-way RMB cash pooling, the group headquarters will probably designate an operating or investing member enterprise (including a finance company), which is incorporated in the free trade zone, and choose a bank to open one RMB dedicated deposit account for undertaking cross-border two-way cash pooling only, the funds in which must be separately accounted for. Each domestic and overseas party participating in cash pooling shall enter into cash pooling agreement, defining their respective duties and obligations in anti-money laundering, anti-terrorism financing, and anti-tax evasion. In the regulation, funds flow from parties whose cash were pooled to parties pooling the cash are considered as "upstream flows"; while funds flow from parties pooling the cash to parties whose cash were pooled are considered as "downstream flows". The RMB funds in the upstream and downstream flows shall be generated from production and operation, as well as industrial investment by enterprises. Cash flows generated by financing activities shall not be pooled for now.

E-Business

The banking institutions in Shanghai are invited to directly provide cross-border RMB settlement services based on genuine e-Business transactions to institutions running cross-border e-Business that are incorporated in the Shanghai Free Trade Zone. The banks in Shanghai are asked to coordinate with pilot free trade zone payment service institutions (including branches) which hold "Internet Payment Business Permit", to provide cross-border RMB settlement services based on genuine e-Business transactions (including transactions by individuals and operating entities engaged in cross-border e-Business exports). The generic bank shall enter into agreements with payment service institutions in respect of processing cross-border e-Business RMB settlement and have to file the agreement with the Shanghai head office of People's Bank of China. The bank must verify the authenticity and compliance status of the underlying transaction of the cross-border RMB settlement business processed through payment service institutions. The cross-border RMB settlement business forwarded to banks by the payment service institutions should be equipped with genuine cross-border e-Business transaction background, in accordance with the relevant state laws and regulations. The payment service institutions perform verification duties concerning anti-money laundering, anti-terrorism financing, and keep corresponding transaction record, as well as coordinate with relevant state departments to undertake inspection.

Even if pre-approvals are no longer required, rules are very strict about reporting cross-border cash movements. All cross-border RMB business and receipt/payment information have to be reported and submitted to RMB cross-border receipt and payment information management system in an accurate, complete, and timely manner, and must be processed for corresponding international payments statistics reporting. When banks provide relevant cross-border RMB services to financial institutions and enterprises in the Shanghai Free Trade Zone, they shall specify in the service agreements that each party shall fulfill the obligations and duties concerning anti-money laundering, anti-terrorism financing, and anti-tax evasion as stipulated in relevant regulations; shall keep relevant transaction records and vouchers; and make sure the original appearance of transaction can be restored, as well as coordinate with the relevant departments to conduct inspections.

To facilitate individual conducting cross-border RMB settlements under current accounts, people working or practicing in the Shanghai Free Trade Zone will probably have to open individual or individual industrial and commercial households bank settlement account in order to make RMB cross-border payments and receipts according to the *Administrative Measures on Renminbi Bank Settlement Accounts* (Order of the People's Bank of China [2003] No. 5) and relevant regulations.

Concluding, reality says that in October 2014 the Chinese currency became the second most used in the world after US dollar, getting over the European currency. Cross-border yuan business has grown with an average of more than 200 % percent annually since China launched its pilot program to settle more cross-border trade in yuan in 2009, and nowadays approximately one quarter of all the total China's international payments have been carried out using renminbi. But until today the trading of the Chinese currency has been possible only in Hong Kong, Macau, Taiwan, and Singapore. Moreover, high-profile projects such as the formal introduction of intercompany loans from Chinese subsidiaries to the parent company, which is an essential condition for cross-border cash pooling, have been hampered by the absence of implementing guidelines, and as long as uncertainty remains, many corporate treasurers are shying away from devoting too much capacity to these projects.

Relaxation of Control on Interest Rates

"Marketing-oriented pricing mechanism will be cultivated, where financial institutions may discretionally determine the price in the Pilot Free Trade Zone, to cope with the development of real economy. The reform of interest rate liberalization will be promoted in a progressive way." Shanghai Municipal People's Government, decree n° 7, art. 21, September 29, 2013.

China thinks it is the right moment to cancel restrictions on the definition of interest rates. In the previous regulation, the central bank fixed a lower and an upper limit to avoid exceptional value of interest rates on the Chinese markets. Limits have been partly removed in order to pass to a system built on market-based interest rates. The People's Bank of China declares that a monitoring mechanism on the market pricing of interest rate for the funds of resident and nonresident FTAs in domestic and foreign currencies have still to be further improved. Consequently a complete openness to interest rates fluctuation actually has not been accepted by policy implementers. Financial institutions have been required to develop advanced procedures to set interest rates basing on supply and demand. Moreover, qualified financial institutions in the Shanghai Free Trade Zone will be added to the list of institutions which may be allowed to issue large-denomination negotiable certificate of deposit with priority.

Foreign Exchange Administration

> A foreign exchange control system in line with the development needs of the Pilot Free Trade Zone will be established to facilitate trade and investment. Shanghai Municipal People's Government, decree n° 7, art. 23, September 29, 2013.

Concerning the foreign exchange administration, the most evident change is the approaching of a registration system rather than an approval one in order to reduce the loss of time for companies to implement investments. The previous regulation discouraged mainly projects that required a fast move to action. These are the main news:

- The management of forex funds pool has been simplified in order to centralize forex management by headquarters of multinational companies.
- The approval from SAFE for outbound investments is no longer required for entities established in the Shanghai Free Trade Zone.
- Banks are responsible for foreign exchange registration for direct investments in the Shanghai Free Trade Zone, not SAFE anymore.
- In the Shanghai Free Trade Zone, cross-border leasing and other offshore credit business activities must be recorded, but not approved anymore.

The foreign exchange registration under direct investments and relevant changes will be delegated to banks, with subsequent supervision being strengthened. Based on the conditions that the authenticity of relevant transactions are ensured and complete information has been collected, foreign exchange funds under foreign direct investment may be converted to RMB according to the enterprise's wishes.

The foreign credits approval requirement on transaction basis for finance leasing companies engaged in foreign leasing is replaced by a registration management system. Subject to approvals, finance leasing companies in financial system (which are under ad- ministration of the Chinese Banking Regulatory Commission) and Chinese-funded finance leasing companies may be permitted to receive rental payments in foreign currencies for domestic finance leasing business. The procedures for prepayments in large finance leasing projects (i.e. aircrafts, ships) will be simplified.

Anti-money Laundering and Anti-terrorist Financing Measures

"Pursuant to relevant laws and regulations, financial institutions and specified non-financial institutions in the Pilot Zone should fulfill their obligations in respect of anti-money laundering, anti-terrorism financing, anti-tax evasion, etc., submit their balance sheets with relevant business information to the PBOC and other financial regulatory departments in a timely, accurate and complete manner, arrange the statistics and reporting of international receipts and payments, and co-operate with financial regulatory departments to closely monitor any irregularities in cross-border cash flows" The People's Bank of China, Opinions to Support China (Shanghai) Pilot Free Trade Zone in Financial Sector, art. 26, December 2, 2013.

The AML Circular is addressed mainly to financial institutions. Briefly it explains that transactions fulfilled by entities in the China (Shanghai) Pilot Free Trade Zone require today less information than in the rest of China. But at the same time banks have to develop an internal supervision department that can refuse to do business with a client that is valuated at high risk (because he didn't provide required information, because he comes from a jurisdiction with weak anti money laundering or anti terrorism system, or simply because of personal information that link him to money laundering or terrorism financing).

Moreover, the Shanghai Municipal Government controls non-financial institutions in the Shanghai Free Trade Zone through a comprehensive information monitoring platform, performs an annual assessment for such institutions, and adopt a categorized administration approach based on the assessment results.

A macro-prudential financial management system is going to be implemented in the Shanghai Free Trade Zone. The People's Bank of China may strengthen the monitoring of short-term speculative capital flows in the free trade zone and take temporary measures due to certain circumstances. The People's Bank of China has surely reinforced the communication and coordination with other financial regulatory departments in order to keep the risk under control and steadily progress the reform.

5.6 Taxation News and Customs

In order to establish an environment suitable for investment and trade with international standard, an innovative supervision model is necessary to facilitate smooth transactions for all goods and services under a highly transparent administrative system and to promote opening up in service sectors and further development in goods trade. Meanwhile, under anyway the premise of keeping a fair, consistent and standardized current tax system, policy makers are working on a functional development of customs supervision to avoid excessive procedures and on tax incentives for trading inside the Shanghai Pilot Free Trade Zone in order to encourage businesses installment.

Import-Export: Tax Incentives

Authorities decided to create some tax incentives and customs simplifications in order to encourage business in the Shanghai Free Trade Zone. Tax revisiting was one of the first topics discussed during the creation of the Shanghai Free Trade Zone, and Chinese government probably was looking to Hong Kong style when woke up with this ideas.

First of all, financial leasing companies registered or project companies set up by financial leasing companies with registration in the China (Shanghai) Pilot Free Trade Zone can enjoy the pilot policies of export tax refund for qualified financial leasing business. A domestic leasing company registered or its project companies with registration in the Pilot Free Trade Zone may enjoy reduced import VAT on an aircraft with empty weight no less than 25 tons, provided that such aircraft is to be leased to a domestic airline with approval from competent authorities. Import VAT and consumption taxes will be applicable in accordance with relevant laws and regulations, on the products manufactured or processed by a company within the China (Shanghai) Pilot Free Trade Zone but sold to the Mainland China outside of the China (Shanghai) Pilot Free Trade Zone. Enterprises will be provided with the option of calculating import duty according to the duty rates applicable to the finished goods or the imported parts. Currently, the imported machines, equipment, and other goods required by manufacturing enterprises as well as manufacturing service companies that are set up in the China (Shanghai) Pilot Free Trade Zone, may be exempt from import taxes, other than those imported by consumer services companies or those which cannot enjoy import taxes exemption as stipulated in laws and regulations.

Briefly, the followings are the tax cuts and exemptions that have already been implemented in the China (Shanghai) Pilot Free Trade Zone:

- *Tax exemption,* import taxes and custom duties for goods moving between the China (Shanghai) Pilot Free Trade Zone and overseas destination are exempt.
- *Tax rebate upon the entry,* domestic goods entering the Yangshan Free Trade Port Area, Shanghai Waigaoqiao Bonded Logistics Zone, and Shanghai Pudong Airport Free Trade Zone are considered like exportations and consequently exporters can have the tax rebate.
- *Exemption of business tax,* revenues from international shipping (and international shipping insurance), transporting and warehousing are exempt from taxation of business income for companies registered in the Yangshan Free Trade Port Area.
- *Tax rebate from home port,* cargos that start from general domestic ports bound for Yangshan Free trade Port Area or Shanghai Pudong Airport Free Trade Zone to be transferred to overseas destinations can ask for their tax rebated as soon as the goods leave the home ports.

Customs Supervision

When people think about a free trade zone, they immediately associate that with customs supervision. It is the most basic function of a free trade zone. The zone has introduced many simplified procedures in terms of customs declaration, clearance, and quarantine inspection. That benefits a lot for companies because the new procedures make customs supervision more efficient.

What is defined in the framework plan of the State Council concerning customs supervision hasn't already been fully implemented, because a new inspection and quarantine system shall be explored and established to further improve quality, guarantee security and promote development with thorough research and bold innovations, based on the new situation of opening up and new requirement for functional transformation of the government, as well as in line with the principle of "import quarantine and relaxed import/export inspection; easily import and export with strict quality and safety risk control." Innovations wants to be encouraged in quality supervision system, and a quality safety guarantee system, a technology-based supporting system as well as an efficient quality and technical supervision service system is being implemented focusing on international standard and practices. Moreover, authorities hope to get great results in the Shanghai Pilot Free Trade Zone in order to replicate and apply the new system elsewhere so as to give full play to quality supervision work for the construction of national economy and society.

The scope of the free trade zone is implementing a new system in which overseas shipments entering the Shanghai Free Trade Zone will not be subjected to customs clearance until a later stage. The current "within the territory of customs" policy applied for special customs supervision bonded area will be substituted with the "inside the territory while outside the customs" policy. It means that the whole process of supervision is simplified in the first line (between overseas and Shanghai Pilot FTZ) while controls are stricter in the second line (with non-PFTZ connections), as adopted by other international free trade ports. The whole customs administration process will be optimized while the administration of "frontier" (goods flow between overseas and the zone) and "second-tier" (goods flow between the zone and other domestic areas) will be coordinated by improvement on e-information network, entry and exit record lists cross check, accounting books management, physical verification, and risk analysis. There is the promotion of an inspection and quarantine model of "easily import and export, with strict quality and safety risk control." Organization departments are also studying how to strengthen the management of electronic customs books and facilitate the flow of goods moving between the China (Shanghai) Free Trade Zone and other domestic places in the charge of different Customs offices.

Enterprises within the China (Shanghai) Pilot Free Trade Zone in principle will be permitted to re-invest and conduct business outside of the zone without geographic restriction, unless specific procedures required under the applicable laws and regulations. The government is enhancing the connection of enterprises' operation information and the government's supervision system, through which effective supervision can be realized through risk monitoring, third-party management and security deposits etc. The government will, through the development and utilization of Shanghai's credit system, accelerate the formulation of policies and mechanism in respect of enterprises' business credit management and exclusive jurisdiction of business activities.

For goods entry and exit between the Shanghai Free Trade Zone and overseas, enterprises within the Shanghai Free Trade Zone may use the information on the import manifests to import the goods into the zone before completing the Customs filing formalities. For goods entry and exit between the Pilot Free Trade Zone and the other areas within China but outside the Pilot Free Trade Zone, the intelligent check point and e-information network management model will be adopted so as to have a sound supervision system for record listing cross check, accounting books management, and goods examination at the check point. Moreover, enterprises within the Pilot Free Trade Zone may apply for goods inspection and examination at their choice of time prior to the goods exiting the zone.

The China (Shanghai) Pilot Free Trade Zone is promoting supervision innovation pilot on new business models and is creating a supervision mode in line with the development of service trade, offshore trading, and new business model of trade. The Pilot Free Trade Zone will proactively develop international transit and distribution services and consequently Shanghai can become also a hub for goods simply in transfer, not with China as their final destination. The approach for "onetime declaration, onetime examination and onetime release" will be adopted. The goods circulation formalities within the Pilot Free Trade Zone will be streamlined. Goods circulation between enterprises within the Pilot Free Trade Zone will be accelerated according to a "consolidated declaration and independent transportation" approach.

Looking forward, because a simplification in the acceptance procedure, there is the necessity to implement an appropriated checking and controlling system, especially for some types of products. Consequently, remote monitoring, whole-process monitoring, and information techniques will be adopted in the pilot free trade zone to facilitate innovations in supervision model and an institution will be established to handle emergencies in respect of special equipment; and the security supervision on special equipment in the Shanghai Free Trade Zone such as boilers, elevators, pressure containers, pressure pipelines, and special motor vehicles for special use within the field (site) will be strengthened. The establishment of a quality supervision model has to be integrated in the free trade zone which mainly deals with self-declaration of quality by enterprises, sample inspection for circulation stage, risk monitoring, treatment of quality-related complaints, and emergent event regarding quality and safety. It is also being implemented a pre-alarming and prevention system for inspection and quarantine. The pre-alarming and prevention system was essential to be established for public health emergencies, animal or plant epidemics, as well as quality and safety of import and export goods; the system of disease vectors surveillance, nuclear, biological and chemical hazardous material monitoring, introduced species monitoring, and risk supervision of food safety have still to be improved to reach better efficiency. Finally to implement all these new systems is reasonable that before proceeding with the creation of the new China (Shanghai) Pilot Free Trade Zone, cooperation with local government as well as relevant authorities was obviously necessary to be improved to provide safety guarantee for the construction and development of the area.

For logistics companies whose activities are located in the Shanghai Free Trade Zone, operational efficiency will be increased thanks to simplified customs, immigration and quarantine procedures, and port management. With a reduction of warehousing and logistics costs, these companies will be able to offer better logistics solution to their clients. It is an invitation for international traders to establish their logistics hub and distribution center in the Shanghai Free Trade Zone.

Briefly here there is a summary of the innovation already implemented about port supervision:

- *Customs,* companies located in the Shanghai Free Trade Zone can make customs declaration for the imported goods collectively. A simpler customs clearance procedure has been adopted for goods that must be sent to waterways, airways, and railroads.
- *Inspection and quarantine,* commodities are preset and some of them can be pre-controlled when they are on the entry record to further shorten the time and reduce the procedures in supervision.
- *Foreign currency,* there isn't any foreign exchange cancellation and companies can fully keep foreign exchange values.

The Pilot Free Trade Zone is still working on formulating and issuing a batch of regional and local standards in line with international standards and practices. Enterprises in the Shanghai Free Trade Zone participate in activities of setting international standards and proactively application of such standards; enterprises in the free trade zone are encouraged to carry out alliance standard innovation pilot.

Corporate Income Tax
During the elaboration of innovations to bring to the new China (Shanghai) Pilot Free Trade Zone, there were rumors concerning a possible reduction of the corporate income tax for entities situated in the Shanghai Free Trade Zone, as what happened previously in Qianhai and Hengqin. On November 15, 2013, the China's Ministry of Finance and the State Administration of Taxation jointly issued the "Circular on Corporate Income Tax Policies for Outbound Investment with Non-monetary Assets and Other Asset Restructuring Transactions by Enterprises in the China (Shanghai) Free Trade Zone," in order to clarify which are the real policies that authorities intend to implement about this topic. The circular doesn't mention any initiative about cutting down the corporate income tax rate, but it explains that there is the possibility for companies to defer the CIT payment for the amount regarding the following activities:

- Establishing a company through capital contributions with non-monetary assets
- Capital contributions with non-monetary assets
- Equity acquisition (an enterprise acquires the equities of another enterprise so as to take control over the latter)
- Asset acquisition (an enterprise purchases the substantive operating assets of another enterprise).

The circular confirms that regarding to the asset appreciation arising from the mentioned type of investments, companies established in the Shanghai Free Trade Zone may pay corporate income tax for the gains from the transfer of non-monetary assets by installment within 5 years. To take advantage of the deferral it is necessary a registration of the outbound investment formalities providing the required documentation to the competent tax authorities within 30 days.

As a conclusion the reduction of the corporate income tax rate persist to be only a rumor and anyway it will be probably a main theme also in the next years.

Encouraging Private Equity
Some policy makers are suggesting to introduce a preferential tax treatment for private equity funds in the China (Shanghai) Pilot Free Trade Zone in order to help them to participate in the global competition with foreign funds. Their main problem is that domestic private equity funds raised on the mainland are subject to corporate income taxes at home and abroad even if they are targeting foreign markets. The proposal is considering registered private equity funds in the Shanghai Free Trade Zone as if they were "offshore funds" with a special tax treatment. The problem is that Shanghai has to convince the national tax authorities, which are not so willing to create this discrepancy between funds in and out the area.

5.7 Investment Liberalization Through the Negative List Approach

Before the creation of the Shanghai Pilot Free Trade Zone, Chinese authorities released a detailed "Negative List" where they established all the industries in which foreign entities cannot invest and do business, even if an establishment of a company in the new Shanghai Free Trade Zone.

The Negative List was officially launched on September 29, 2013, and first critics were that it seemed just a replacement of the already existing Foreign Investment Industrial Guidance Catalog, with also some additional restrictions. Then, the Negative List was subsequently newly revised at the beginning of 2014 reducing the number of restrictions.

For the Chinese government, the "Negative Lists" is a new approach that aims to simplify the access into the Chinese market for foreign enterprises: if nothing is mentioned in the "Negative List," it means that a foreign company has the same rights and requirements of a domestic company regarding that sector. Because this principle, the policy makers elaborated the list specifying detailed prohibitions and requirements. In fact there isn't a strict division between the sectors in which strangers can invest or not: in some industries (the ones that the Chinese government considers absolutely strategic) foreigners absolutely cannot completely access, in other ones they can access only through joint ventures with local partner, sometimes there are limitations concerning the percentage of equity that can be held by foreign entities, and finally in some sectors it is absolutely allowed by the presence of wholly foreign-owned enterprises (WFOE).

Negative list is a more open and efficient management method for its abandoning the redundancy approval processes and eliminating the risk of scrapped prophases cost and other misuse issues. To replenish, file system has been created to strengthen post-registration supervision and serves the foreign investment projects out of the negative list.

Anyway the following activities in the Pilot Free Trade Zone shall comply with relevant regulations: mergers and acquisitions by foreign investors, strategic investments in listed companies by foreign investors, foreign investors' using equity interest in domestic enterprises for capital contribution purpose; if a national security or anti-monopoly investigation is involved, relevant regulations shall be applied.

Shanghai Municipal People's Government is elaborating the new project filing procedures. The approving requirement on foreign investment contracts and Articles of Association is replaced by a filing procedure with Shanghai Municipal People's Government, with the same follow up procedures finished according to the current laws and regulations. An optimization of the overall system is however required. National security review system must be improved, and pilot national security review on foreign investment projects will be trialed in the China (Shanghai) Pilot Free Trade Zone to create a safe and efficient open economic system.

The Negative List also applies to investments in the Pilot Free Trade Zone by investors from the Hong Kong Special Administrative Region, the Macao Special

Administrative Region and Taiwan. Regulation specifies that if more favorable treatment (if applicable in the Pilot Free Trade Zone) is available for qualified investors according to the *Mainland and Hong Kong/Macau Closer Economic Partnership Agreement* and their supplements, the *Cross-Straits Economic Cooperation Framework Agreement* and the follow-up *Cross-Straits Agreement on Trade in Services,* and other free trade agreements signed by China, such treatment shall prevail over the Negative List.

Finally, it must be underscore that, apart from the special administrative measures listed in the Negative List, foreign investors are prohibited (or restricted) from investment in industries which are prohibited (or restricted) by China, or by international agreements/treaties China concluded with other countries/jurisdictions. Foreign investors are also prohibited from investment in projects which would compromise China's national or social security, and from business operations which would compromise the public interest.

It is evident that China still persists to not be really inclined to open completely its market to international investors, and moreover the Negative List approach is valid only in the Shanghai Pilot Free Trade Zone. As every change implemented in the free trade zone, Chinese authorities are considering all these new innovations in Shanghai as an experiment that will be evaluated in the long term. If good results for the Chinese economy will arise in the next years, probably the experience of the China (Shanghai) Pilot Free Trade Zone will be translated gradually to the rest of China. Anyway it will be surely a very long process to see the latest changes in the FTZ applied in Mainland China.

Then, apart restrictions defined by the Negative List, there is a particular filing procedure for outbound investments. An outbound investment is prohibited if it:

- Endangers Chinese sovereignty, security and public interest, or violates Chinese laws and regulations
- Impairs the relations between China and relevant countries/regions
- Potentially violates the international treaties entered by China
- Involves technologies or goods the export of which are prohibited by China.

Outbound investment projects in sensitive countries/regions or sectors must still be subject to the preliminary review by the Shanghai Development and Reform Commission, and final approval by the National Development and Reform Commission or the State Council, regardless of the amount of investment. Sensitive countries/regions include countries that do not have a diplomatic relation with China or suffer from international sanctions, countries/regions where wars or upheavals are taking place, and other sensitive countries/regions designated by the National Development and Reform Commission. Sensitive sectors include industries in respect of basic telecommunication services, development and utilization of cross-border water resources, large scale land development, electricity transmission grids and news media, and other sensitive sectors designated by the National Development and Reform Commission.

After the necessary explanation of the concept of Negative List and the change from an approval based system to a filing one, we can focus on the typology of sectors that China is opening up to foreigners investors in the new China (Shanghai) Pilot Free Trade Zone, in particular we will see that the openness of China is mainly in the service industry.

Taking China's special traits of its composition of GDP into consideration, it would be more challenging for China to fulfill its promises on the service trade part than trading of commodities. Trade in service has always been distinct from goods because of its nonphysical feature. A misunderstanding of what service had been defined as a flow that could not be storable and therefore required the proximity of both sides of dealing for exchange (Hill, 1977) had resulted into a biased view that services were untradeable, consequently becoming the constraints of services. Nevertheless, trade in services was an essential indicator in the economic landscape (Francois and Hoekman, 2010), whose increasing status was driven by both demand factors and striking evolution in the trade and production patterns (Clark 1940, Baumol 1967 and Panagariya, 1988). Put it another way, Melvin (1989) claimed that services were inputs into productivities for its promoting transactions through space-saving and time-saving such as transportation, telecommunications, and financial services. Moreover, services also are closely intertwined with manufacturing activities and sometimes are the direct inputs like labor. To prove that, Triplett and Bosworth (2004) once calculated and concluded that increasing on productivity in distribution and financial services fueled the post-1995 overall expansion in U.S. productivity. Once realizing the significance meaning of trading in services, Chinese economic policy makers devoted themselves into accelerating the process of economic reform by shifting to the tertiary industry from the second industry. To some extent, the agreement on trade in services (GATS) became a guideline for China to optimize her services market. However, all the promises of removing specific entry barriers that were expected to be accomplished at the end of 2007 could be a challenging task for China under the temporal economic situation. Using the U.S. as a benchmark, the employment percentage of the tertiary industry accounted for more than 70 % in the late 1990s while that of China amounted for only 26.9 % and people who were occupied in the primary industry still dominated the labor force with a proportion of 50 % (Table 1). Main reason of the unbalanced development of the industrial structure was a preferential policy regime on the second industry, and as Mayes and Wang (2003) identified, there were non-tariff barriers in Chinese agriculture trade policies. Other askew structures existing in the openness level of different provinces were due to a strong support of the eastern coast cities from the central government.

The resolution to construct Shanghai into a metropolis of trading is reflected in breaking the old trading pattern and escalating international transportation services provided in Shanghai Pilot Free Trade Zone. For the former, core competency of global trading would be rebuilt in technology, brand and services etc. to attract headquarter economy, while the latter would be achieved by adequately taking advantages of Shanghai port, upgrading international shipping services and encouraging shipping financial services simultaneously (Lee et al. 2013). For example, tightly controlled by Chinese government, telecommunication sector is up to the present highly dominated by state-owned companies and foreign capital is bounded for 50 % ownership. Local authority only claims that they do not eliminate the role of wholly foreign-owned telecom companies and the domestic market would be more opening in the near future. By contrast, shipping sector is evolving based on the GATS. Chinese-funded companies are allowed to hold shares of ship hanging five-starred red flag and to carry on cabotage business among domestic maritime ports. Noting the business is only available to domestic enterprises, compared with the reform benefit for foreign investors is the permission to establish foreign-owned shipping management corporations. But the policies on shipping finance have been considered profoundly. Financing, insurance, fund settlement, and shipping price derivatives are required to be launched to coordinate with an incubating financial center and an international leading shipping center. Outsourcing is another effective way to discard laggard trading pattern for a reduction of distraction from peripheral activities. As discussed earlier, services are nonphysical and therefore do not have high standard on spatial sources. Besides, Chinese government has been intended to step forward in trade in services to optimize economic structure, which could be delivered by outsourcing because it is the medium of international services transactions (Hertel et al. 2001). Similarly, offshore services provided also serves the mission of building Shanghai into an international metropolis.

Other ordinances associated with the investment in Shanghai Free Trade Zone that consolidate the liberalization in services sector including permission of foreign sole-capital medical institutions' registrations, repeal the 2-year restriction on foreign travel agencies which is the item on the GATS. As for the lawsuit services, foreign law firms are allowed to set up their businesses in China by their Chinese offices. Despite that China once committed to abolish a series of restrictions that imposed on foreign law firms, to date, foreign law firms outside Shanghai Free Trade Zone could only set up representative offices which are not allowed to conduct profitable businesses. Unlike the deregulation in other sectors, foreign investors have to submit applications to Shanghai competent department of culture for running commercial entertainment venues within the Shanghai Free Trade Zone. Finally, improving legal system to guarantee the reform system is also contained in the scheme.

Concluding, we briefly summarize the main innovation for every kind of service in Pilot Shanghai Free Trade Zone.

Banking
Foreign financial entities will be permitted to set up foreign own banks; qualified private capital and financial institutions will be allowed to create joint venture banks; domestic banks can look overseas for seeking offshore business.

Health and Medical Insurance
Only on a pilot basis, investments in the area by foreign health and medical insurance institutions will be permitted.

Financial Leasing
The minimum threshold requirement of registration capital and expanding business scope has been removed.

Ocean Shipping
Limitations on foreign participation in international shipping business are relaxed: foreign investors are allowed to set up Sino-foreign equity joint ventures and Sino-foreign cooperative joint ventures to operate international shipping business with more than 49 % participation. The foreign investment in entities which may have their ships registered in China will not be limited to 50 %, and the ship registration will proceed in accordance with relevant laws and regulations and other relevant rules.

International Ship Management
Foreign investors will be allowed to set up wholly foreign-owned enterprises in the China (Shanghai) Pilot Free Trade Zone to engage in international ship management business.

Telecommunication
Foreign investment companies will be allowed to do engage in certain telecommunication services.

Law Firms
There is the intent to increase the collaboration between foreign and local law firms.

Credit Investigations
Foreign investments are permitted.

Travel Agency
Expansion of the business scope of the foreign equity joint venture travel agencies.

Engineering Design
Relaxation of application criteria.

Investment Management
The creation of joint-stock foreign investment companies is permitted.

Headhunting Service
The limit of equity ratio of foreign investors will be increased up to 70 %; otherwise also equity wholly owned by investors from Hong Kong or Macau is permitted; the minimum threshold requirement of registered capital will be reduced.

Entertainment
Wholly foreign-owned enterprises are permitted to enter in this business. In particular, foreign invested enterprises are allowed to engage in the production and sales of gaming consoles in the China (Shanghai) Pilot Free Trade Zone which may be sold to mainland market after passing the content examination by the competent culture authorities.

Artists Agency
Restrictions about the equity ratio between foreign and domestic funds will be removed; wholly foreign-owned enterprises are allowed to engage this sector.

Where a business entity of performance or entertainment artist agency places in the form of an equity joint venture, a cooperative joint venture, or a wholly foreign invested company hold commercial performances in a place managed by the entity, an application shall be filed to Shanghai culture authorities. For commercial performances with the participation of mainland cultural and art performance organizations as well as mainland actors and actresses, the authorities shall make decisions within 3 days from the date of accepting the application.

Education and Training Employment
Sino-foreign cooperative joint ventures (joint venture agreement between a Chinese and foreign company that gives to the foreign company much more flexibility than a Sino-foreign equity joint venture) can enter in this business.

Medical Services
There is the allowance for establishing wholly foreign-owned enterprises medical institutions.

Going back to the Negative List, it is divided in 16 sections linked to the following sectors:

- Agriculture, forest, husbandry, and fishery
- Mining
- Manufacturing
- Electricity, heating, gas and water production and supply
- Construction
- Wholesale and retail
- Transport, warehouse, and postal service
- Information transmission, software and IT service
- Financial services
- Real estate
- Leasing and business service
- Scientific research and technology service
- Management of water conservancy, environment and public facilities
- Education
- Health and social activities
- Culture, sports, and entertainment

The first version of the Negative List was established on September 29, 2013, and as mentioned previously it was of some disappointment to many foreign investors, since it included virtually all of the restrictions and prohibitions on foreign investment set out in various Chinese regulations and policy documents, like the current *Foreign Investment Industrial Guidance Catalogue* which governs foreign investments nationwide. But hope for more change was kept alive by promises that the restrictions and prohibitions would be reduced in subsequent editions of the negative list that would be periodically issued by the Shanghai Municipal Government.

The first of these subsequent editions of the negative list, the *Special Administrative Measures on Foreign Investment Access into the China (Shanghai) Pilot Free Trade Zone*, was issued by the Shanghai Municipal Government on June 30, 2014 (2014 Negative List). With a total of 139 listed items, it is about 27 % shorter than the 2013 Negative List, although it bears noting that many of the reductions appear to result from reclassification and elimination of items which were duplicated on the 2013 Negative List.

The reductions include removal of restrictions from 14 items which were on the 2013 Negative List. Almost half of them relate to manufacturing and processing. The others relate to professional services, transportation, entertainment, trading, and real estate.

In the areas of manufacturing and processing, removal of restrictions will now, in principle, allow foreign investors in the Shanghai Free Trade Zone to engage in cotton seed processing, pulp and paper production, the manufacture of all types of ordinary level bearings and parts (steel balls and retainers), and the production of more than 20 pharmaceuticals (including penicillin G, vitamin B1, vitamin B2, vitamin C, vitamin E, and multiplex vitamins). However, it is not clear whether some of these changes will be meaningful, since there is very little room for new manufacturing or processing activities in the Shanghai Free Trade Zone and since these sorts of manufacturing and processing activities do not seem to be really encouraged by the Shanghai Free Trade Zone authorities.

The changes in the 2014 Negative List which relate to professional services, transportation, entertainment, trading, and real estate may be more significant. They include the following:

- Professional Technology Services: foreign investment is now allowed for the establishment of imported and exported goods certification companies, and the qualification criteria for foreign certification institutions are now removed.
- Transportation Services: restrictions on foreign investment in international cargo handling, international marine shipping container station, and yard operation or air transportation agency (permitting only Sino-foreign equity or cooperative joint ventures) have been removed.
- Entertainment: foreign investment is now permitted for the establishment of Internet cafes.
- Trading: foreign investment is now allowed in trading companies which engage in vegetable oil and sugar wholesale, retail, and distribution.
- Automotive Electronics R&D: restrictions on foreign investment in the research and development of automotive electronics (permitting only Sino-foreign equity joint ventures) have been removed.
- Real Estate: foreign investment in project companies is now allowed in the secondary property market and for investments in high-end hotels, office buildings, and international exhibition centers.

The 2014 Negative List does not indicate whether foreign-invested companies engaged in the activities mentioned above will be able to do business or operate branch offices outside the Shanghai Free Trade Zone.

It bears noting that although some of the restrictions on foreign investment in banks, financial firms, trust firms, and currency brokers appearing in the 2013 Negative List have been removed from the 2014 Negative List, it is likely that they will remain in effect, since a statement was added to the 2014 Negative List to the effect that investments in banking-style institutions will be subject to existing regulations.

Also, although some restrictions on the minimum investment threshold and the maximum operation period of foreign-invested medical institutions have been removed from the 2014 Negative List, these restrictions will likely remain in effect since they now appear in the *Tentative Measures for the Administration of Wholly Foreign-Owned Medical Institutions in the Shanghai FTZ*, promulgated on November 13, 2013.

Finally, although prohibitions on gambling have been removed from the 2014 Negative List, it would be imprudent to assume that foreign investment is now permitted in these activities, since they are prohibited nationwide by Chinese criminal laws and regulations.

In conclusion, it appears to us that, although the 2014 Negative List takes a few modest steps toward the reduction or elimination of restrictions on foreign investments in the areas of professional services, entertainment, trading, and real estate, it leaves many existing restrictions on foreign investment untouched. It's possible that other new version of the Negative List will be elaborated in order to reduce restrictions by the time.

Here below the complete latest version of the Negative List released on July 1, 2014, by the Shanghai Municipal People's Government, from an unofficial translation operated by Deloitte.

A – Agriculture, forest, husbandry, and fishery	
A01 – Agriculture, A02 – Forest, A03 – Husbandry, A04 – Fishery, A05 – Agriculture, forest, husbandry, and fishery services	
1	Planting/breeding for traditional Chinese medicine (equity or cooperative joint ventures only)
2	Breeding of new crops, seeds production (restricted, equity controlled by Chinese party)
3	For investing in crops seeds, equity or cooperative joint ventures only, with minimum registered capital of US$ 0.5 million; seeds of grain, cotton, and oil crops enterprises (Chinese participation over 50 %; minimum registered capital of US$ 2 million)
4	Processing of logs derived from rare species of woods (restricted, equity, or cooperative joint ventures only)
5	R&D, breeding, cultivation of rare or peculiar species, and production of relevant propagation materials including superior genes in crops, husbandry and aquatic sectors; R&D in genetically modified organisms (GMO) and production of genetically modified crop seeds, animal, and aquatic breeds (prohibited)
6	Fishing of aquatic products of sea areas and inland waters within China (prohibited)

B – Mining	
B06 – Coal exploitation and cleaning	
7	Prospection and exploitation of special and rare type of coal resources (restricted, equity controlled by Chinese party)
B07 – Oil and natural gas exploitation	
8	Coal bed gas exploration and exploitation, and comprehensive utilization of mine gas (equity or cooperative joint ventures only)

(continued)

B – Mining	
9	Junior exploration and exploitation of oil and natural gas (equity or cooperative joint ventures only)
10	Exploitation of low permeability oil and gas reservoirs (fields) (equity or cooperation joint ventures only)
11	Exploration and exploitation of unconventional oil resources such as oil shale, oil sands, heavy crude oil, and extra-heavy crude oil (equity or cooperative joint ventures only)
12	Exploration and exploitation of unconventional natural gas resources such as shale gas and submarine natural gas (equity or cooperative joint ventures only)
B08 – Ferrous metal mining	
13	Pyrites exploitation and ore dressing/beneficiating operations; and ludwigite exploitation (restricted)
B09 – Non-ferrous metal mining	
14	Szaibelyite exploitation; lithium exploitation and ore dressing/beneficiating operations; exploration and exploitation of noble metals (gold, silver and platinum group) (restricted)
15	Exploration and exploitation of tungsten, molybdenum, tin, and antimony; exploration, exploitation, and ore dressing/bene-ficiating operations of rare earth, radioactive minerals (prohibited)
B10 – Non-metals mining	
16	Exploration and exploitation of barites (restricted, equity, or cooperative joint ventures only)
17	Exploration and exploitation of important non-metal ores such as diamond, high-aluminum fireclay, wollastonite, graphite; phosphorite exploitation and ore dressing/beneficiating operations; refinery of salt-lake brine resources; and exploitation of celestite (restricted)
18	Exploitation of marine manganese nodules and sea sands (restricted, equity controlled by Chinese party)
19	Exploration and exploitation of fluorite (prohibited)
B11 – Ancillary mining activities	
20	Processing of ludwigite ores (restricted)

C- Manufacturing	
C13 – Farm and sideline food processing	
21	Processing of rice and flour (restricted)
22	Processing of edible oils such as soy oil, rapeseed oil, peanut oil, cottonseed oil, camellia oil, sunflower oil, palm oil (restricted, equity controlled by Chinese party)
23	Production of biological liquid fuels (ethanol fuel, bio-diesel) (restricted, equity controlled by Chinese party)
24	Corns deep-processing (restricted)
C15 – Alcohol, drinks, and refined tea manufacturing	
25	Production of yellow rice wine ("huangjiu"), famous and high-quality Chinese spirits (restricted, equity controlled by Chinese party)
26	Processing and production of green tea with Chinese traditional handicraft (equity controlled by Chinese party only); processing and production of special tea (including white tea, yellow tea, oolong tea, dark tea, pressed tea etc.) (prohibited)

(continued)

C- Manufacturing	
C16 – Tobacco products manufacturing	
27	Processing and production of leaf tobacco (i.e. threshing and redrying) (restricted)
28	Processing of cellulose diacetate or tow (equity or cooperative joint ventures only)
C23 – Printing and reproduction of recorded media	
29	Printing of publications (restricted, equity controlled by Chinese party with minimum registered capital of RMB 10 million)
30	Read-only CD reproduction (equity or cooperative joint ventures only, and equity controlled or dominated by Chinese party)
C24 – Culture and education, arts and crafts, sport and entertainment products manufacturing	
31	Ivory carving, tiger bone processing, production of bodiless lacquer ware, enamelwork, Chinese art paper and ink ingot (prohibited)
C25 – Oil processing, coking, and nuclear fuel processing	
32	Smelting and processing of radioactive minerals (prohibited)
C26 – Chemical raw material and chemical products manufacturing	
33	Production of polyvinyl chloride (through acetylene method only), ethene with limited capacity and post-processing products, calcined soda, caustic soda, sulfuric acid, nitric acid, potassium carbonate, and inorganic salt (restricted)
34	Production of butadiene rubber (excluding high cisbutadiene rubber), emulsion polymerized styrene butadiene rubber and thermoplastic styrene-butadiene-styrene rubber (restricted)
35	Production of precursor chemicals (ephedrine, 3,4-methylenedioxyphenyl-2-propanone, phenylacetic acid, 1-phenyl-2-propanone, piperonal, safrole, isosafrole, and acetic anhydride), hydrogen fluoride and other low-end chlorofluorocarbon or chlorofluoro-compounds, and photosensitive materials (restricted)
36	Arms and ammunition manufacturing (prohibited)
C27 – Pharmaceutical manufacturing	
37	Production of narcotic drugs and active pharmaceutical ingredients for first class of psychotropic drugs (restricted, equity controlled by Chinese party)
38	Processing of materials for traditional Chinese medicines as listed in the *Regulations on Protection of Wild Medical Resources* and the *Catalogue of Rare and Endangered Chinese Plants* (prohibited)
39	Processing of traditional Chinese medicines (through steaming, frying, moxibustion, calcination, etc.); and production of traditional Chinese medicine patent drugs with secret formulas (prohibited)
40	Production of blood products and vaccines which fall inside the scope of the national immunization plan (restricted)
C32 – Non-ferrous metal smelting and rolling processing	
41	Rare earth metal smelting and separation (restricted, equity, or cooperative joint ventures only)
C34 – General equipment manufacturing	
42	Production of wheeled or crawler cranes (400 tons below) (restricted, equity, or cooperative joint ventures only)
C35 – Specialty equipment manufacturing	
43	Design of deep water (more than 3,000 m) marine engineering equipment (equity or cooperative joint ventures only)

(continued)

C- Manufacturing	
44	Manufacturing of bulldozers (≤320 horsepowers), hydraulic excavators (≥15 tons; ≤ 30 tons), wheeled loaders (≥3 tons; ≤ 6 tons), graders (≤220 horsepowers), rollers, forklifts, electric drive off-highway self-dumping trucks (≤135 tons), hydraulic mechanical transmission and off-highway self- dumping trucks (≤60 tons), asphalt concrete mixing and paving equipment and aerial work machinery, garden machinery and equipment, and concrete machinery (pump, mixer vehicle, mixing station, pump vehicle) (restricted)
45	Manufacturing of large-scale coal chemical equipment (equity or cooperative joint ventures only)
46	Manufacturing of air traffic control system equipment (equity or cooperative joint ventures only)
C36 Automobile Manufacturing	
47	Manufacturing of automobiles, special purpose motor vehicles, and agricultural transportation trucks (equity joint ventures only, with Chinese participation reaching 50 %).
	For a listed company as a manufacturer of automobiles, special purpose motor vehicles and agricultural transportation trucks, if its shares were sold by a corporate shareholder, the company must still be controlled by one of its Chinese corporate shareholders and whose shareholding must exceed the total shareholdings by foreign corporate shareholders.
	One foreign investor may establish up to two equity joint ventures to manufacture automobiles in the same category (note: two categories – passenger vehicle and commercial vehicle), but this restriction may not apply to the case of acquiring other domestic automobile manufacturing companies together with its Chinese partners.
48	Manufacturing, R&D of embedded electronic integrated system (equity or cooperative joint ventures only)
49	Manufacturing of energy-type power cells of clean energy vehicles (energy density ≥ 110 Wh/kg and cycle life ≥ 2,000 times) (foreign participation within 50 %)
C37- Rail, vessel, aviation, and other transportation equipment manufacturing	
50	Rail transportation equipment (equity or cooperative joint ventures only):
	R&D, design and manufacturing of trains used in high-speed railway, passenger dedicated railway line, intercity railway, main railway line and urban rail transportation and their key components (traction drive system, control system and braking system)
	R&D, design and manufacturing of passenger service facilities and equipment used in urban rail transportation, as well as R&D and design work relating to information systems used in high-speed railway, passenger dedicated railway line, inter-city railway, and urban rail transportation
	R&D, design and manufacturing of communications and signal systems of rail transportation, R&D of rail noise, and vibration control technology; manufacturing of safety monitoring equipment for railway transportation
51	Design of low- and medium-speed diesel engines for vessels and their components and manufacturing of yachts (equity or cooperative joint ventures only)
52	Manufacturing of low- and medium-speed diesel engines and crankshafts for vessels (equity controlled by Chinese party)
53	Manufacturing of machinery for ship cabins (comparatively equity controlled by Chinese party)
54	Design, manufacturing and repair of vessels (sub-block included) (restricted, equity controlled by Chinese party) Manufacturing and repair of marine engineering equipment (module included) (equity controlled by Chinese party)

(continued)

C- Manufacturing	
55	Design, manufacturing, and repair of civil aircraft for general aviation purpose (equity or cooperative joint ventures only)
56	Design, manufacturing, and repair of aero-engines and aviation auxiliary power systems (equity or cooperative joint ventures only);
	Design and manufacturing of airborne equipment for civil aviation (equity or cooperative joint ventures only)
57	Design and manufacturing of civil helicopters (<3 tons) (equity or cooperative joint ventures only); design and manufacturing of civil helicopters (≥3 tons) (equity controlled by Chinese party)
58	Design, manufacturing, and repair of civil aircrafts for trunk line and feeder line (equity controlled by Chinese party)
59	Manufacturing of ground effect and water surface effect aircrafts as well as design and manufacturing of unmanned aerial vehicle and aerostat (equity controlled by Chinese party)
60	Manufacturing of high engine displacement motorcycles (displacement>250 ml) (Chinese participation reaching 50 % in the equity joint venture)
	For a listed company as a manufacturer of high engine displacement motorcycles (displacement > 250 ml), if its shares were sold by a corporate shareholder, the company must still be controlled by one of its Chinese corporate shareholders and whose shareholding must exceed the total shareholdings by foreign corporate shareholders
	One foreign investor may establish up to two equity joint ventures to manufacture motorcycles, but this restriction may not apply to the case of acquiring other domestic automobile manufacturing companies together with its Chinese partners.
C38 – Electrical machinery and materials manufacturing	
61	Manufacturing of key supporting machineries used in 1 million KW supercritical thermal power units (equity or cooperative joint ventures only): safety valves, control valves
62	Manufacturing of electric transmission and transformation equipment (equity or cooperative joint ventures only): amorphous metal transformers, 500+ KV high voltage switch operating mechanisms, arc-control devices, large disc insulators (1000 KV+, 50 Ka+), outlet devices used in transformer of 500 KV+, casing pipes (AC 500, 750, 1000 KV, all type of DC), voltage regulation switches (AC500, 750, 1000 KV on-load and no-load voltage switch), air core smoothing reactors used in AC power transmission, ±800 KV converter valves used in AC power transmission (water cooling equipment, DC field equipment)
63	Manufacturing of large pumped-storage aggregate with rated power of 350 MW and above (equity or cooperative joint ventures only): accessory equipment like pump turbines and governors, large variable speed reversible pump turbine aggregates, generator-motors, and excitation and starter gear
64	Manufacturing of vented lead-acid batteries (i.e. direct acid mist discharge), silver oxide batteries with mercury button, alkaline zinc-manganese batteries with mercury button, paste zinc-manganese battery, and Cd-Ni battery (prohibited)
C39 – Computers, communications, and other electronics manufacturing	
65	Design and manufacturing of commercial satellites; manufacturing of commercial satellite payloads (equity controlled by Chinese party)
66	Manufacturing of ground satellite TV broadcasting receiving facility and key parts (restricted)

D – Electricity, heating, gas and water production and supply	
D44 – Electricity and heating production and supply	
67	Construction and operation of nuclear power stations (equity controlled by Chinese party)
68	Construction and operation of power grid (restricted, equity controlled by Chinese party), and heat-supply, gas-supply, water-supply, and drainage pipe network in cities with populations greater than 500,000 (restricted, equity controlled by Chinese party)

E – Construction	
E48 – Civil engineering construction	
69	Construction and operation of feeder railways with relevant bridges, tunnels, ferry facilities, and station facilities (equity or cooperative joint ventures only)
70	Construction and operation of railway networks (equity controlled by Chinese party)
71	Comprehensive maintenance of infrastructure of high-speed railways, passenger dedicated railway lines and inter-city railway (equity controlled by Chinese party)
72	Construction and operation of city subways and light railways (equity controlled by Chinese party)

F – Wholesale & retail	
F51 – Wholesale, F52- Retail	
73	Purchase of grain (restricted), food enterprises which are responsible for operation and management of grain reserves and supplying military food (controlled by the State), wholesale of grain and cotton (restricted), construction and operation of large wholesale markets of agricultural products (restricted)
74	Wholesale, retail, and distribution of tobacco (restricted)
75	Qualified service suppliers from Hong Kong and Macao are permitted to invest in the business of distribution of audio and video products (including post-movie products) in the form of wholly owned enterprise, equity, or cooperative joint venture
	Distribution of audio and video products (excluding movies) (restricted for non-Hong Kong/Macao investors, co- operative joint ventures only)
76	Wholesale and distribution of pesticide, agricultural film, bonded oil (restricted)
77	Auction of cultural relics and cultural relic shops (prohibited)
78	Retail and distribution of pesticide, agricultural film (restricted; chain stores with more than 30 branches and selling goods of different kinds and brands from multiple vendors – equity controlled by Chinese party)
79	Chain stores retailing books, newspapers and periodicals
	Qualified Hong Kong/Macao service suppliers: participation rate of a single investor must be within 65 %;
	Investors from other jurisdictions: no controlling interest is permitted if the number of chain stores is more than 30
80	Establishment and operation of gasoline stations (restricted; chain stations with more than 30 branches and selling processed oils of different kinds and brands from multiple vendors – equity controlled by Chinese party)
81	Direct selling (restricted; investors with experiences in oversea direct selling of more than 3 years; minimum paid-in capital of RMB 80 million)
	Online retailing (excluding online retailing of general goods) (restricted)

G – Transport, warehouse, and postal service	
G53 – Railway transport	
82	Investment in railway passenger transport companies (restricted, equity controlled by Chinese party)
G54 – Road transport	
83	Investment in highway passenger transport companies (restricted; equity joint ventures only), passenger transport shifts or lines, tourist transport, and passenger transport chartering (foreign participation within 49 %; one of major investors engaged in the business of road passenger transport in China for more than 5 years); operation of road passenger transport station (yard) (equity joint ventures with foreign participation within 49 %, or cooperative joint ventures)
84	Investment in motor transport companies engaged in cross-border road transport business (restricted)
G55 – Water transport	
85	Investment in domestic waterway transport business (restricted, equity controlled by Chinese party); international maritime transport, whether scheduled or not (equity or cooperative joint ventures only)
86	Shipping agency (restricted, equity controlled by Chinese party – except for public international shipping agency where foreign participation may be up to 51 %)
87	Cargo tally (restricted, equity, or cooperative joint ventures only)
G56 – Air transport	
88	Investment in air transport (equity controlled by Chinese party, the legal representative must be Chinese national, and operation period must be within 30 years), for public air transport, a single foreign investor's participation (including that of its related parties) must be within 25 %
89	Investment in general aviation companies in the sectors of farming, forestry, and fishing industry (equity or cooperative joint ventures only, the legal representative must be Chinese national, and operation period must be within 30 years)
90	Investment in general aviation enterprises in the sectors of business flight, sightseeing flight (equity controlled by Chinese party), investment in general aviation enterprises for aviation photography, mining exploration and industry purposes (restricted, equity controlled by Chinese party), the legal representative must be Chinese national, and operation period must be within 30 years
91	Qualified service suppliers from Hong Kong and Macao are permitted to provide, in the form of wholly owned enterprises, seven air transport ground services, namely, agency services, assembling and disassembling control services, communication and departure control system services, ULD management services, passenger and luggage services, commodity and airmail services, apron services and aircraft services
	Investing in air transport ground services by non-Hong Kong/Macao investors must be only in the forms of equity or cooperative joint ventures.
92	Aviation fuel project (equity controlled by Chinese party)
93	Investing in computerized airline reservations system (prohibited) – except for WTO members' qualified service suppliers which are permitted, by free trade agreements concluded by China and the WTO member, to establish equity joint ventures with local Chinese service supplier of computerized airline reservations system, with equity controlled by the local Chinese enterprise; economic demand tests are required for related investments
94	Construction and operation of civil airports (comparatively equity controlled by Chinese party)
95	Investment in air traffic control companies (prohibited)
G60 – Postal service	
96	Domestic courier business of delivering letters, investment in postal service companies (prohibited)

I – Information transmission, software and information technology (IT) service	
I63 – Telecommunication, radio/TV, and satellite transmission service	
97	Basic telecommunication services (restricted, foreign participation within 49 %)
98	Investment in any radio station, TV station, radio and TV channel, and transmission network (transmitting station, relay station, broadcast satellite, satellite uplink station, satellite receiving and broadcasting stations, microwave station, monitoring station, and cable TV network) (prohibited)
I64 – Internet and related service	
99	Information service (other than app stores) (foreign participation within 50 %)
100	Domestic internet virtual private network (VPN) service (foreign participation within 50 %)
101	News websites, online audio-visual program service, venues to provide internet access (i.e. cybercafé), and internet culture-related services (excluding music service) (prohibited)
102	Direct or indirect participation in online game operation (prohibited)
I65 – Software and IT service	
103	E-commerce business (foreign participation within 55 %); other online data and transaction processing service (foreign participation within 50 %)
104	Internet data center service (prohibited)

J – Financial services	
J66 – Monetary financial service	
105	Investment in banking financial institutions must comply with the current regulations
J68 – Insurance	
106	Investment in insurance companies (including group companies, foreign participation in a life insurance company within 50 %), insurance intermediary institutions (including insurance brokers, agents and assessment companies) and insurance asset management companies (restricted)
J67-Capital market services	
107	Investment in securities companies (restricted; foreign participation within 49 %), initial business scope including underwriting and sponsorship of shares (A shares and foreign invested shares) and bonds (government/corporate bonds), brokerage of foreign-invested shares, trading and brokerage of bonds; business scope to be expanded upon application after 2-year operation given other conditions qualified); securities investment fund management companies (restricted; foreign participation within 49 %); securities investment consulting institutions (restricted; foreign participation limited to Hong Kong/Macao securities firms and within 49 %); futures companies (restricted; foreign participation limited to qualified Hong Kong/Macau service suppliers and within 49 %)
J69 – Other financial services	
108	Investment in financial leasing companies (total assets of the foreign investor reaching US$ 5 million; minimum registered capital of US$ 10 million for the leasing company; senior management with required expertise and professional experiences of no less than 3 years)

K- Real estate	
K70- Real estate	
109	Investment in luxury hotels, high-class office buildings, international conference centers must be in the form of project companies
110	Construction and operation of villas (prohibited)
111	Investment in real estate transaction in secondary market must be in the form of project companies

L – Leasing and business service	
L72 – Business service	
112	Requirements to set up an investment company: the registered capital of the investment company is no less than US$ 30 million, the foreign investor should be a foreign company, corporate or other economic organization, total assets of the foreign investor reached US$ 400 million in the year preceding the application, and such investor has established enterprises in China with more than US$ 10 million of paid registered capital; *or* the foreign investor has established more than ten enterprises in China with more than US$ 30 million of paid registered capital
113	Legal consultation (restricted), foreign law firms can provide legal services only by setting up representative offices
114	Accounting firms (partnerships only)
115	Market research (restricted, equity or cooperative joint ventures only)
116	Social research (prohibited)
117	Except for qualified Hong Kong/Macao service suppliers which are permitted to set up wholly-owned HR agencies, non-Hong Kong/Macao investors may only set up HR agencies in the form of equity joint ventures with 70 % foreign participation or below, minimum registered capital is US$ 125,000, the foreign investor must be a foreign company, enterprise or other economic organization with at least 3 years of experience in HR agency service
118	Overseas travel agencies (excluding tourism business in Taiwan) (equity joint ventures only)
119	Security companies engaged in armed security service (foreign participation within 49 %)
120	Rating service (restricted)

M – Scientific research and technology service	
M73 – Research and experimental development	
121	Development and application of technologies in respect of human stem cells (prohibited)
122	Development and application of gene technologies in diagnosis and medical treatment (prohibited)
M74 – Special technology service	
123	Investment in surveying and mapping companies (restricted, equity controlled by Chinese party); geodetic surveying, marine charting, aerial photography for surveying and mapping, surveying and mapping of territorial boundaries of administrative divisions, compiling topographic, world political map, national political map, political map of province level and below, national teaching maps, local teaching maps and real three-dimensional maps and navigation e-maps as well as other surveying and mapping activities stipulated by the administrative department in charge of surveying and mapping under the State Council (prohibited)
124	Special photography service such as aerial photography (restricted, equity joint ventures only)

N – Management of water conservancy, environment and public facilities	
N76 – Water conservancy management	
125	Construction and operation of comprehensive hydro projects (equity controlled by Chinese party)
N77 Ecological and Environmental protection	
126	Construction and operation of nature reserves and inter- nationally important wetland (prohibited)
127	Exploitation of wildlife animals and plants originating from China and protected by the State (prohibited)

P – Education	
P82 – Education	
128	Investment in profit-seeking education and training institutions, profit-seeking vocational skills training institutions (cooperative joint ventures only)
129	Investment in non-profit education institutions (preschool education, secondary vocational education, normal high school education and higher education), non-profit education and training institutions, non-profit vocational skills training institutions (cooperative joint ventures only; no branch is permitted)
130	Investment in compulsory education, as well as special education institutions focus on military affairs, policemen, political, religions and Party school (prohibited)
	Investment in profit-seeking education institutions (pre-school education, secondary vocational education, normal high school education and higher education) (prohibited)

Q – Health and social activities	
Q83 – Health	
131	For investment in a medical institution, no branch is permitted

R – Culture, sports and entertainment	
R85 – News and publishing	
132	Investment in news agencies (prohibited)
133	Publishing of books, newspapers, and periodicals (prohibited)
134	Production and publishing of audio-visual products and electric publications (prohibited)
R86 – Production of radio, television pro- gram, film, and relevant audio recording	
135	Except for service suppliers from Hong Kong and Macao, construction and operation of movie theaters (restricted, equity controlled by Chinese party)
136	Production of radio, TV program (works), and films (restricted, cooperative joint ventures only)
137	Investment in production companies of radio and TV program (works), film-making companies, film distribution, and marketing companies (prohibited)
R88 – Sports	
138	Construction and operation of golf courses (prohibited)
R89 – Entertainment	
139	Construction and operation of large-scale theme parks (restricted)

5.8 Safety, Information Systems, and Anti-monopoly Investigation

A project like the new China (Shanghai) Pilot Free Trade Zone requires a strong regulation in terms of fair competitions, information and communication transparency, environment protection, security and dispute resolution.

The China (Shanghai) Pilot Free Trade Zone will carry out law enforcement examination and made it public pursuant to laws and regulations. Where the food and drug security, public health, environment protection, and safe manufacturing issues involved, the dealing process shall be publicized with necessary warnings, preventive advice, or other messages.

Relevant mechanism for security review and anti-monopoly investigation is being established in the Shanghai Free Trade Zone. Where the investment projects or enterprises fall within the scope of security review and anti-monopoly investigation, the Administration Committee propose to carry out security review and anti-monopoly investigation in a timely manner.

Intellectual property protection in the Shanghai Free Trade Zone will be enhanced. Professional institutions are encouraged and supported to provide services such as intellectual property related conciliation assistance and other services in intellectual property protection.

An annual report of the enterprises in the China (Shanghai) Pilot Free Trade Zone will be publicly announced. Enterprises in the Pilot Free Trade Zone shall submit annual reports to the industry and commerce authority. The annual reports shall be publicly released, except for commercial secret related contents. Enterprises shall be responsible for the authenticity and legitimacy of the annual reports.

A system of the recording, publicizing, sharing, and using of the credit information of enterprises in the Pilot Free Trade Zone will be established to advance credit incentive and credit-cracked penalty mechanism.

The Administration Committee shall establish a supervision information sharing mechanism and platform in the Pilot Free Trade Zone to achieve the communication, exchange, and sharing of supervision information for government authorities such as Customs, inspection and quarantine, marine affairs, financial, development and reform, commerce, industry and commerce, quality supervision, finance and tax, environment protection, safe manufacturing supervision and port shipping, so as to optimize administrative procedures, provide services with high efficiency, and enhance the support for mid-event control and subsequent supervision.

Shanghai will establish a comprehensive evaluation mechanism for industry information tracking, supervision, and collection. The Shanghai development and reform authority as well as relevant other authorities and the Administration Committee shall establish a working mechanism to carry out comprehensive evaluation on pilot implementation and risk prevention for the entire industry and enterprises; put forward relevant evaluation report and expand the opening up areas, pilot contents and systematic innovation measures.

Where commercial disputes arise between enterprises in the Pilot Free Trade Zone, they can bring them to the People's Courts or apply for arbitration or commercial conciliation pursuant to the agreement. The arbitration institution of Shanghai will be supported to improve the arbitration rules, and promote the professional standard of commercial dispute arbitrations in accordance with laws, regulations, and international practices.

5.9 Infrastructures Improvements

The last task we approach talking about the new China (Shanghai) Pilot Free Trade Zone is transportation and connections.

The Ministry of Transport declared to consider the construction of the China (Shanghai) Pilot Free Trade Zone as an opportunity to accelerate the construction of the Shanghai international transport center, further deepen the reform, expand the opening up, lead the way, and explore new paths, enrich and expand the functions of the comprehensive pilot zone for the development of international transport.

There is the willingness of creating innovative transport policies:

- Create a linkage mechanism among the ports: proactively leverage on the Waigaoqiao Port, Yangshan Deep-Water Port, and Pudong International Airport to form a development system and operation model that will have strong global competitive advantages.
- Create a new international ship registration system: by utilizing the geographic advantages of Shanghai and the preferential taxation on Chinese "flag of convenience" ships, qualified ships will be encouraged to register in Shanghai. Based on the ship registration policy of "China Yangshan Port," relevant policies will be studied to promote the establishment and implementation of a convenient and efficient international ship registration system, simplify the application process on permitting international shipping, properly relax the registration conditions such as entities subject to registration, age range of vessel, etc., improve the registration items such as crew manning, type of registration, registration fee, navigation zone and so on, optimize the procedures in relation to ship operation, inspection and registration, so as to encourage qualified ships to register in Shanghai.
- Proactively and orderly promote the construction of port infrastructure: the fourth stage construction project of Yangshan Deep-Water Port will be accelerated to meet the demand of the increasing shipping volume. Railways (including Hutong railway, Huzha railway, etc.), the preliminary preparation and construction of container transportation infrastructure for inland waterways will be accelerated. Shanghai port's capacity of centralization and distribution transportation, such as maritime and railway combined transport, transit between waterways and so on, will be improved. The construction of berths on the mainstream and tributaries will be orderly promoted to mitigate the structural conflicts of berths on the mainstream and tributaries of Shanghai port and optimize the

functions of the port. Soil from dredging the Yangtze estuary deep-water channel will be comprehensively utilized to better serve the development of Shanghai international transport center.

- Guide the structural and functional optimization of centralization and distribution transportation: the advantages of inland and Yangtze river waterway transport will be fully taken to promote the construction of an integrated transportation system, enhance the interaction between Waigaoqiao Port and Yangshan Port, elevate the size and efficiency of water transport, increase the proportion of transit between waterways, and promote the sustainable development of Shanghai port. Researches on standards of ship type, management and fees for river-sea transportation will be supported to lower the costs of river-sea transportation and encourage a wide application of ships for river-sea transportation.
- Accelerate the development of safe and green shipping: it is encouraged to construct a safe sea area and put in efforts to improve the capability for rescuing human lives, property, environment in and around the Shanghai port, and the capability for preventing and controlling ship pollution. The construction of anti-collision facilities for key bridges in the navigable waters will be strengthened to guarantee important channels safe and unblocked. "Sunshine Piloting" will be earnestly organized and implemented to gradually eliminate the compulsory piloting for the domestic trade ships from sea to rivers. Relevant technical specifications and standards will be established and improved to promote the wide application of LNG fueled ships in inland waterways.
- Enhance and improve the regulatory system of international maritime transportation market: the Shanghai Shipping Exchange will be authorized to administer the freight price filing for container liner companies and non-vessel operating carriers in international and domestic shipping markets and the shipping market across the strait. In addition, it will cooperate with and assist related authorities to inspect and supervise the freight price filing. The role of relevant industry associations for ship owners and ports will be further utilized for self-discipline within the industry.

Water Transport Department of the Ministry of Transport and Shanghai Urban Construction and Communications Commission are responsible for taking the lead in contacts and carry-out of relevant tasks, for tracking and studying new situations and problems occurred during the implementation of policies, and for communication and tasks promotion.

5.10 Observations About the Implementation of the New Shanghai Free Trade Zone

The establishment of the Shanghai Pilot Free Trade Zone has been recognized as a crucial economic reform initiated by China's new leadership. How the area will affect businesses in China and throughout Asia is top of mind as multinational corporations and local Chinese companies seek to benefit from more relaxed financial and investment controls. As of mid-October 2013, 36 new companies had already set up operations in the new China (Shanghai) Pilot Free Trade Zone in various sectors covering banking, leasing, logistics, e-commerce, and trading.

The new free trade zone is now entering its second year in operation. It shoulders the responsibility of implementing some of China's most ambitious reforms to put the economy on a more market-based footing. If the experiment proves successful, it's expected to be rolled out across the nation.

So far, policies in the zone to reduce red tape, simplify customs procedures, limit government interference, widen market access across service sectors, and deregulate financial markets have drawn considerable attention and guarded praise. Foreign investors, already operating or planning to expand operations in China, seem to be optimistic about opportunities that the Shanghai Free Trade Zone could bring. They are also studying the released policies and planning their business strategies around measures widely anticipated to be announced. Foreign investors should start assessing the impact of the Shanghai Pilot Free Trade Zone on their existing or potential business plans and operations in China. If the reform is implemented smoothly, foreign investors will be able to operate more efficiently throughout the Shanghai Pilot Free Trade Zone with the creation of treasury centers, shared service centers, regional headquarters, distribution hubs, as well as trading and investment platforms.

International investors in the Shanghai Pilot Free Trade Zone are expected to make relevant changes to their future business models. Investors are also encouraged to start open dialogues with relevant stakeholders and Chinese government authorities to better understand the new policies and regulations. Both local enterprises and multinational corporations need to start developing a systematic strategy and step-by-step plan to take advantage of the policies implemented in the Shanghai Pilot Free Trade Zone.

It is also important to note that the Shanghai Pilot Free Trade Zone should be seen as a testing model with policies that could be replicated in other regions in China. This pilot free trade area provides investors with an idea of the changes that could come about in terms of the investment administrative system, financial and foreign exchange control system, international trade model as well as the further opening up of service sectors across China and beyond Shanghai.

The most positive responses related to the introduction of the negative list as a measure to open up investment options. It was a breakthrough in the zone that has been adopted in many areas outside the zone. The move is a signal that China is willing to embrace foreign investment. The latest 2014 version of the list is much shorter, and companies still expect more relaxation to come. Compliance with international practices is the major issue and restrictions need to be relaxed further. The positive impact of the negative list will ripple through many sectors, transforming government's role. Investor look forward to more details to be specified in the list, and they hope the government will involve more companies in that process.

Moreover, companies are feeling "relatively strong" about changes in government functions. Measures to replace some administrative approvals with simpler registration mark a transformation from a controlling to a service government function. These are the most important innovations in the Free Trade Zone in the past year. They streamline the government's role in the market and conform to international practices.

Compared with industrial innovation, changes to adjust government functions are relative more outstanding. In this aspect, improvements can be done to get a better interface between companies and government. For example, procedures are now simplified concerning start-ups, but maybe it's necessary to introduce after-event regulations on issues such as deregistration and mergers so that companies experience more convenience throughout their life cycles. However, the public opinion is still confident that the government will continue to deregulate its role in the market.

Concerning the finance sector, the most prominent financial reform is the establishment of the free trade account system, allowing separate management of capital in the zone. The accounts facilitate cross-border money flows and trade financing. Around 70 % of companies interviewed in a workshop operated by PwC, said they can actually lower borrowing costs by using the account to access yuan offshore. The bilateral cash pool business can enhance the efficiency of asset management. The major task for policymakers is to settle details for policies now applied in the zone, especially when it comes to cross-department regulations. Financial reforms are now being carried out in a cautious way. It may help if a comprehensive regulatory body is set up to avoid overlaps and loopholes in terms of financial regulation.

In order to attract directly companies' headquarters, the area would be even more appealing if it could offer more incentives, a better regulatory environment, and simpler administrative procedures.

Regarding the establishment of a legal system specific for the China (Shanghai) Pilot Free Trade Zone, the zone has a basic law, but some companies are concerned that details are not specific and supporting laws are insufficient. The challenge is to build a sound legal environment in the zone to support business operations. Breakthroughs need to be made to solve contradictory legal issues inside and outside the Shanghai Free Trade Zone. Another task is introducing a comprehensive assessment mechanism for government officials that focus not on GDP.

Referring to customs, the Shanghai Free Trade Zone has an essential regulation called "opening-up the first border and controlling the second border." That refers to opening up offshore activities while still restricting domestic activities. Easier customs clearance rules can indeed shorten time and save costs for companies. It is evident that credit systems need to be unified across customs, quarantine, and quality inspection departments. Otherwise, companies will still have to deal with various departments and won't be able to enjoy the simplified procedures introduced in the zone. The zone can act as a pilot area to trial a new credit system for companies. It can be expanded in China afterward.

Previously, import and export activities in a bonded zone involved goods in China. Now, goods can go through the Free Trade Zone from one country to another even if they don't relate to the domestic market. Ports like Hong Kong and Singapore handle a lot of transshipment business. It is important that Shanghai's free trade zone become more active in that.

In terms of tax, companies feel the system is quite clear and plausible. Tax regulations in the zone are more simplified than actual incentives. Companies said the rules help lift efficiency and improved the services of the tax authority. However, companies still wish for incentives in the zone. But it is not sure that authorities can continue to simplify tax management and introduce targeted tax incentives for some business operations, such as offshore businesses and headquarters. Authorities may also consider a tax regime to support corporate overseas expansion.

Going back to the *Opinions and Circulars on Financial Reform,* these opinions further refine the reforms in the areas of finance and foreign exchange based on the Plan and will have a profound influence on the reform of Chinese financial system, further reflecting the determination of the Chinese government for financial system reform. Restrictive terms such as "qualified" and "when conditions permit" are frequently mentioned in the *Opinions*, which aims to raise the entry requirements for China (Shanghai) Pilot Free Trade Zone risk control. Meanwhile, instead of issuing detailed implementation rules, the opinions are only a rudimentary reform framework. A series of new regulations in future are highly anticipated and it is necessary to continue to pay close attention to further movements.

Circular of the PBOC Shanghai Head Office on Supporting the Expansion of RMB Cross-border Business in China (Shanghai) Pilot Free Trade Zone This circular further simplifies the procedures of direct investment and RMB cross-border use under current accounts in the China (Shanghai) Pilot Free Trade Zone. For the first time, innovative business including the scale and use scope off offshore RMB borrowing, cross-border e-Business settlement, RMB trading services is specified. The circular reflects a preliminary development of macro-prudent regulatory supervision. It should help enhance the innovative capability of banks' cross-border RMB services, reduce financing costs for multinational enterprises, and provide strong support in facilitating trade and investment in the China (Shanghai) Pilot Free Trade Zone.

Circular of the PBOC on removing the ceiling of interest rate for small-denomination deposits in foreign currencies in China (Shanghai) Pilot Free Trade Zone This circular underscores the China (Shanghai) Pilot Free Trade Zone becoming a pioneer in the full liberalization of interest rate for foreign currency deposits in China. Based on the interest rate liberalization path designed and promoted by the PBOC, a "four-step" strategy featuring "loans followed by deposits and foreign currencies followed by local currencies" has been confirmed, with the Circular being welcomed as a critical step. Meanwhile, it also lays a solid foundation for driving interest rate liberalization reform across the nation in future. As interest rate liberalization has just commenced, its healthy development should rely on risk prevention. The opening of small-denomination deposits in foreign currencies means the matching with overseas markets. Therefore, the interest rate trend links to both the market pricing of neighboring countries and regions as well as to the supply and demand status of foreign currencies in domestic markets. As an export-oriented trading economy, the China (Shanghai) Pilot Free Trade Zone has witnessed tremendous demand for foreign currencies, with fierce price competition. This circular serves as an effective monitoring and preventive measure against unscrupulous competition and sharp fluctuations in interest rates during the liberalization process, hence laying a tone of stable development for interest rate liberalization.

Circular of the State Administration of Foreign Exchange Shanghai Branch on Issuing Implementing Rules for Foreign Exchange Control to Support the Construction of China (Shanghai) Pilot Free Trade Zone

Foreign enterprises are used to settling exchange based on demand and providing evidence of payments. However, this limit has been cancelled upon the publication of this circular. The circular provides investors with many new options in anticipation of an RMB appreciation. In the medium term, owing to the exchange fluctuations, enterprises should determine settlements based on a more international and market-oriented perspective. This circular reflects a new idea of financial regulation, namely the concept of after-event supervision, representing the new direction of financial reform. The circular plays a prominent role in facilitating trading and investment, financial leasing, and the trading of commodities. Therefore, it will be more convenient for enterprises and banks in the China (Shanghai) Pilot Free Trade Zone to conduct foreign exchange business. Furthermore, this circular contributes to the development of the real economy and better supports the national strategy, as well as accelerate the transformation of the supervision model of foreign exchange.

Circular of the PBOC Shanghai Head Office on Practically Conducting the Anti-money Laundering and Anti-terrorism Financing Work in China (Shanghai) Pilot Free Trade Zone

This circular confirms that anti-money laundering and anti-terrorism financing efforts have significant implications for the steady and healthy development of the China (Shanghai) Pilot Free Trade Zone. The progress of those works helps to cultivate an internationalized and legalized market environment for the China (Shanghai) Pilot Free Trade Zone, make reasonable assessment and effectively control the potential implicit money laundering risks of business in the zone. The circular also requires various institutions to bear the anti-money laundering obligation, to fully carry out various regulations and measures for anti-money laundering obligation, to fully carry out various regulations and measures for anti-money laundering and anti-terrorism financing and to pioneer and innovate as well as proactively explore creating replicable and promotable anti-money laundering experiences in the China (Shanghai) Pilot Free Trade Zone.

The worldwide investment bank HSBC was one of the first foreign banks to raise its flag in the Shanghai Free Trade Zone pilot project. "There are benefits in being there first", Helen Wong, deputy chairman, president and chief executive officer of HSBC China, told Shanghai Daily on November 11, 2014. From the point of view of a bank, first of all, the procedures of yuan transactions should be simple and easy, including payments to suppliers and fund transfers between subsidiaries. Secondly, the money market needs to supply ample liquidity so that clients can raise funds or get a bank loan in yuan when needed. Thirdly, if a dispute occurs, there needs to be a competent legal system to handle it. For example, there must be reliable arbitration procedures. Lastly, the clients want to be dealing with local professionals who are efficient, have high standards and are generally nice to do business with. It's all about convenience, liquidity, risk controls, legal protection, and professional business partners.

The internationalization of the yuan has made tremendous progress. Now, almost a fifth of China's international trade is settled in yuan. On the investment side, interbank market participants, foreign sovereign funds, and central banks can invest in the domestic market through the RMB Qualified Foreign Institutional Investors (RQFII) program. Participants include Hong Kong, the United Kingdom, Singapore, France, South Korea, and Germany. It is expected to further expand to other countries such as Australia. For a global currency, free convertibility is important, but interest rates and foreign exchange markets are also vital. To make the Chinese yuan a global currency, the markets need to provide effective interest rates and foreign-exchange hedging tools. The China (Shanghai) Pilot Free Trade Zone Master Plan is aimed not only at boosting yuan internationalization, but also at the development of financial services. Previously, cross-border yuan settlement involved heavy paperwork. "The client had to fill out a pile of forms and produce lots of documents to complete transactions. Financial innovations in the FTZ including centralized cross-border yuan cash management solution simplified those procedures and lowered transaction costs for the clients. For example, let's say Company A needs to make 50 separate payments to Company B. Previously, we needed to do 50 transactions for the client, one by one. Now we can bundle the transactions and do it in one single transaction. It makes the operation a lot easier," said Helen Wong, deputy chairman, president and chief executive officer of HSBC China. "Establishing the FTZ sub-branch allows us to be closer to our clients. Companies can visit our sub-branch at any time to get information about new developments in the zone. We find many foreign companies are interested in the FTZ and want to know more. We held a forum in Shanghai recently, attended by many of our global clients. They made a tour to the FTZ and stayed at our sub-branch there for about 2 h because they were eager to discuss exciting new opportunities with our bankers."

Multinational companies in electronics, medical devices, and high-end consumer goods have established distribution centers in the zone and become involved in related financial leasing projects. UPS, DHL, and FedEx, the world's top three express companies, have set up branches in the zone and helped it developed a strong business chain of air freight distribution, financial leasing, express transit, and exhibitions of Asia-Pacific trade. Anyway companies wish that the government would better understand their needs. It is crucial that the government continue to enhance its services for companies beyond simply issuing new regulations. More coordination is expected among various government departments. In terms of opening up investment, foreign companies said they hope rules in the zone will be made more compliant with international practices. The zone will be more appealing to foreign investors if it does things the way they are done in other major economies.

After the beginning period of the FTZ launch, many analysts say the trade zone has fallen well short of expectations. While the project is thought to still enjoy the support of Beijing, reforms have been slow to materialize. On the thorny issues of how to loosen capital controls and liberalize interest rates, almost no progress has been made. "I think that [the Shanghai Free Trade Zone] was oversold. And in many ways, it was overbought," said Patrick Chovanec, chief strategist at Silvercrest Asset Management. Chovanec said that confusion reigns over what exactly can be done in the zone, a problem that has plagued the project from the day it opened. "I'm confused and I follow it. Maybe there are some lawyers out there who aren't confused, but I doubt it," he said. "I think everyone's confused about exactly what the latest rules that have been promulgated mean in practice". Peng Zhenwei, an economist with the Shanghai-based research firm CEBM Group, says the zone has been targeting low-priority reforms like removing red tape and easing the exchange of goods, rather than capital. Long, the business owner, agrees. "The flow of currencies is still not as easy as we thought," he said. For now, many companies appear content to register and open small offices in the zone as a bet that future reforms will fulfill the project's promise. Amazon, for example, plans to open a single warehouse. "A foreign company might want to establish some kind of presence in the Shanghai Free Trade Zone, so that if some day actually there's a rule that allows you to do something interesting, you're there," Chovanec said. "You don't lose anything by doing that."

The transition to a more market-based economy is by no means easy. We have seen this successfully implemented in other free trade zones around the globe such as in Singapore or Dubai. But given the sheer size of China's economy, this is a major undertaking. And it involves enormous levels of risks that need to be taken into account. The government is prudent about these risks and it is reasonable why they are doing it in the form of a pilot first. It is clear that while we are seeing a number of striking reform advances today in the China (Shanghai) Pilot Free Trade Zone, we will need to see more in the future. The question is how fast every program will be implemented. One of the most important things about every international financial center is regulatory oversight. It takes time to build a solid foundation. A platform built on short notice can easily collapse in one or two risk events. Surely authorities have taken cautious steps in establishing the regulatory framework of the China (Shanghai) Pilot Free Trade Zone. For example, free trade accounts were launched 9 months after the Shanghai Free Trade Zone was established. It took that long because the system requires a very high degree of accuracy in order to distinguish zone transactions from other transactions. It's a specialized system, and it needs to be quick and effective. That's not easy. But once passing this stage, everything else will follow through very quickly. The first step is always the hardest. We saw China's astounding ability to manage rapid change in the past, as such the expectations for the Shanghai Free Trade Zone are very high. But we also have to keep in mind that China can't make hasty decisions when the economic fortune and well-being of a whole nation is at stake. The reform must be implemented the right way.

Appendix 1: Highlights Toward the New China (Shanghai) Pilot Free Trade Zone

December 2003	Mr. Siwei Cheng, former National People's Congress Vice Chairman, proposes that China is ready to set up a reform pilot for the transformation from bonded zones to free trade zones. The selected date of the reform pilot is soon to be advised
At the end of March 2013	Mr. Keqiang Li, Premier of the State Council, during his research trip to Shanghai's Waigaoqiao Bonded Zone encourages the city to establish a pilot free trade zone on the basis of the existing comprehensive bonded zone
May 14, 2013	The China Shanghai Pilot Free Trade Zone is approved to become a national-level project
June 2013	Having been revised and improved, the *General Plan for China (Shanghai) Pilot Free Trade Zone* is submitted for approval to the Ministries and Commissions under the State Council
July 3, 2013	The *General Plan for China (Shanghai) Pilot Free Trade Zone* is approved in principle by the State Council executive meeting
July 10–11, 2013	At the fifth round of China-US Strategic and Economic Dialogue, China State Councilor Yang Jiechi and US Secretary of State John Kerry agree to take measures to deepen bilateral trade and investment relations, as well as to establish an open environment for trade and investment
August 22, 2013	The Press Office of the Ministry of Commerce announces that the State Council has approved the establishment of the China (Shanghai) Pilot Free Trade Zone and that the *General Plan for China (Shanghai) Pilot Free Trade Zone* (the "Plan") would be published after the completion of relevant legal procedures.
September 18, 2013	Circular of the State Council on the Framework Plan for the China (Shanghai) Pilot Free Trade Zone (Guofa 2013 n° 38)
September 24, 2013	Circular of the State Administration for Industry and Commerce on Authorizing the Administrative Authority of Foreign-invested Enterprises Registration to the Branch of Shanghai Administration for Industry and Commerce in Pilot Free Trade Zone
September 26, 2013	The State Administration for Industry and Commerce of the People's Republic of China releases its Opinions on Supporting the Establishment of the China (Shanghai) Pilot Free Trade Zone and Reply for Approving the Trial Implementation Plan of New Business License Template in the China (Shanghai) Pilot Free Trade Zone
September 27, 2013	The State Council publishes the Plan on its official website in its release of Guofa (2013) n° 38
September 27, 2013	The General Administration of Quality Supervision, Inspection and Quarantine releases its Opinions on Supporting the Establishment of the China (Shanghai) Pilot Free Trade Zone
September 27, 2013	Implementation Opinions of the Ministry of Transport and Shanghai Municipal People's Government on Implementing the "Framework Plan for the China (Shanghai) Pilot Free Trade Zone" and Accelerating the Construction of the Shanghai International Transport Center
September 27, 2013	Circular of Ministry of Transport concerning Trial Implementation of Coastal Shipping of Chinese-invested Foreign Ships of International Sails

(continued)

September 28, 2013	Circular of China Banking Regulatory Commission on Issues Concerning Banking Supervision in China (Shanghai) Free Trade Zone.
September 29, 2013	The Shanghai Government publishes the Administrative measures for China (Shanghai) Pilot Free Trade Zone in *Shanghai MPG Order (2013) n° 7*
September 29, 2013	The China Securities Regulatory Commission releases Polices and Measures on Capital Market for Supporting and Promoting China (Shanghai) Pilot Free Trade Zone
September 29, 2013	China Insurance Regulatory Commission releases its Opinions to Support China (Shanghai) Pilot Free Trade Zone
September 29, 2013	Circular of the Ministry of Culture on Implementing the Policies of Cultural Market Administration for the China (Shanghai) Pilot Free Trade Zone
October 15, 2013	The Ministry of Finance, General Administration of Customs, and State Administration of Taxation edits the Circular on Relevant Import Tax Policies for the China (Shanghai) Pilot Free Trade Zone
November 2013	The Third Plenum of the 18th CPC Central Committee proposes to relax its restrictions on admittance of foreign investment and to speed the development of the China (Shanghai) Pilot Free Trade Zone
November 15, 2013	Circular of the Ministry of Finance and the State Administration of Taxation on Enterprise Income Tax Policies Concerning Asset Restructuring Activities Such as Using Non-monetary Assets for Investment Purposes by Enterprises in the China (Shanghai) Pilot Free Trade Zone
December 2, 2013	The PBOC releases: *Opinions of the People's Bank of China to Support China (Shanghai) Pilot Free Trade Zone in Financial Sector*
January 6, 2014	The Chinese Central Government's Official Web Portal publishes: *Decision of the State Council on Temporary Adjustments to the Administrative Approval Items or Special Administrative Measures on Access Prescribed in Relevant Administrative Regulations or State Council's Documents in China (Shanghai) Pilot Free Trade Zone*
February 20, 2014	The PBOC Shanghai Head Office issues: *Circular of the People's Bank of China Shanghai Head Office on Supporting the Expansion of RMB Cross-border Business in China (Shanghai) Pilot Free Trade Zone* and *Circular of the People's Bank of China Shanghai Head Office on the opinion of Shanghai payment institutions conducting Cross-border RMB payment business*
February 25, 2014	The PBOC Shanghai Head Office issues: *Circular of the PBOC on removing the ceiling of interest rate for small-denomination deposits in foreign currencies in China (Shanghai) Pilot Free Trade Zone*
February 28, 2014	The State Administration of Foreign Exchange Shanghai Branch issues: *Circular of the State Administration of Foreign Exchange Shanghai Branch on Issuing Implementing Rules for Foreign Exchange Control to Support the Construction of China (Shanghai) Pilot Free Trade Zone* The PBOC Shanghai Head Office issues: *Circular of the People's Bank of China Shanghai Head Office on Practically Conducting the Anti-money Laundering and Anti-terrorism Financing Work in China (Shanghai) Pilot Free Trade Zone*
March 5, 2014	At the Shanghai group discussion of the second session of the 12th National People's Congress, President Xi Jinping stresses the construction China (Shanghai) Pilot Free Trade Zone as a national strategy and should "construct bravely, try boldly, reform freely" as long as in accordance with international rules. And, thereafter, summarize the experiences learned on constructing China (Shanghai) Pilot Free Trade Zone which can be promoted nationwide

(continued)

March 8, 2014	The Shanghai Stock Exchange obtains the approvals from regulators in order to establish an international trading center in the Shanghai FTZ
March 23, 2014	Shanghai Branch of the State Administration of Foreign Exchange releases Implementation Regulations concerning Foreign Exchange Administration to Support the Construction of the China (Shanghai) Pilot Free Trade Zone
June 18, 2014	Industrial and Commercial Bank of China (branches of Bank of China), China Construction Bank, Pudong Development Bank, and the Bank of Shanghai open the first free trade accounts for companies in Shanghai FTZ for facilitating cross-border money transfers
June 30, 2014	Bulletin of the Shanghai Municipal People's Government on Special Administrative Measures (Negative List) on Foreign Investment Access to the China (Shanghai) Pilot Free Trade Zone (2014 Amended Version)
September 19, 2014	The Shanghai Gold Exchange officially launches its international trading platform in the Shanghai FTZ

Appendix 2: Organization Structure of the China (Shanghai) Pilot Free Trade Zone

For any clarification about topics and issues regarding the New China (Shanghai) Pilot Free Trade Zone, ten related office has been established in order to manage the new free trade zone. These are the General Office, the Human Resource Bureau, the Police and Regulation Research Office, the Economic Development Bureau, the Fiscal and Financial Services Bureau, the Construction Planning and Environmental Management Bureau, the Comprehensive Supervision and Execution Bureau, the Yangshan Free Trade Port Office, the Waigaoqiao Free Trade Zone Office, and the Pudong Airport Free Trade Zone Office.

Here attached the information available on the China (Shanghai) Pilot Free Trade Zone Website:

1. The General Office
The General Office is responsible for the management of the secretarial pool, confidential files, archives, publicity, information collection, foreign affairs, reception, news releases, communications, and support facilities. It coordinates the creation of digital services and emergency management. It is also responsible for the promotion of social and political development for the Party and other groups within the administration.

2. The Bureau of Human Resources
The Bureau of Human Resources is responsible for recruiting, retaining, and serving professionals. It undertakes to optimize the environment for professional development, to attract and assist professional talent from overseas, and to coordinate smooth employer-employee relations.

3. The Office of Policy and Regulation Research
The Office of Policy and Regulation Research is responsible for studying how to promote and expand institutional innovation. It conducts research to determine where ideas successful in one place can be replicated elsewhere. It assists departments in the drafting and revising of laws and rules related to the pilot free trade zone. It is also responsible for auditing administrative documents, evaluating development progress, and managing the zone's legal publicity.

4. The Bureau of Economic Development
The Bureau of Economic Development is responsible for fostering innovation in investment management and trade supervision, in the further opening the services sector and in the expansion of the zone's functional roles. It implements the approval, verification, and filing of foreign investment documents and coordinates the "one-stop shop" services for approvals.

5. The Bureau of Fiscal and Financial Services
The Bureau of Fiscal and Financial Services is responsible for financial supervision and financial policy innovation. It assists financial authorities in implementing innovation in the financial system and accelerating the opening-up process for financial services. It coordinates the introduction of financial institutions and trading entities to nurture a multi-layer market serving both domestic and foreign interests. It conducts research on fiscal policy, adopts international standards, and produces annual plans and analysis of economic growth. It coordinates city and district authorities in allocating fiscal resources and in implementing supportive fiscal policies. It is also responsible for budgetary, fiscal, and accounting management in the administration.

6. The Bureau of Construction Planning and Environmental Management
The Bureau of Construction Planning and Environmental Management is responsible for compiling, revising, and implementing construction within the zone. It manages land planning and management, housing management, construction, civil defense, outdoor maintenance, environmental protection, and transportation.

7. The Bureau of Comprehensive Supervision and Execution
The Bureau of Comprehensive Supervision and Execution is responsible for comprehensive oversight. Its aim is to establish a supervision model. It coordinates the development and application of platforms for information sharing and sharing of services. It explores ways of integrating social policies into supervision and assists with interdepartmental coordinates related to security review, anti-trust monitoring, and social-credit evaluation.

8. The Office of Yangshan Free Trade Port
The Office of Yangshan Free Trade Port is responsible for undertaking administrative works in the port, accelerating innovation in trade supervision, and nurturing a headquarters environment. It is responsible for attracting and retaining investment, facilitating trade, and fostering regional headquarters. It is also responsible for contact and coordination between operational departments and for monitoring the economic targets of the port.

9. The Office of Waigaoqiao Free Trade Zone
The Office of Waigaoqiao Free Trade Zone is responsible for undertaking administration in the Waigaoqiao Bonded Area, the Waigaoqiao Logistics Park, and the Senlan Zone. It is responsible for attracting and retaining investment, facilitating trade, and fostering regional headquarters. It is also responsible for contact and coordination between operational departments.

10. The Office of the Pudong Airport Free Trade Zone
The Office of the Pudong Airport Free Trade Zone is responsible for undertaking administrative works in the zone, accelerating their innovation in trade supervision, and nurturing an efficient headquarters environment. It is responsible for attracting and retaining investment, facilitating trade, and fostering regional headquarters. It is also responsible for contact and coordination between operational departments and for monitoring economic targets of the zone.

References

Baumol WJ (1967) Macroeconomics of unbalanced growth: the anatomy of urban crisis. Am Econ Rev 57(3):415–426

Clark C (1940) The conditions of economic progress. Macmillian, London

Francois J, Hoekman B (2010) Service trade and policy. J Econ Lit 48(3):665–679

Guofa (2013) General Scheme regarding the free exchange in pilot FTZ, Governmental Decree, no° 38, Shanghai Government

Hertel TW, Walmsley T, Itakura K (2001) Dynamic effects of the "new age" free trade agreement between Japan and Singapore. J Econ Integr 16(4):421–444

Hill TP (1977) On goods and services. Rev Income Wealth 23(4):315–338

Lee B, Zhou F, Sun (2013) Construction Of China Free Trade Zones. China Machine Press

Mayes and Wang (2003) Effects of WTO membership on income distribution and labour movement in China – BOFIT discussion papers 18/2003

Melvin JR (1989) Trade in producer services: a Heckscher-Ohlin approach. J Polit Econ 97(5):1180–1196

Panagariya A (1988) A theoretical explanation of some stylized facts of economic growth. Quart J Econ 103(3):441–463

Triplett JE, Bosworth BP (2004) Productivity in the U.S. services sector: new sources of economic growth. Brookings Institution Press, Washington, DC

Wei Y, Leung C (2005) Development zones, foreign investment, and global city formation in Shanghai. Growth Change 36(1):16–40

Wu W (1999) City profile: Shanghai. Elsevier Sci 16(3):207–216

Chapter 6
Steps Forward to an Open System

6.1 The New Company Law

On December 28, 2013, the sixth meeting of the 12th Standing Committee of National People's Congress (NPC) amended the "Company Law of the People's Republic of China" turning into the New Company Law. The amendments to the PRC Company Law focus on the registered capital, being involved with three types of companies, namely limited liability companies, one person limited liability companies and companies limited by shares.

The New Company Law takes effect from March 1, 2014, and revamps the company establishment system with the purposes of streamlining the registration formalities and relaxing the threshold for setting up a company in China. By doing so, it is expected to encourage more entrepreneurs to start their own business resulting in fostering the growth of the individual economic sector. The aim of this new amendment of the PRC Company Law is to boost the economy, removing several major hurdles, which discouraged domestic and foreign investors from investing and establishing their new businesses in China.

More importantly, the New Company Law provides sound legislative protection in the vigorous economic development in China. The amendments to the former PRC Company Law formally introduced the new capital regime also providing a reformed public regime that will allow a more harmonized and transparent company registration with a greater freedom of action than in the past.

6.1.1 Major Changes in Amended Chinese Company Law

The New Amendments substantially change certain basic requirements for forming and capitalizing a company. They include the minimum amount of registered capital, the form, and the schedule for contributing registered capital and the registration process.

L. Riccardi, *Investing in China through Free Trade Zones*,
DOI 10.1007/978-3-662-47354-2_6

These changes make the establishment of companies in China easier and faster for several reasons. Requiring investors to contribute certain amounts of registered capital (usually cash) by certain deadline, the former regulation forced them to undertake the difficult goal of anticipating a company's capital needs years in advance. Furthermore, investors were forced to subscribe for a statutorily required minimum registered capital even for companies that did not require such capital. Additional burdens regarding capital contributions and hiring accountants certificating and verifying payment of capital contribution have been removed. Following discussion is aimed at analyzing the most important changes occurred to PRC Company Law one by one.

Cancellation of Minimum Registered Capital
The New Amendments repeal the statutory requirements for a minimum amount of registered capital, which previously were RMB 30,000 for a limited liability company, RMB 100,000 for a single-shareholder limited liability company, and five million for a joint stock limited company.

Before the reform, the PRC Company Law required that companies have a "paid-in capital" that is no less than the minimum amount of registered capital required by law. Under the New Amendments, companies must "have a capital contribution in compliance with the provisions of the Articles of Association." The Company Law gives initial shareholders (promoters) of a company, substantial discretion in deciding the contents of the company's Articles of Association. That discretion will also now apply to determining the "right amount" of equity to be contributed to a new company. This exercise of discretion will involve consideration of several factors that are familiar with U.S. companies and their legal counsel, including the risk of "piercing the corporate veil" and the ability to obtain third-party financing. Similarly, when companies wish to reduce their registered capital, there will no longer be any lower limitation on the registered capital after reduction.

Deregulation of Form and Schedule of Capital Contribution
Under the New Amendments, the form and the payment schedule of paid-in capital subscribed by the shareholders can be determined by the shareholders as set forth in the article of association. Removal of such barriers substantially reduces the cost and the time in setting up these companies. Almost all statutory restrictions on the payment of registered capital have been eliminated. These constrains regarded for limited liability companies the contribution in cash no lower than 30 % of registered capital and the initial payment of contribution no less than 20 % of registered capital; for single-shareholder limited liability company, the capital contribution was required to be paid in a lump sum; for a joint stock limited company, the initial payment of contribution by the promoters was required to be no less than 20 % of the total registered capital and finally the shareholders or promoters, irrespective of type of company were required to pay in the remaining amount of registered capital within 2 years after the company's incorporation (limit extended to 5 years in case of investment company).

Simplifying Registration
Consistent with the above changes, the New Amendments also simplify the registration process for companies. "Paid-in capital" will no longer be recorded on the

business licenses of companies. Capital verification reports, which verify the amount of paid-in capital, will not be required to be submitted for incorporation. The companies will be not required to register the amount of paid-in capital actually contributed by each shareholder with the governmental agency in charge of company registration (e.g. the State Administration for Industry and Commerce – SAIC). SAIC is currently addressing administrative issues in order to accommodate the implementation of the new Amendments. All the mentioned elements clarify the shift from a "paid-in capital" to a "subscribed capital" approach.

Amended PRC company law in brief

Issue	Former company law	Amended company law
Registered Capital	RMB 30,000 for a limited liability company	No longer required
	RMB 100,000 for a single-shareholder limited liability company	
	RMB 5 million for a joint stock limited company	
Contribution Schedule	For a limited liability company, contribution in cash not less than 30 % of the registered capital and initial contribution not less than 20 % of the registered capital and not less than the statutory minimum amount of registered capital	No longer required
	For a single-shareholder limited liability company, capital contribution require to be paid in a lump sum	
	For a joint stock limited company, initial payment of contribution not less than 20 % of total registered capital	
	Equity-holders are required to fully pay up their contributions within 2 years after the company's incorporation	
Minimum Cash Required	Not less than 30 % of registered capital contribution in cash	No longer required
Capital Verification	Capital contribution verification and related reports are required; the amount of verified paid-in capital is required to be stated on a business license	No longer required

With New company law, the format of business licenses will be reviewed.

In the most obvious changes, the redesigned business licenses are in portrait orientation (rather than landscape, as previously) and contain an embedded QR code linked to the company listing in the National Enterprise Credit Registry. Most important change will be the removing of paid-in capital from the new licenses, this shown the percentage of registered capital that a company has actually contributed to its operations in China. The removing of this indication is unclear, as paid-in capital is a useful diagnostic for assessing company performance. This doesn't mean that no one is keeping track of this information anymore, it can still be found through local AIC records, but it does make due diligence more difficult than it used to be.

Two other minor changes consist of permitting multiple entities to list the same registered address on their respective business licenses and switching over from a system of multiple types of licenses for different types of commercial entities to a standardized license including a "Type" criterion.

Any company founded on or after March 2014 will have to hold the new licenses, for all companies the deadline to switch over to a new business license is February 28, 2015. In the meantime, a dual system is in place during the circulation of both kind of licenses, old and new.

6.1.2 *What Will Remain Unchanged*

All these amendments are undoubtedly welcome moves. However not everything is changing and so it is worth to keep in mind several points which are left untouched. First the new capital regime will not change shareholders' civil liability in relation to capital contribution. The amount of capital paid, and the form in which is paid, will be reflected in the company annual AIC report. A shareholder who fails to contribute capital in accordance with the articles of association will continue to be liable for that amount to the company and fellow shareholders, as well to creditors if the company is unable to satisfy its contracted debts.

Second the relaxed and simplified requirement on registered capital finds an exception in situation where there are requirements in other relevant laws and regulations. In fact the financial sector as well as other specific-industry sectors is not within the scope of the new regime, as they fall within the jurisdiction of the respective industry regulators, with different policies concerns applying to the manner in which they are regulated. Industry specific minimum registered capital requirements therefore continue to apply for these cases.

6.1.3 *Implications of Amended Company Law and Further Observations*

For all these points to be taken into account, let us make some consideration regarding the extent to what the reform of PRC Company Law will infer over companies' setting up activities and governance.

First, the statutory minimum capital requirement for registered capital has been a legal hurdle in China that was unfamiliar to companies and lawyers from Common Law jurisdictions. The Chinese laws used to set various thresholds on the amount of registered capital and also specified the payment schedule of capital contribution for foreign investment entities. Before the New Amendments, registered capital requirements were, in many cases, arbitrary and varied among different regions and industries. The local government often required high registered capital to secure large capital investment in order to improve the local government's performances in attracting foreign investment and lifting local GDP statistics. Under such mindsets, projects with lower capital investment were often not welcome. With the repeal of statutory requirement of registered capital and deregulation of capital contribution, the legal basis for such practice is shaken. Hopefully this will bring a substantial and positive impact on starting foreign investment projects. The abolishment of the above-mentioned requirements will likely result in an increase in the number of companies established in China, which would presumably encourage entrepreneurship. It is also a shared belief that these changes simplify structuring considerations and reduce execution costs and expenses for strategic investors.

Second, the relaxation on registered capital under the New Company Law, such as removal of minimum registered capital and waiver of capital verification, does not mean there will be relaxation in the supervision on investment and business operation by government authorities. Instead of procedural examination, government authorities will now focus more on the overall administration and supervision on the shareholders, directors, and executives, as well as company's operations and compliance. In the view that a refined system of credibility for both individuals and companies is expected to play an important role in China, companies are recommended to pay more attention to the corporate governance system, to elevate their compliance level and to take on more social responsibilities.

Third, as previously mentioned, under the new regime, shareholders will be able to agree among themselves the amount of capital to be subscripted, form of capital contribution and timeline for making the contribution. These details are required to be recorded in the company's articles of association, and will be captured in the nationwide corporate information database as new companies are established. The State's Council reform plan specifies that the enterprise annual inspection system, which involves an annual process of renewing SAIC's seal on a company's business license following the filing of various documents by the company, is being replaced with a new annual reporting system.

Whilst the new details to be filed are awaited in the form of further rules, it seems that, at a minimum, the details of shareholder's capital contribution and the assets of the company must be included in an annual report, to be filed by the end of June each year with the SAIC and which will be publicly accessible through the new nationwide corporate information database. The burden of complying with the current annual reviewed procedures should be reduced. That means in turn no more annual inspections, rather more transparency.

Under the new regime, if a company fails to publish its annual SAIC report by a specific time, the relevant SAIC in the locality of the company's registration will publicly categorize the company as an "abnormal business operation." The company can apply for have its name removed from the list once it has complied with its annual reporting obligations for at least 3 years from the time of breach. However, if a company is in breach for more than 3 years, its name will stay in that category permanently and the company will be "blacklisted." The consequences of this punishment can be severe, affecting all aspects of an enterprise's operation. For instance, a company may face restrictions in its own business operations, and its shareholders will be monitored by the regulatory authorities and be restrained from making further investments in China. Its legal representative may also face potential administrative penalties.

Finally, the State Council's reform plan is a further step in implementing the PRC Company Law revisions. It is expected to be followed by China's other government authorities developing further new rules and reviewing and amending their existing procedures, many of which are based on the previous requirements of minimum capital contribution and filing of the accountant's verification of capital contribution with the SAIC.

6.1.4 Impact to Other Regulations and Legal Aspects

The amendment of PRC Company Law is expected to lead several amendments in others laws and regulations in order to apply it as better as possible in the China system.

The State Administration for Industry and Commerce of the PRC has announced the intention to propose some changes and amendments in order to adjust the "Administrative Regulations of the PRC on Company Registration." The intention of SAIC is to develop a public information system to control the credibility of market participants, to improve and simplify the registration system, and to standardize the documents used in the registration procedure.

The Ministry of Commerce (MOC) is working on the draft amendment of the "foreign-funded enterprises", which is already part of the legislative scheme of the 12th NPC Standing Committee. Furthermore, the MOC is also trying to speed up the process through the release of the new company law.

The current "criminal law of the PRC" is also expected to be adjusted with attention to offences related to acts of "fraudulent capital contribution" and "surreptitious withdraw of capital."

Finally, it is expected to have changes in judicial interpretation of the new company law by the Supreme Court. Changes will include the interpretation of the obligation and liability of directors and executives in ensuring shareholders making their capital contribution in time and honoring their commitments given in the subscription.

6.2 "Decision on Major Issues Concerning Comprehensively Deepening Reforms"

On November 12, 2013, in Beijing, during the third plenum of the 18th Central Committee of the Communist Party of China (CPC), it was approved the first important step by Xi Jinping's new leadership, a document entitled "Decision of the Central Committee of the Communist Party of China on Some Major Issues Concerning Comprehensively Deepening the Reform" also called "Decisions." The Party also issued Explanatory Notes for the "Decision of the Central Committee of the Communist Party of China on Some Major Issues Concerning Comprehensively Deepening the Reform" under Xi's personal signature.

The document includes a range of several reforms and measures: reduction of regulatory and administrative burdens and reform taxation, reforms of economic system and role of the government, tax reforms, urban-rural development, ever-greater opening to the outside world, political reform, the rule of law, the supervision and checks and balances of power, China's cultural system, social services, the environment and national defense.

The document is organized in an unusual scheme for economic policy design; it includes over 300 instructions grouped in 16 subheadings:

The 16 Subheadings of the *Decisions*

i. The Significance of and Guiding Thoughts on Deepening the Reform Comprehensively
ii. Adhering to and Improving the Basic Economic System
iii. Accelerating the Improvement of the Modern Market System
iv. Accelerating the Transformation of Government Functions
v. Deepening the Reform of the Fiscal and Taxation Systems
vi. Improving Mechanisms and Institutions for Integrated Development of Urban and Rural Areas
vii. Building a New Open Economic System
viii. Strengthening Building of the Socialist Democratic System
ix. Promoting the Rule of Law
x. Strengthening Check and Oversight System of Exercise of Power
xi. Promoting Innovation in Cultural Systems and Mechanisms
xii. Promoting Reform and Innovation of Social Undertakings
xiii. Making Innovations in Social Governance System
xiv. Accelerating Ecological Progress
xv. Deepening Reform of National Defense and Armed Forces
xvi. Strengthening and Improving the Party's Leadership in the Course of Comprehensively Deepening the Reform

The meeting of Politburo Standing Committee held in May 2013 worked on an eight-category taxonomy for high-priority economic reforms. After, the State Council meeting held on May 6, 2013, issued a nine-points program for economic work:

1. Central fiscal reform
2. Competition policy reform
3. Financial system reform
4. Foreign trade and investment reform
5. State-owned enterprise reform
6. Land policy rationalization
7. Labor and welfare reform
8. Environmental policy reform
9. Innovation policy reform

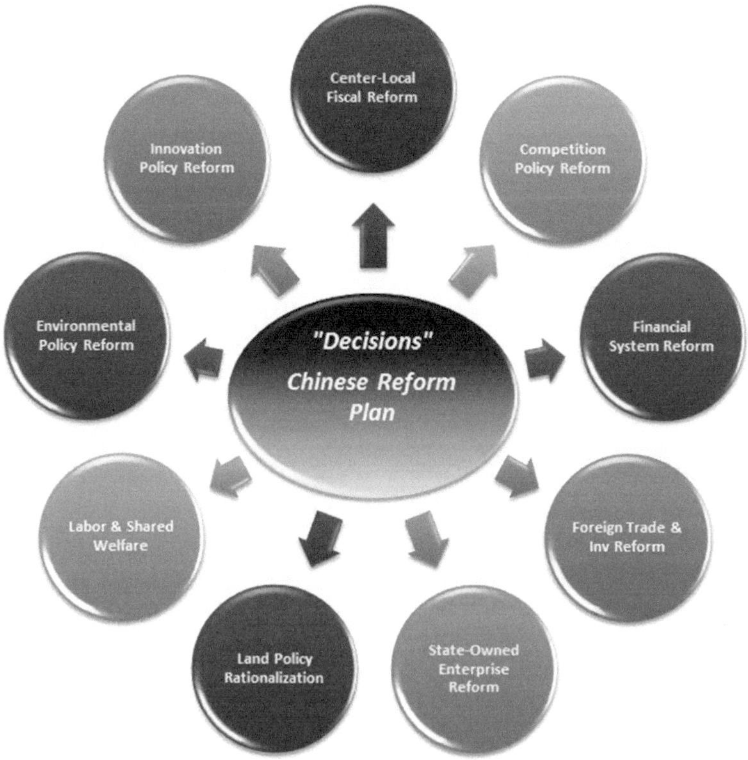

Central-Fiscal Reform

Central-local reform is fundamental for the China's fiscal affairs and for a correct division of power between central and local authorities, the Decisions pledged to realize this, but in general terms, not specifics.

In order to speed up the process of reform, in June 2014, Party leaders approved a top-level national plan for deepening fiscal and tax reforms specifying reform priorities and setting an interim deadline of 2016 to complete the major tasks. The three most urgent tasks for fiscal and tax reforms, in the order they should be carried out, are to: (1) improve budget management; (2) improve the taxation system; and (3) rationalize the center-local fiscal system to match governments' administrative responsibilities with financial resources.

Competition Policy Reform
In China, Competition policy was introduced progressively, starting in 1980 when the State Council emitted its first competition policy instrument. In 1982, they started the elimination of price controls. Whilst in 1992 took place the most significant switch from a planned economy to a "socialist market economy," when the "basic" role for the market and protection for private sector enterprises were introduced into Party doctrine.

In 2007, China created its Anti-Monopoly Law (AML), the most important among several competition laws in force today, which went into effect on August 1, 2008, after 14 years of preparation.

With the new competition policy, China will move from its traditional policy, reducing its range of interventions and allowing to the market to fortify its competition regime. The competition is the principal attribute of an advanced economy system and the Third Plenum aims to reach this goal and want to remove the opposition to competition common in the China's economy.

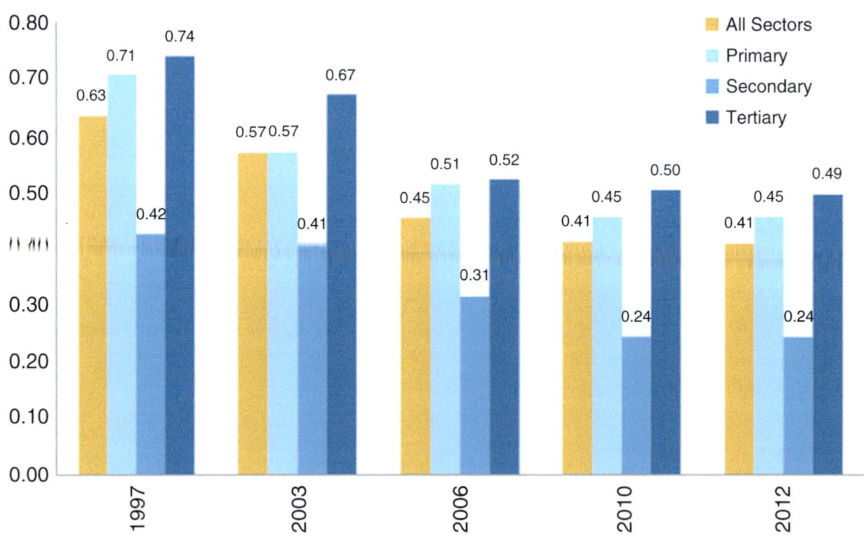

Formal FDI restrictiveness in China, 1997–2012 (Note: 0 means completely unrestricted market access; I means completely restricted. Source: OECD: more detailed breakdown available at: http://www.oecd.org/investment/fdiindex.htm)

Financial System Reform

The fundamental aim of financial reform is to give carte blanche to market forces. Key points regarding financial system reform are:

- Open up the financial sector further both inwardly and outwardly. Authorize establishment of small privately owned banks and other financial institutions that meet certain conditions. Reform policy financial institutions.
- Optimize multi-tier financial market structure. Reform equity issuance registration system. Promote equity finance via many channels. Develop and regulate bond markets. Increase direct finance's prevalence.
- Improve insurance's economic compensation mechanism. Develop mega-disaster insurance scheme.
- Develop inclusive finance.
- Encourage financial innovations. Diversify financial market strata and products.
- Improve renminbi exchange rate formation mechanism through market forces. Accelerate interest rate liberalization.
- Improve the government bond yield curve to better reflect the market's supply-demand balance.
- Open up capital markets both inwardly and outwardly. Further liberalize cross-border capital and financial transactions.
- Establish and optimize a regulatory system for external debt and capital flows under a macroprudential regulatory framework. Accelerate renminbi capital account liberalization.
- Steadily implement financial regulatory reforms and moderation standards. Improve regulatory coordination.
- Clarify financial regulation and risk mitigation responsibilities between national and sub-national governments.
- Develop deposit insurance scheme. Improve financial institutions market exit mechanism.

The intent behind the Third Plenum's is to improve the efficiency of resource allocation by allowing market forces to play bigger role in setting factor prices. Potential financial reform includes liberalization of interest, exchange rates and deposit rate, but market-led liberalization of interest rates in particular is already well under way.

The governor of China's central bank, the People's Bank of China (PBOC), has expressed hopes of completing deposit rate liberalization by 2016, and by the end of 2014, regulators intend to implement a deposit insurance scheme.

Foreign Trade and Investment Reform

Nowadays the China's partners claim for more reciprocity in trade and investments and more facility to enter in the Chinese market. They want that investment approvals for foreign investors are handled in the same ways that domestic businesses are handled. To do that, important steps are made in order to enforce the same laws and regulations on domestic and foreign investment, and to put market forces at the center of the economy. In May 2014, the State Council issued opinions giving a policy guidance on the trade front and third plenum implementation, imports is the first issue of the document.

In order to rationalize the China's foreign trade structure, government has to withdraw from interfering in commercial decision making allowing the market forces to play a decisive role. State Council Opinions suggest a several special policies for tweaking the situation: manage the ratio of export-processing trade to trade for final consumption, promote Chinese companies going abroad to trade, stimulate and improve trade exchanges, growth rates for imports and exports, accelerate efforts to "improve the trade structure," and set the pace at which services imports should grow.

The new company law and the Shanghai Free Trade Zone will be other important steps in order to reform the sector. Rules are to be fair, open, and conducive to provide a level playing field for all firms. About this reform Decision 9 of Third Plenum, says:

> We will make the business registration system more convenient by reducing the number of items that require qualification verification, turning certification before licensing into licensing before certification, and gradually changing the paid-in capital registration system into a subscribed capital registration system. … We will reform the market oversight system, implement uniform market oversight, tidy up and annul all sorts of regulations and methods that impede the national unified market and fair competition, strictly ban and punish all unlawful acts extending preferential policies, combat regional protection, and oppose monopoly and unfair competition.

Foreigners welcome (Source: China's state administration of foreign exchange The Wall Street Journal)

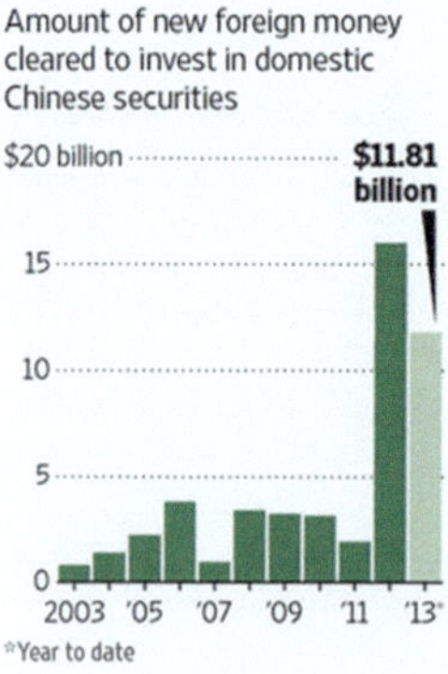

State-Owned Enterprises Reform

State-owned enterprises (SOEs) and state shareholding are a smaller part of China's economy today than in the past, but these sectors still dominate the marketplace in many ways. With this reform Beijing push for a "mixed ownership," one of the reasons is because the gap between state-owned and non state-owned enterprises is getting wider, based on fixed targets such as return on equity, state-owned enterprises are not performing very well. Now, for the health of the China's economy, Beijing has to understand how to redirect the resources from inefficient state-owned sectors and companies to efficient ones.

The goals of reform include dilution of state shareholding through the introduction of private shareholders; extracting more profit from SOEs to finance public expenditures; specifying which industries legitimately require state control; and understanding that the normal market competition should apply, when the state remains a non-controlling shareholder in a competitive industry.

The reform wants to reduce political interference in the management of SOEs by designing the holding companies to focus on maximizing shareholder value rather than advancing the government's policy goals.

In the late August 2014, the State Asset Supervision and Administration Commission (SASAC) in Beijing was broadening implementation of governance reforms at central SOEs, and more than 20 provinces had published SOE reform plans that involved listing or selling off assets in up to 70 % of provincial SOEs by 2017.

Better private than red (Source: Gavekal Dragonomics)

Land Policy Rationalization

Actually, in China, local authorities can expropriate land and other properties without permit of rural residents for the aim of "public interest," the expropriated holders receive an indemnity often much lower than normal market rates. Recent surveys shown that Local authorities sell the expropriated land to property developers at the price 10 times higher than the compensation paid to farmers. This situation developed constant social protest and violent conflict. A new land policy could solve this problem; it would be a key to achieving social stability and sustainable growth in agricultural sector.

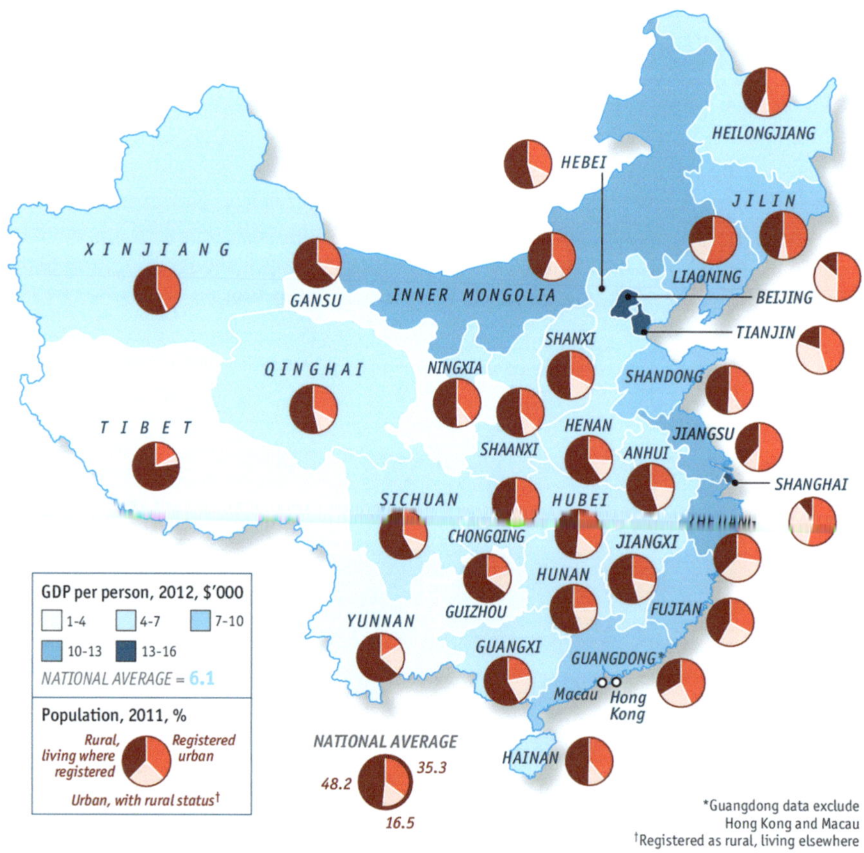

Sources: Haver analytics; The Economist estimates

In addition, without reform Beijing can't realize its purpose to support the urban labor pool with as many as 300 million permanent new workers, 200 million of whom are already in towns and cities but are reluctant to relinquish their ties to rural land and commit to urban futures. In August 2014, Beijing announced a land registration system, with interim deadlines for 2014, 2015, and 2016 along the way to a complete national database by 2017. This system would help improve the foundation for property rights and due process and get incentives to urbanize back on track.

Labor and Shared Welfare

From 1982 China's working-age population increased by 375 million people, to just over 1 billion. Today, this demographic growth has run its course, and China's labor force size is decreasing. In addition, the incorporation of rural workers into cities has brought China to a turning point with several implications for competitiveness and social stability.

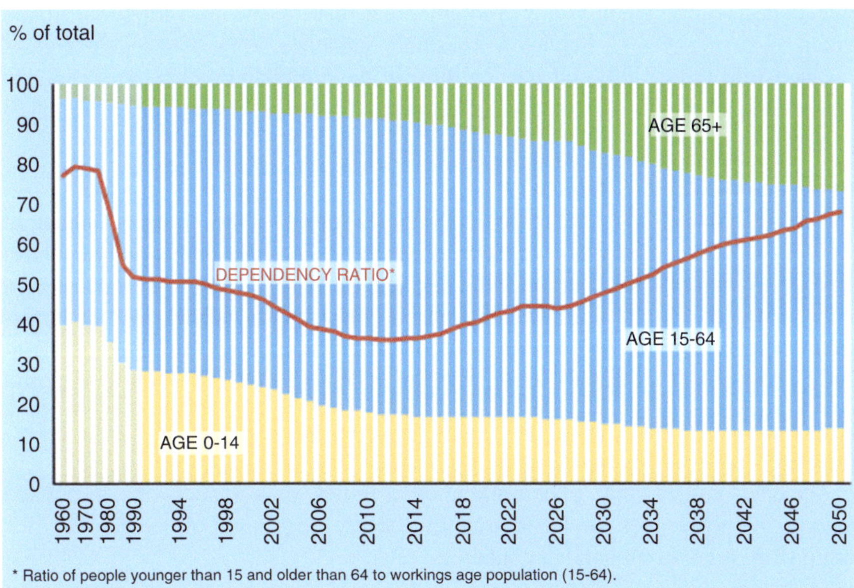

China's population structure by age group (Source: China Statistical Yearbook. U.S. Census International Database (1991–2050), Rhodium Group estimates)

The decisions address labor and shared welfare in many aspects: education, health care, worker rights, minimum wage, and income inequality, with particular focus on incoming disparities between urban and rural areas.

Hukou system introduced in 1950s, which ties people's access to services and benefits to their residential status, will be improved.

In June, 2014, the "Deepening Reform Small Leading Group" discussed steps Beijing can take on urban-rural dynamics to transform the economic development pattern, build a fair and unified market, and promote equal access to basic public services, during the meeting of June it was reviewed a comprehensive hukou and rural land system reform program.

It describes formalization of urban residency for irregular 200 million workers now temporarily in urban areas, an additional transfer of 100 million people out of agricultural work into towns and cities, and up to 100 million new formal urban hukou permits. In March 2014, Shandong province issued its 2014 hukou reform policy, which permits migrants to obtain hukou by meeting two requirements: a stable job and a stable residence.

In May 2014, Jiangsu province announced a more liberal urban and rural development policy, wherein migrants to counties and small-to-medium cities may obtain hukou by having either a stable job or a stable residence.

One Child Policy will end for one-third of the population, allowing couples to have a second child if one of parent is an only child, the first major easing of its respective birth policy.

Environmental Policy Reform

The permissive Beijing's environmental policy allowed to build a strong industrial economy in China, many firms have been attracted from this policy and they have generated outsized profit, but, now, the negative impacts of that policy are reflected in the quality of life in China. The imperative to reform China's environmental management is stated in the first sentence of the first decision in the Third Plenum manifesto. The goals of reform are to improve the management of natural resources and to establish lines in ecological protection, with stronger ecological compensation for pollution victims.

The environment could play a role in other issues, such as social instability and poverty, the government understood that its economic plans could be derailed if it fail to stop its environmental degradation.

In order to do that, Beijing established key points to watch including: cleaning up China's notorious system of Environmental Impact Assessments, strengthening the Ministry of Environmental Protection and giving it authority over the provincial and local Environmental Protection Bureau, and creating a system of sanctions for polluters.

In January 2014, the Ministry of Environmental Protection (MEP) began to negotiate requisites for particulate matter reductions with each of China's provinces. It also implemented a plan for emphasizing public disclosure by making available to the public real-time air and water pollution emissions for 15,000 Chinese industrial firms. The data have also been made accessible to application designers who have developed public interfaces for viewing them.

On March 25, 2014, the MEP started reporting national ambient pollution data based on a measurement program begun in 2013, and it announced that at least 30 million Chinese were breathing polluted air on a typical day.

In addition, Beijing amended the environmental protection law to allow non-government organizations to bring public interest lawsuits, and many industrial firms are showing their emissions to the public on smartphone apps.

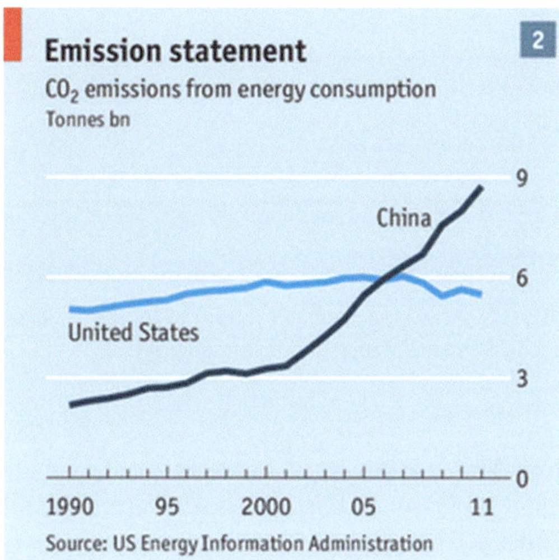

Innovation Policy Reform

Innovation does not come from guidelines or subventions; it comes from creativity, experimentation, and entrepreneurial initiative with toleration of mistakes and failures. Third Plenum set up the key points to reform this sector including, increasing vitality and creativity of the non-public sector; building an innovative and service-oriented industry. The reform will give priority to empowerment of market mechanisms to improve innovative capacity and initiative spirit in China.

Beijing want to build basic framework conditions in order to stimulate and protect the innovation, such as a functioning legal system, protection of intellectual property, a strong educational system, and access to financial support. During its meeting in June 2014 meeting, the Deepening Reform Small Leading Group established a Program Regarding Establishing Intellectual Property Rights Court, which was a step toward realization of the "explore establishing IPR courts" provision of

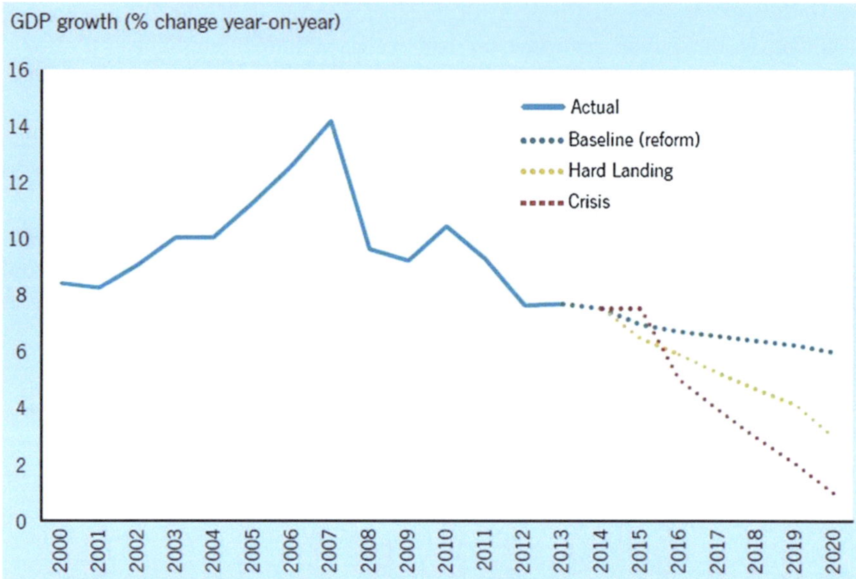

Fig. 6.1 China's GDP outlook with and without reform (Sources: Chinese National Bureau of Statistics, Rhodium Group estimates. Projections begin after 2013)

the Decisions. The program says Jiangsu, Guangdong, Beijing, and Shanghai have been formulating pilot programs in this area since December 2012. Separately, on May 1, 2014, an amended Trademark Law came into force, with accompanying State Council amendments to the trademark Law Implementing Regulations.

The new law makes useful improvements on trademark protection and administrative processes.

In addition, Beijing wants to reform and improve entrepreneurship education by universities. In May 2014, education officials announced changes in the content of the national college admission examination, or *gaokao*, beginning in 2017. The emphasis on English language proficiency will be dropped.

On August 18, 2014, the Deepening Reform Small Leading Group reviewed and passed Measures on Test-Based Admission moving this reform ahead (Fig. 6.1).

In addition to "Decisions" issued by the Third Plenum, with the goal to carry out a new economic system based on a open economy system and on consumption, the China's National Development and Reform Commission released on March 2014 a new set of economic reform measures: "Opinions on Key Tasks for Deepening Economic Structural Reform in 2013." It includes 22 major duties in different fields:

Fiscal and Taxation System

1. Improving the fiscal budget system and establishing an open, transparent, standardized, and complete budget system
2. Adjusting the scope and rate of consumption tax, and including the products that seriously pollute the environment or consume large volumes of resources under the taxable scope
3. Expanding the scope of the pilot program for property tax on individual housing
4. Expanding the scope of ad valorem collection of resource taxes to cover coal and other taxable items, and cancelling relevant fees or funds in coal exploitation and sale
5. Improving the fiscal and tax policies for the growing, technologica, and export-oriented small or micro-sized enterprises
6. Expanding the scope of business tax (BT) to value-added tax (VAT) pilot conversion

The BT to VAT pilot conversion shall be carried out in the transportation industry and some modern service sectors nationwide, and the railway transportation, post and telecommunications, and other relevant industries shall be incorporated into the scope of the pilot program.

Financial System

1. Expanding the scope of the pilot program for the small and medium-sized enterprise share transferring system
2. Promoting the formulation of the plan for implementing the deposit insurance system and establishing a risk compensation and sharing mechanism for financial institutions
3. Promoting the interest and exchange rate liberalization:
    - The range for deposit and lending interest rates floating shall be expanded and the market benchmark rate system shall be established and improved.
    - The system for the formation of RMB exchange rate shall be improved.
    - The convertibility of RMB under capital accounts shall be pushed forward steadily.
    - The system for the qualified domestic individual investors to make investments overseas shall be set up.
    - Research shall be done to push forward the domestic issuance of RMB bonds by qualified overseas institutions.

Investment and Financing System

1. Cleaning up the policies and regulations that hinder fair competition, thereby pushing forward the effective entry of private capital into the areas of finance, energy, railways and telecommunications
2. Reforming the railway investment and financing system

The compensation system for public-benefit transport and a proper pricing mechanisms for rail operations shall be established, thereby creating conditions for the introduction of private capital into the railway sector.

Prices of Resource Products

1. Pushing forward the electricity fee reform and simplifying the price classification in the sales of electricity
2. Facilitating the construction of a nationwide market system for coal trading
3. Establishing a ladder-price mechanism for electricity, water, and natural gas to charge higher per-unit prices for extra usage

Administrative system

1. Deepening government institutional reform
2. Streamlining governmental administration and delegating powers to lower levels
3. Innovating government public services

Basic Livelihood System

1. Facilitating the critical illness insurance for urban and rural residents
2. Establishing and improving the system on guaranteeing minimum living standards
3. Establishing the strictest regulatory system for food and drug safety to cover various stages of production, circulation, and consumption
4. Establishing the strictest environmental protection supervision and administration system and the standardized and scientific ecological compensation system:

   - Formulating comprehensive measures to strengthen prevention and control of air, water, and rural (soil) pollution.
   - Implementing the pilot trading program on pollution-discharge rights and carbon emission rights.
   - Conducting research to set up a national trading market for pollution-discharge rights and carbon emission rights, and implementing the pilot program for compulsory liability insurance for environmental pollution.
   - Formulating measures on investigating and handling environmental emergencies and conducting research on the ecological compensation regulation legislation.

In conclusion, if correctly implemented the Reform will permit to achieve a 6 % potential GDP growth in 2020, with a moderate decline from current levels to deliver a $14.4 trillion Chinese economy in that year. Several analysts believe that 6 % growth in 2020 is what China needs in order to have an economic and social stability. This potential GDP would allow a significant growth in two-way flows of trade and finance with the world; the annual two-way trade would be $2.6 trillion higher by 2020, the stock of cross-border assets and liabilities rises by $10 trillion during this interval. Abandoning the trade surpluses, China can expand Chinese net foreign asset position leads from today's net Chinese investment income payments to the world to a net income inflow from foreign investments of almost $150 billion a year, along with considerably increase domestic growth. Without reform, the Chinese economy would see, just 1–3 % annual GDP growth in 2020, and drastic lower flows of trade, corporate FDI, and investment.

The speed of reform and organization improvement happening in China today is slower than was predicted in 2013, or than most people believe. The target of 2020 for the complete application of reforms is ambitious.

In 2014, many interim deadlines between now and 2020 were announced, with specific milestones. In order to make these targets more significant, reports are being issued, and public interests are being invited to scrutinize results. Many enterprises are reporting their daily pollution, and non-government advocacy groups are now authorized to bring an action against these companies if they are not complying with emissions restraints.

Chapter 7
Further Developments

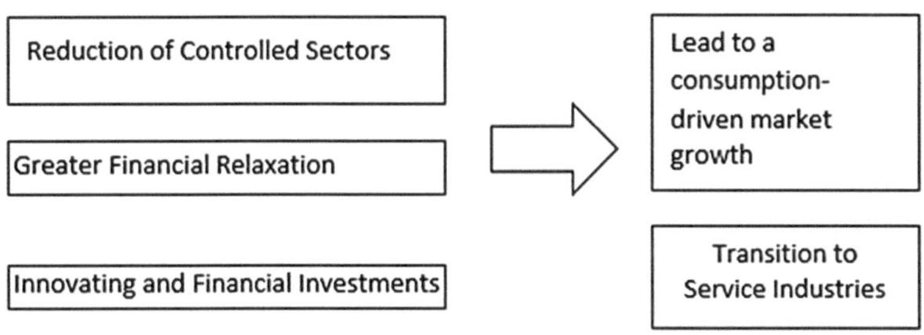

While growth, until today, has been strongly driven by exports and traditional industries such as fixed asset investments and low-end manufacturing, China now needs to change its strategy and step up the game to compete on the same field of the most developed countries. In 2013, China performed the lowest GDP growth in 12 years, and the expectations for 2014 are that growth target of 7.5 % will not be met. China is stuck in the middle of industrialization as the cardiotonic effect from the late 1970s reform has been fading away, resulting in a diminishing growth rate, reflected by the fluctuated performance in the tertiary sectors. The decade from 1982 witnessed a rapid advance in Chinese services sector. However, the tertiary industry occupied in China GDP figure began to shrink from 2002 and then kept fluctuating rather than an increasing momentum. A strand of literatures ascribed that to the abnormal dilatation of the second industry while the others thought it had something to do with the inner structure of the tertiary industry. For the former, after entering the twenty-first century, the central government intended to pull up Chinese economic using administrative measures. Ma and Zhao (2008) claimed that the politic regime had been focusing on simulating GDP growth in an unhealthy way that ignores the development in long run. Policy in the last decade before twenty-first century preferred to invest in projects that could gain great magnitude profits within a relative short period such as manufacturing and construction industry, and

L. Riccardi, *Investing in China through Free Trade Zones*,
DOI 10.1007/978-3-662-47354-2_7

the radical progression then resulted in less support in investment in the tertiary industry. For the latter, urging issues includes insufficient economic aggregate and unreasonable constitutions have been covered under a fast growth superficial phenomenon. Except that the tertiary industry's contribution to GDP is smaller than the average of developing countries, traditional services sectors (e.g. catering and transportation) compose the most significant part of Chinese tertiary industry. In order to upgrade the economic structure and therefore break the sluggish situation, China needs to adjust investment regime for times, gradually reducing the threshold for foreign investment to enter Chinese market and to focus on new growth drivers; with the 12-years-plan, China identified the main areas of focus that need to be quickly developed such as industrial sector, green and high tech development, domestic consumption, and service sector. Opaque corporate governance, heavy state involvement, red tape, closeness of financial markets, and the negative list make it extremely hard and frustrating for foreign investors to do business in China. Following these premises, it's understandable why the project of Shanghai Free Trade Zone is receiving wide approval, with the premier Li KeQiang in the first row of supporters, and why many other regions are asking Beijing the approval for establishing bonded zones on their territories.

7.1 Opening the Services Market Is an Irresistible Trend

Shanghai pilot FTZ is expected to help China to find a path out of the stagnant situation by seeking for a universal principle that can be adopted cross the country. In other words, Shanghai is an experimental field for China to try new controversial regulation on a pilot basis. The ban on gambling is a supportive point of that because gambling is a special case to attract capital and is not appropriate for other Chinese inland cities Besides, Chinese top leaders indicates that there would not be another FTZ before Shanghai FTZ succeeds, which also reveals the special nature of Shanghai FTZ.

Bonded zones, bonded logistic parks, bonded ports, and export processing zones are not newly introduced concepts in China, many areas already grant fiscal benefits, but the pilot area is revolutionary because of its different purpose: while the absence of tariffs on manufacturing is aimed at raising GDP and therefore serving a short-term growth objective, openness in the service sector, on the other side, would introduce long-lasting sophisticated management systems and human resources. Shanghai Free Trade Zone is therefore aimed at providing a genuine free trade zone for financial and foreign exchange and encourages cross border financing and fund management. By analyzing the neighborhood, it's possible to understand how paramount are the service functions, especially in terms of financial sector, for free trading to expand further. Singapore, for instance, was born mainly as a logistic center but to maintain a high level of competitiveness it achieved with attractive fiscal benefits and a high level of liberalization, it had to develop an efficient financial system that would not only serve the incentive purpose but would also tow other trading fields. Like Singapore, also Japan and Hong Kong initially started out as logistic centers but eventually became main global financial centers. Offshore services are another pillar of financial development and another area on which Shanghai needs to focus in the future. Although still undeveloped, offshore funding can be boosted if Shanghai Free Trade Zone will manage to exploit some advantages it already benefits from: easy facility of cross-border business, taxation benefits, and lower operational costs. It's the purpose that diversifies the Shanghai Free Trade Zone from the other bonded area in China; the area is in fact conceived as a platform for testing concepts that have always been controversial in the Chinese economy: full convertibility of the RMB, the opening up of financial services, and duty free trade. With this experimental area the Government wants to reduce the number of controlled sectors, attract innovating and efficient investments and achieve a high degree of liberalization in the service market by loosening the operating environment for foreign capital steps further than WTO GATS in order to achieve a domestic-driven consumption growth and transition toward service industries. Mr. Ai Baojun, head of the free trade zone's administrative committee, emphasized the broader significance of the Shanghai free trade zone, saying it was being used by China's top leaders as a vehicle to experiment with aggressive reforms that are designed to be rolled out on a nationwide basis if successful; the main purpose is to experiment with administrative innovations rather than to implement preferential policies.

The special experimental nature of Shanghai Pilot Zone is such that on the success of it will depend on the approval by Beijing of further bonded areas in China. Not many 28 square meters of land are subject to the same pressure.

So far China has been hesitating to reduce administrative measures to reduce the risk of jeopardizing the financial system since a massive amount of foreign loans could easily lead to a debt crisis. On the other side, Free Trade Zone optimists claim that heavy infusion of foreign capital would break the monopoly and introduce a competitive status that would make Chinese financial market look more attractive worldwide, transition of administrative government functions will redefine relationships between government and the market and reforms will help China to certify to the latest standards of international trade to enhance investors' confidence.

As we previously discussed, February 2014 saw two important regulatory reforms for Shanghai Free Trade Zone take place, reforms that will change the Chinese economic scenario: the relaxation of capital restrictions for corporate registration and the permission accorded by the five third-party payment firms to handle yuan-denominated cross-border payment in Shanghai's free trade zone. The relevance of these reforms is not overestimated and the outcome will be a disruptive change on what currencies we use, how money flows, and how financial institutions dominate global finance.

7.2 Sectors Undergoing Structural Change

Pursuant to the general plan, restrictions on foreign investment are wholly or partially waived for a total of 17 industries within the Free Trade Zone. Six are expected to be the sectors that will experiment the biggest structural changes.

7.2.1 Financial Sector

The Free Trade Zone is built by following the guideline of "complete deregulation of first tier, safe and efficient full-control of second tier and free flow of goods within the Zone." "First tier" refers to the relationship between the Free Trade Zone and abroad, which goods can freely exit from and enter into China free of customs supervision; "Second tier" refers to the relationship between the Zone and the rest of mainland China, which movements of goods shall be subject to applicable taxes and regulation.

The above guidelines are fairly easily understood when applied in physical trade; however, they are confusing when applied in the financial industry. These guidelines seemingly borrowed directly from the experience of other international free trade zones, but Shanghai appears to be an exception where its financial reform has been much more laggard than other free trade zones. The definitions have also given rise to various speculations and uncertainties on the financial reform, such as should one financial institution have to open a branch or subsidiary in the Free Trade Zone (with area of only 28.78 km^2) to benefit from the financial reform? Does complete deregulation of first tier mean full liberalization of financial operations within the Free Trade Zone? How full-control of second tier concerning financial industry will be ensured once first tier is deregulated?

One of the main targets of the Shanghai FTZ is the opening to foreign competition of financial sector through freely convertible capital accounts and opening of financial services. Under current PRC foreign exchange regulations, conversion between RMB and a foreign currency is permitted for current account transactions, but is subject to approval for capital account transactions, such as foreign equity investment and foreign debt. In addition, FIEs are generally not permitted to convert foreign currency into RMB for investments in other PRC companies or the real estate market in China. If foreign currency is allowed to be freely converted into RMB in the Free Trade Zone and flow to other regions of China and transmitted overseas for investment or other purposes, cross-border transactions through the Free Trade Zone will undoubtedly increase.

China's foreign exchange policy and capital controls have been highly controversial over the last decade. Whether the discussion centers on the apparent undervaluation of the Renminbi (RMB) or the stringent control of currency flowing in and out of China, it seems quite certain that these issues will continue to receive considerable attention in the foreseeable future.

Amidst the controversy and accusations, what is often overlooked or ignored are the great efforts already made to internationalize the RMB. China has gradually increased the convertibility of its currency over the last decade as it pledged it would do upon joining the World Trade Organization in 2001. In fact, it is true at this very moment that companies can engage in limited trade, hedging and even cross-border trade settlement in RMB.

China keeps a firm grip on currency flows in and out of the country. However, the severity is highly dependent on whether the currency flows are associated with a current account or a capital account.

A current account in China includes categories such as the sale of goods, provision of services, interest payments, and repatriation of dividends. For domestic Chinese companies, foreign currency received by such means may be retained or sold to financial institutions permitted to engage in foreign currency conversion; whereas, on the other hand, foreign companies receiving profits in RMB may convert them into foreign exchange through a process by which certification is obtained from the State Administration of Foreign Exchange (SAFE).

Foreign exchange restrictions on the capital account items, however, are far stricter. In broad terms, any transaction whose purpose is to create or transfer capital will be regarded as a capital account item. Examples of such items include foreign direct investment (FDI), outbound direct investment (ODI), cross-border or cross-currency loans, capital markets investments, and derivative transactions.

Foreign companies interested in FDI must obtain approval through SAFE and other Chinese government authorities and may thereafter inject capital into their China-based entities and operations. Chinese investors interested in ODI must obtain approval from the National Development and Reform Commission (NDRC) and Ministry of Commerce, among other agencies, and are then permitted to invest abroad.

As we previously stated, International capital markets investors may invest in domestic Chinese capital markets only through Qualified Foreign Institutional Investors (QFII). Domestic Chinese are permitted to invest in global capital markets only by means of Qualified Domestic Institutional Investor (QDII).

These restrictions present some serious obstacles to capital markets participants and corporate investors. On the one hand, it may be rather difficult for foreigners to gain exposure to Chinese capital markets, and, on the other hand, global companies may face intriguing challenges when seeking to hedge their exposure to the RMB. While such challenges can only be truly overcome when there is a freely convertible RMB, the Chinese government has already initiated measures that in part may solve the problem.

Hong Kong as Proving Ground

Because of its position as a global financial center and strong legal framework, Hong Kong has time and again served as a laboratory for China's newest financial and currency policies. This was the case in 2003 when the Chinese government sought to develop an offshore RMB-market as part of the currency's internationalization process.

RMB transactions began in 2004 with an arrangement that allowed Hong Kong banks to develop an offshore deposit market for RMB. In 2007, the Chinese government took another major step in liberating its capital accounts when it allowed companies to issue RMB denominated debt in Hong Kong – the so-called "Dim Sum Bonds."

Although Hong Kong's offshore market allowed both non-Chinese individuals and companies to own RMB, the Chinese currency still had a long way to go before it could claim to be truly convertible. A very strenuous approval process was required to transfer the offshore RMB back into Mainland China. In fact, because of these stringent capital controls, the Chinese government had effectively fostered and developed two parallel markets for the RMB, the onshore RMB market and the offshore RMB market.

Another milestone was reached in 2009, when a pilot program allowed cross-border trade to be settled in RMB. Initially, this program only included the Chinese cities of Shanghai, Guangzhou, Shenzhen, Zhuhai, and Dongguan, the territories of Hong Kong and Macau, and the ASEAN countries. The program was gradually expanded, and in 2012 all Chinese provinces were permitted to conduct international, cross-border trade as long as the Chinese participant had obtained an import-export qualification in its business license.

The pilot program for the cross-border settlement of RMB complemented the bilateral currency swaps that China had signed with selected partner countries after December 2008. Essentially, these swap agreements allowed foreign governments to offer local importers RMB financing when purchasing Chinese goods. Among the countries that have entered into these RMB swap agreements are Japan, Russia, Singapore, Australia, Hong Kong, and Brazil.

The bilateral currency swap agreements with national trading partners, the cross-border trading program for Chinese companies, and the offshore RMB-market are very important steps forward toward the ultimate goal of liberating the RMB.

Cross-Border Arbitrage

At present foreign and domestic companies can access the RMB-debt markets in both Hong Kong and Mainland China through the issuance of Dim Sum and Panda bonds, respectively. They can also conduct cross-border transactions, and they can trade in RMB offshore with minimum restrictions. So how come there are two different RMB markets with separate quotations?

Again the issue relates back to China's stringent capital controls. Corporations will have a natural incentive to buy RMB in the cheapest market and sell them in the priciest, which will limit the divergence between the domestic Yuan (CNY) and the offshore Yuan (CNH). However, as transactions can only be conducted against the background of approved corporate activity, there is no clean cut arbitrage relationship between the two markets.

Thus, as long as the cross-border arbitrage can be based on current account items such as trade and profit repatriation, companies can move RMB relatively easily across the Chinese border and potentially take advantage of the spread between the two markets.

However, the cross-border arbitrage becomes difficult to implement when transaction relates to China's capital accounts. Under normal circumstances it takes 2 or 3 months for a foreign company to inject new capital into a Mainland China foreign-invested entity and the process may potentially be extended by another month when the capital to be injected comes in the form of offshore RMB. Investors have to undergo a similarly cumbersome process when funds are transferred through the QFII and QDII schemes.

Thus, for non-Chinese companies and individuals the capital controls do not put severe restrictions on the currency flow out of the country; the problem is rather getting capital into the country.

But why does it have to be so complicated? Why bother to establish offshore RMB hubs? Wouldn't it be more feasible simply to remove the capital controls? The answer to these questions can be traced back to what economists have dubbed "The Impossible Trinity". Ideally a country's central bank would like to be able to (1) fix a country's exchange rate, (2) allow a free capital flow, and (3) lead an independent monetary policy. However, in praxis this is hardly possible and the central bank will have to forfeit one of these three items. While countries such as the United Kingdom and United States of America largely have relinquished their exchange rate controls to maintain free movement of capital and an autonomous monetary policy, the Chinese government chose to sacrifice the free cross-border flow of capital to keep a fixed exchange rate and control money supply.

The Impossible Trinity also highlights the connection between China's recent moves to lessen capital controls while expanding the daily trading band of the RMB. China may be at a point where it needs to let capital flow more freely in order to facilitate a more efficient distribution. A prime example in this regard is the country's overheated real estate market, where considerable amounts of Chinese have put their savings due to the lack of alternative investment options. Allowing Chinese companies and individuals to invest more freely abroad could not only help China to deflate some of the domestic asset bubbles, but could also deliver some of the much needed capital for struggling western economies like the ones of Europe.

Furthermore, if Chinese investors and enterprises were less constrained with regards to outbound investments, the People's Bank of China – China's central bank – would be less dependent on buying US treasury bonds and could thereby more easily diversify its holdings into other asset classes. The extra outbound investments would most likely cause the RMB to depreciate against the Dollar. In fact, this process may already have begun, as China's stock of outbound investments continues to increase while its foreign exchange reserves slowly are starting to decline. This development has so far been accompanied by two percent depreciation of the USD/RMB exchange rate since the beginning of May 2012.

China may have a long way to go before it can claim a truly international currency. Meanwhile, the primary obstacles to convertibility are associated with capital accounts restrictions and lack of access to the Chinese capital markets. The ability to raise capital and hedge risk is consequently restricted. Arguably the offshore RMB financing services in Hong Kong and elsewhere are fit to aid companies raising capital to be injected in Mainland entities or to settle trade. Hong Kong also provides sophisticated services to manage risk.

Besides a US Dollar settled non-deliverable CNY forward market, Hong Kong also offers deliverable USD-CNH forwards, swaps and foreign exchange options. The interest rate risk can be managed through CNH interest rate swaps or alternatively through cross-currency swaps that under normal circumstances provide higher liquidity. Hypothetically, this means that companies with access to both markets potentially may benefit from the interest differentials.

While the process of liberating the country's capital account has been rather slow, it seems imminent that capital flows in and out of China will be less constrained in the near future. Looser capital controls and a less constricted RMB exchange rate may in fact not only turn into a win-win situation for China, but also for the global community as a whole.

To gain competitiveness in the financial sector, China must act on two fields: innovation and strength. In order to accelerate innovation China is going to use the Free Trade Zone as an experimental platform for controversial reforms such as the liberalization of the interest, yuan-denominated cross border transactions and full convertibility of yuan-denominated capital accounts. To liberalize cross border funding and make it easier, companies will be encouraged to use both domestic and overseas resources and markets and the model for managing foreign debt will be reformed. The liberalization of interest rate that will generate an independent pricing mechanism in line with the development of the real economy.

Cross-border financing and use of RMB will facilitate trade investing and relaxation on foreign debt control. The foreign debt management reform will make it easier for a group to cross-border finance its operation and pool cash from its subsidiaries located worldwide. Easier access to capital, domestic or foreign, lowers financing costs with the banks, thus resulting in a more efficient capital allocation.

Subsidiaries established by the financial leasing companies in the Pilot Zone which only hold one aircraft or one vessel will no longer be subject to the minimum registered capital requirement; financial leasing companies will be allowed to engage in factoring business as a major or sideline business.

In order to strengthen and make financial markets more functional, the financial services system is being opened completely to foreign capital and the generation of foreign capitalized banks and Chinese-foreign banks joints are being encouraged. On 28 September, the CBCR (China Banking Regulatory Commission) published the Notice on Banking Regulation in China Free Trade Zone Area where it is outlined its expectations to reshape the financial sector by supporting the establishment of non-bank financial institution, the development of foreign banks and offshore business, the entrance of private capital into banking sector, cross-border investments and financing services (such as commodity trade financing, supply chain trade financing, offshore shipping financing, modern service sector financial support, domestic loans under overseas guarantee, and commercial papers).

Investment banks, financial companies, trust companies, and currency brokerage companies have been removed from revised list so foreign investments are now allowed. Related to the liberalization of yuan-denominated capital accounts noted earlier, the State Council Notice removes the restrictions in the Shanghai Free trade Zone on Chinese banks providing offshore services, designing a model close to the JOM, the Japanese offshore market, wherein trading is conducted through an offshore account established within the financial institution. This regulation opens the door for many opportunities and, of course, new risks. In order for these measures not to jeopardize the financial system, it's paramount to implement a good internal credit risk system and a transparent and honest disclosure procedure in collaboration with Shanghai Head Office of the People's Bank of China. According to the "Opinions of the People's Bank of China on Providing Financial Support for the Development of the China (Shanghai) Pilot Free Trade Zone," Shanghai municipal financial institutions shall follow the requirements of "separate identifiers, separate accounting, independent statements, special reporting and seeking self-balance" to carry out free trade separate accounting business. A separate account management system will be established for convertible transactions under capital items to facilitate investing and financing.

Although the CBCR measures for the establishment of foreign banks are predicated on certain conditions being met, in the Shanghai FTZ, branches can be established and sub-branches can be promoted to branches. The Government is always been conservative about the number of branches allowed and this rule will make it's going to encourage a big number of offices to upgrade to the branch status. Moreover, partially licensed banks are now admitted, meaning that also new banks that don't adhere to the traditional business model focused on deposits and loans could now operate side by side with traditional banks.

By looking at these reforms, it's evident as convenience for companies to set up in the FTZ lies not only in the lighter red tape burden but also in the financial advantages.

The establishment of privileges in the Free Trade Zone will particularly benefit some sectors:

Offshore Insurance Market

The Shanghai FTZ will be positioned as the offshore insurance market test zone, the insurance innovation test field, and the insurance fund overseas investment base.

The test zone will mainly develop the areas of shipping insurance, high-end health and medical insurance, liability insurance and credit insurance, and will also explore the construction of an insurance market (exchange). The main goals of the zone are to further internationalize China's insurance industry and introduce a more efficient and transparent insurance supervisory system that can be applied domestically at a later stage.

With respect to the overseas investment base for the insurance fund, the Shanghai FTZ will study the two-way (outward and domestic) investment with insurance funds and expand the overseas investment scope of the insurance fund.

In terms of the shipping insurance business, the CIRC (China Insurance Regulatory Commission) Shanghai Branch is working on further promoting the construction of shipping insurance services and introducing more companies to establish shipping insurance centers in Shanghai.

Pei also revealed that a shipping insurance association is expected to be established before the end of this year, and the CIRC Shanghai Branch is now cooperating with the local government to include the insurance industry information under the supervision of the Shanghai FTZ.

Financial Leasing
The State Council notice has eased minimum registered capital restrictions for leasing companies established in the Shanghai FTZ and removed the minimum threshold required. In step with the ease on restrictions, some tax breaks and fiscal benefits will be also granted. In addition, financial leasing companies will also be allowed to engage in the factoring business. For nonbanks, CBRC measures provide support for global corporations to establish financing subsidiaries, autofinancing companies, and consumer finance companies in the Shanghai FTZ, as well as for Shanghai registered trust companies to move to Shanghai FTZ and nationwide financial asset management companies to establish branches there. The banks that have already received approval to open sub-branches are both domestic and global such as Citibank and Singapore based DBS Bank, HSBC, and Bank of East Asia.

Another interesting point is the admission of foreign companies into credit research. The administration of credit histories of corporations and individuals by foreign companies will potentially encourage consumer finance and supply of funds to growth sectors.

Trade Financing
The People's Bank of China (PBOC) is considering setting up a trading platform for bill of exchange trade financing at the Shanghai FTZ, according to Pan Yingli, professor at Shanghai Jiaotong University.

After establishment of the platform, trade financing tools such as letter of credit will be able to be traded on the platform and the traders thereof will be the major banks, including foreign-invested banks and Chinese banks.

Trade financing refers to short-term financing or credit facilitation related to the import and export trade settlement provided by banks to importers or exporters. The main methods include factoring, letter of credit, outward bill, and import bill advance.

As of now, China does not have a nationwide trading platform, which largely hinders the development of the bill of exchange market in the country. Pan believes setting up a trading platform of bill of exchange in the Shanghai FTZ will largely facilitate the RMB financing of overseas trade.

Future Market
The security industry is being liberalized as the CSRC (China Securities Regulatory Commission) published on 29 September 2013 its policy measures for the capital market to support and promote the Shanghai Free Trade Zone declaring it will support qualified entities and individuals in the FTZ to make investments in foreign and domestic securities and futures markets and to carry out over-the-counter transactions of commodities and financial derivatives for domestic clients. Also the OTC trading of commodity futures and derivatives is being liberalized for domestic investors through securities and futures brokerage companies. Moreover, the CSRC will consent foreign companies to issue RMB bonds in domestic markets and to set up subsidiaries in the FTZ.

The Shanghai Futures Exchange (SFE) will establish a bulk commodity trading platform on a pilot basis at the Shanghai FTZ, as part of the continuous efforts to further open up China's financial market and facilitate the construction of a multitiered capital market system.

The CSRC Measures support the establishment of securities and futures brokerage subsidiaries in the Shanghai FTZ, and list specific examples of future companies (Haitong Futures, Hongyuan Futures, GF Futures, and Shenyin & Wanguo Futures) and asset management companies (huaan Fund) that have either established, or are preparing to establish, risk management and asset management subsidiaries.

The International Energy Trading Center in its notice has been preparing for trading in international crude oil futures and has already registered in the Shanghai FTZ with a registered capital of RMB5 billion opening up to the full participation by nonresident investors. This marks the first time for both the listing of crude oil futures and the participation of nonresident investors in trading on futures markets within China.

RMB Cash Pooling

Article 12 of the Circular states that RMB and foreign currency positions arising from the exchange services provided by the FTU of a financial institution to their free trade account shall be closed within the Pilot Zone or abroad. The foreign currency balance of the free trade account, pooled by the FTU of the financial institution, shall not be deposited in a domestic financial institution, except where it is necessary to be deposited in a domestic financial institution due to the need of clearing. Such balance that is deposited in a domestic financial institution due to the need of clearing shall be included in the foreign debt management of the financial institution with which the clearing account is opened. Cross-border RMB cash pooling will provide financial institutions advantages by facilitating the allocation and management of the funds at home and abroad through bidirectional cross-border RMB communication, realizing integrated cash management with centralized RMB netting payment and collection and flexible use of money within the cash pool to relieve the funds lack of member companies thus reducing the financing cost. The flexible allocation of debt, if done properly, can help reduce the total fiscal burden in terms of passive interests, more efficiently manage resources, deploy liquidity, and obtain a better deposit rate that the revenue's country of origin.

A Wholly Foreign Owned Enterprise can use cash pooling to remit undistributed profits to a foreign related company with which it has an equity relationship. The WFOE's interest income will be subject to 25 % CIT and 5.6 % BT, and the CIT paid in China can be later used to offset income tax liability incurred in the foreign country if there is a DTA in place.

The procedure for establishing a cash pool differs between RMC and foreign exchange denominated transfers. In both cases, the participating enterprise must sign a contract with a bank in China stipulating the terms of the inter-company loan and describing the enterprises' size, revenue, and the purpose of the loan. While a term limit of 1 year applies, this may be extended with permission from the bank. To obtain this agreement, the company will need to submit a copy of its business license and a board resolution in favor of establishing the cash pool. In case of RMB cash pooling, an agreement must be signed between the cash pool header and a bank in China, through which the participating enterprise may open a special domestic header account for RMB cash pooling. The funds used in the cash pool can only be obtained from business operations and industry investment rather than financing. The cash pooling arrangement must then be recorded with the People's Bank of China, following which funds may be freely transferred. The participating enterprise will be asked to sign an agreement on obligations/liabilities in relation to money laundering, counter-terrorism financing, and tax evasion. On the other side, foreign exchange cash pooling may only be completed by a company registered in the Shanghai FTZ and must be filed in advance with the State Administration of Foreign Exchange (SAFE), in addition to the bank agreement as required for RMB cash pooling. The participating enterprise must open two special bank account: a domestic header account and an international header account. During a cash pool transfer, funds must first be placed in the domestic account, and then transferred into the international account pending SAFE approval.

7.2.2 Shipping Services

The new regulation is going to have a significant impact on how goods enter and exit China. The 11,000 trade and logistic-related enterprises located in the city's four designated bonded areas show how FTZ is just as relevant for logistic purposes than for transforming the city into a financial center.

With its amalgamation of four bonded zones: the Waigaoqiao Free Trade Zone, Waigaoqiao Free Trade Logistics Park, Yangshan Free Trade Port Area, and Pudong Airport Comprehensive Free Trade Zone—the FTZ has been shaking the traditional concentration of logistics operations in the city's Hongkou District, where more than 3,500 companies in related industries contribute roughly 28 % of the district's GDP.

According to CBRE, high-quality warehousing space in the FTZ totaled 780,000 m^2 in October 2013, and this figure is expected to increase by 210,000 m^2 by 2015 with the completion of several high-profile projects. As of 2013 Q3, there remained a strong discrepancy in vacancy rates between logistic properties in Puxi (1.4 %) and Pudong (22.4 %).

In relation to shipping, the reform mostly impacts ocean shipping and international ship management. The Framework Plan relaxes the restriction of the equity ratio between foreign funds and domestic funds for joint venture international marine business. For what concerns international ship management, wholly foreign-owned enterprises are allowed in the Free Trade Zone. More recently, the revised negative list introduced further liberalizations to the industry, mainly in transportation, warehouse and postal services.

Ship Transport

In terms of ship transportation, Shanghai retains a wide margin in its title as the world's busiest port in terms of cargo volume (seven of the ten busiest are located in China). In 2013, container throughput at Yangshan Port rose 3.3 % to a record 33.6 million TEUs, having previously surpassed Waigaoqiao Port in late 2012. As an indication of the potential for further growth in the industry, only 5.5 of cargo was classified as international transshipment, compared with over half of shipments in Hong Kong. With the simplified Customs procedures adopted in the FTZ, this imbalance is likely to correct itself over the coming years.

One of four bonded zones comprising the FTZ, Yangshan Free Trade Port Area offers state-of-the art facilities and exemptions on import tariffs as long as goods remain within the zone. The port features 16 modernized berths with a total quay length of 5.6 km and is joined to the mainland by the 32.5 km Donghai Bridge. Expansion of the port to a total area of 14.16 km^2 is to be completed by December 31, 2015, adding seven additional 50,000–70,000 ton berths. All companies registered before this date engaged in domestic carriage, warehousing, or loading and unloading services can obtain an immediate refund of the levied taxes.

While Waigaoqiao Port remains a crucial part of the broader logistics framework of Shanghai and China, there is indication that the area has reached its saturation point, with warehouse rents significantly higher than Yangshan and little room for future construction. However, the savings on logistics costs offered by Waigaoqiao's centralized location and its one-stop shop for international freight forwarders to arrange and organize shipments will ensure that it remains a competitive alternative to Yangshan well into the future.

Air Transshipment

Air Cargo into the FTZ flows through the Pudong Airport Comprehensive Free Trade Zone, where giants such as China Cargo Airlines, Lufthansa Cargo, and UPS have all established operations. DHL was selected as the first company to set up international transshipment operations in the Pudong Airport Comprehensive FTZ (part of the larger Shanghai Free Trade Zone), including a new international transit air route linking Leipzig to Tokyo.

This entails 24-h processing of overseas cargo (receiving, sorting, and dispatching), in cooperation of Shanghai Airport Customs and Shanghai International Airport Entry-Exit Inspection and Quarantine Bureau. Similar to elsewhere in the FTZ, air shipments through Pudong Airport are unimpeded by customs procedures or import duties. With international transshipments surging as a result, companies like DHL plan to add more routes in the coming years to keep up with demand.

The FTZ offers several customs policies to benefit logistics operations in the zone. Companies are afforded the option of delivering overseas shipments to the zone using just a shipping bill, rather than a formal customs declaration. As of March of this year, Shanghai Customs has offered a paperless declaration system in the FTZ, allowing companies to submit electronic documentation rather than apply in person. Enterprises importing goods into the zone may decide on the timing of the declaration and inspection process—reduced from 3 days to 1 day (or even a half day)—before goods are transferred outside the Zone. Conversely, the FTZ allows for exemptions on export goods to be obtained faster when goods are delivered to bonded warehouses within the zone. Whereas previously, China Inspection and Quarantine (CIQ) monitored cargo from multiple angles, in the FTZ only the status of the cargo (bonded or not bonded) is monitored, and goods with different status can be placed together in one warehouse. The requirement to move goods outside of the zone within 6 months of entry, as applying to other bonded areas in China, has been abolished in the FTZ. Lastly, in April of this year, the General Administration of Customs launched a "single window" pilot project at Yangshan Port integrating functions which outside the zone are separately executed by CIQ, Border Control, and Customs.

7.2.3 Commercial and Trade Services

The Pilot Free Trade Zone allows foreign investment enterprises to engage in certain value-added telecommunication services such as cloud computing and, more specifically, e-commerce. However, since the release of the Opinions in January 2014, the government has taken a cautious regulatory approach in approving the establishment of FITEs in the FTZ. In the approval process, the government authorities will consider the investor's reputation and creditworthiness in the industry, as well as the potential influence of the project. Consequently, up until the FTZ FITE measures were issued, the government rarely granted FITEs with VATS licenses in the FTZ.

On January 6, 2014, the Ministry of Industry and Information Technology ("MIIT") and the Shanghai Municipal Government issued the *Opinions,* which introduce a number of new initiatives that increase participation by foreign investors in the telecom industry.

For example, the *Opinions* open up seven types of VATS services to FITEs that are incorporated in the FTZ and that have all their service facilities located in the FTZ. More specifically, a FITE incorporated in the FTZ is authorized to provide:

- Five kinds of telecom services without any restrictions on foreign investment, i.e. the foreign investor can make up to 100 % investment in the FITE, including in (1) application store services, (2) store-and-forward business services, (3) call center services, (4) internet access services (provision of internet connection services to online users), and (5) domestic multi-party communication services;
- two kinds of telecom services, subject to restrictions on foreign investment, including (1) online data and trade processing services (i.e., operating e-commerce businesses), subject to a 55 % investment restriction, and (2) domestic internet virtual private network (VPN) services, subject to a 50 % investment restriction.

All of the above mentioned services can be provided on a nationwide basis, except internet access services which are only allowed to be provided to customers in the FTZ. Since the FTZ is a pilot zone to test reform initiatives that may significantly impact China's relevant markets, the *Opinions* serve as an important signal to show that the government is moving towards liberalizing the telecom industry.

In general, the new FTZ regulations open up foreign investment to various businesses involved in the Chinese telecom industry, e.g., cloud computing, and more specifically, e-commerce. However, since the release of the *Opinions* in January 2014, the government has taken a cautious regulatory approach in approving the establishment of FITEs in the FTZ. In the approval process, the government authorities will consider the investor's reputation and creditworthiness in the industry, as well as the potential influence of the project. Consequently, up until the FTZ FITE measures were issued, the government rarely granted FITEs with VATS licenses in the FTZ.

E-commerce Market

In recent years, foreign investors have shown increasing interest in the Chinese e-commerce market – in particular in operating online platforms to sell third party goods in China. However, this is considered to involve a type of VATS ("online data and trade processing services"), which is generally subject to a 50 % restriction in foreign investment under China's WTO commitments.

In theory, the opinions bring good news to foreign investors that seek to gain a foothold in the e-commerce business as they can now hold majority shares (55 %) in e-commerce businesses based in the FTZ. However, as mentioned above, the government has currently adopted a strict regulatory approach that makes it difficult for foreign investors to obtain the relevant license(s) in practice.

Cloud Computing

China's cloud computing industry has experienced fast and dynamic growth in recent years, which has attracted an increasing amount of interest from foreign investors. Although there is no specific telecommunication legislation that covers cloud computing yet, the majority of cloud computing services fall under the PRC Telecommunication Regulations as VATS, which are tightly restricted in China. Since cloud computing services encompass a wide range of services, market suppliers may need various kinds of VATS licenses to provide these services (depending on the type of their cloud computing services).

The opinions open up several kinds of VATS businesses to foreign investment in the FTZ that may allow foreign investors to provide certain cloud computing services (if they can obtain the corresponding VATS license(s)). For example, foreign investors may now provide "domestic multi-party communication services" (e.g., audio/visual conference call services) through a FITE business structure within China.

Nevertheless, against many expectations, certain key VATS businesses that are required to provide certain cloud computing services remain closed to foreign investors. For example, internet data center services ("IDC"), which are largely used as the fundamental IT infrastructure in the provision of cloud computing services, are still closed to foreign investors. As a result of the existing restrictions, foreign investors tend to use other structures to enter China's VATS markets.

One of the ways foreign investors can enter the VATS market is to partner up with Chinese companies that can obtain (or already have obtained) the relevant VATS licenses required to provide cloud computing services. In June 2013, Microsoft launched 'Microsoft Azure' in China, together with Chinese partner 21Vianet, to provide businesses with computing, storage, database, integration, connectivity, and support for open-source software over the internet. In December 2013, Amazon.com signed a memorandum of understanding with the Beijing and Ningxia governments to develop cloud computing services in China. To do so, Amazon.com will partner up with several Chinese providers, including

ChinaNetCenter and SINNET, who will provide the IDC and ISP services required to deliver the relevant cloud computing services in China. On the exact same day of the Amazon.com announcement, IBM also announced its agreement with Chinese partner, 21Vianet, to provide 'IBM SmartCloud Enterprise', private cloud infrastructure and managed services in China.

7.2.4 Professional Services

The following sectors open up to foreign investment:

- Credit investigation agencies.
- Travel agencies (Sino-foreign equity joint venture travel agencies registered in the FTZ that will be allowed to provide travel services to overseas locations except to Taiwan).
- Recruitment agencies (as long as the foreign equity interests do not exceed 70 % of the whole investment, Sino-foreign equity joint ventures can set up human resources agencies. Investors from Hong Kong and Macau will be allowed to establish wholly foreign-owned human resources agencies. The minimum registered capital for foreign-invested human resources agencies will be lowered from $300,000 USD to $125,000 USD.).
- Engineering and construction agencies servicing Shanghai: foreign investment limitations are removed; for foreign-invested engineering design companies registered in the FTZ (excluding engineering survey companies), the criteria on past engineering design experience will be waived when they apply for the qualification to provide service in Shanghai for the first time. Wholly foreign-owned construction enterprises registered in the FTZ will be allowed to conduct Sino-foreign joint construction projects in Shanghai without any equity restrictions.
- Foreign-invested equity investment companies: they may be structured as companies limited by shares, allowing for possible listings on the A-share market in the PRC. For what concerns headhunting service, the threshold for foreign equity ratio is raised to 70 %.
- Mainland Chinese law firms: they are expected to enhance cooperation with "foreign law firms." For the purpose of this provision, law firms in Hong Kong, Macau, and Taiwan are also considered foreign law firms.

7.2.5 Cultural Services

A disruptive change is going to happen in the cultural sector since entertainment opens for the first time to WFOE. With the promulgation of the rules, the relevant policies in respect of the cultural market in the FTZ have become more developed and complete. The lifting of the 14-year ban on gaming consoles in China, originated in June 2000, as well as the liberalization of foreign investment policy with respect to the entertainment sector, etc., will certainly bring new business opportunities in the FTZ and will no doubt boost the prosperity and development of the media and entertainment industry in Shanghai and even the whole of China.

It should be pointed out that although the FTZ now allows for foreign investment in the sale and service of gaming and entertainment consoles, foreign investment with respect to gaming software development is still prohibited. In particular, there is no sign that the online gaming market will be opened to foreign investment any time soon.

Moreover, equity restrictions for foreign-invested performance agencies will be removed and wholly foreign-owned performance agencies will be allowed to provide services in Shanghai.

7.2.6 *Social Sector*

Education

For-profit education and training institutions and for-profit professional training institutions may be jointly formed by foreign investors and PRC persons.

Outside the FTZ, the scope of the regulatory regime only covers Sino-foreign education institutions, which are public undertakings and therefore not-for-profit. The relevant national regulations, referred to here as the National Sino-Foreign School Rules, do not apply to profit-making education institutions (usually referred to in laws as "operational education institutions").

The National Sino-Foreign School Rules themselves state that the State Council will eventually issue regulations applicable to profit-making institutions, which are to be registered with the Administration of Industry and Commerce (the "AIC"). However, no such separate regulations have been issued to date, a decade after the issuance of the National Sino-Foreign School Rules.

There have always been arguments within the Ministry of Education and outside it about whether foreign investment in education should be allowed to develop freely. Those who oppose profit-seeking foreign investment argue that education is sacred and should not be tainted by commercialism. And those who support investment ask why, without market incentives, anyone would provide the various skills (and the cash) that China's school system needs.

To date, neither side has won outright, but the pro-investment team scored a goal with the FTZ.

While there are no nationwide regulations on Sino-foreign profit-making training institutions, in some locations (including Jiangsu, Hangzhou, and Shanghai), local AICs have not waited for the national government and have already issued rules governing the registration of private profit-making training institutions. These rules arguably apply not only to domestic entities but also to those that have foreign investment. The practice varies from place to place: some provinces restrict the business scope of Sino-foreign institutions to vocational skills training and do not allow "cultural" education, while some provinces allow both forms. The qualification and approval/registration procedures also differ from one province to another.

This new rule in Shanghai FTZ, although also a local regulation, is the first one that specifically regulates Sino-foreign profit-making training institutions. It confirms that foreign investment is allowed in this area and clarifies the qualification and approval procedures.

The opening-up of the sector follows the Overall Plan for the China (Shanghai) Pilot Free Trade Zone approved by China's State Council. It provides that Sino-foreign cooperative profit-seeking education institutions and vocational training institutions are allowed to be established in the FTZ.

After that, the Interim Administrative Measures on Sino-Foreign Cooperative Training Institutions in the FTZ (dated November 13, 2013, the "Interim Measures") formulated by Shanghai Municipal Education Committee and another three local authorities took effect from the date of publication and marked the reform of the administration of foreign-invested private training institutions.

The legal status of profit-seeking training institutions, either domestic or Sino-foreign cooperative, has remained vague for a long time. Related laws expressly provide as follows:

- No organization or individual may found a profit-seeking school or other educational institution.
- Private education must be in the interests of the public both for domestic education and for Sino-foreign cooperative education. Sino-foreign cooperative education institutions and Sino-foreign cooperative vocational training institutions and education projects are prohibited from undertaking profit-seeking activities.
- The sponsors of education or vocational training institutions are entitled to "reasonable returns"; however, "reasonable returns" does not mean "profit distributions".

Thus, outside the FTZ, training institutions are still categorized as "non-profit-seeking training institutions" and cannot be operated as profit-seeking enterprises. However, the various laws and regulations did not rule out the promulgation of rules allowing profit-seeking training institutions, provided that any such rules would need a special regulation from the State Council, which, so far, has not promulgated any such rules.

Local rules applicable in different provinces and cities generally categorize private non-degree education institutions and private vocational training institutions as non-profit-seeking organizations.

Shenzhen promulgated rules on Private Vocational Training Institutions back in 2006 and they provided that the administration of private profit-seeking training institutions must be subject to State Council rules.

In 2013, Shanghai promulgated certain regulations on private profit-seeking training institutions outside the FTZ, dealing with domestic companies.

Sino-foreign training institutions attempting to do the same thing would still be subject to the regulations on Sino-foreign Cooperative Education. In conclusion, there are no laws or regulations clearly applicable to profit-seeking Sino-foreign cooperative training institutions outside the FTZ.

The new rules in the FTZ allow for corporate enterprises to be jointly established by qualified foreign enterprises (or other economic organizations) and Chinese enterprises (or other economic organizations) with the purpose of providing non-pro-bono cultural, educational, or vocational training services to the public. These "cultural and educational cooperative training institutions" are subject to the administration of the Bureau of Education. Cooperative vocational training institutions are subject to the Bureau of Human Resources and Social security.

The biggest breakthrough in the Interim Measures is that it permits "profit-seeking" Sino-foreign training institutions, which, as we have seen were not prohibited but remained in a grey zone while the State Council remained silent. Outside the FTZ, laws applicable to "profit-seeking" Sino-foreign training institutions are still not available.

Medical Service/Healthcare

Wholly foreign-owned medical institutions may be established by foreign investors.

China is the third largest healthcare market in the world and this is growing by double-digits. Despite the country's spending on healthcare per capita is only about 5 % of its GDP—versus around 10 % in Japan and Europe, and 18 % in the U.S, the Chinese government is expanding its healthcare budget and has said it welcomes foreign investment and aims to double the share of private hospital beds from 9 % currently to 20 % by 2015. Healthcare investment opportunity in China appears to be sizzling.

Healthcare foreign investors in China have followed a "begin or buy" approach, employing either greenfield/organic growth or M&As to achieve their investment targets. Referral services such as International SOS and International Medical Center (IMC) represent early out-patient entrants into the Chinese healthcare market established to service expatriates in China. They have integrated forward into laboratory work and vaccinations. As private entities they do not publish financial results but appear to be well staffed, equipped, and visited. In complex cases, they utilize ambulances to take patients to premier urban hospitals such as Beijing's premier-ranked Xiehe (Peking Union) in Wangfujing.

Joint ventures and outright acquisitions represent the largest potential opportunity and the greatest challenge. It has been difficult for healthcare firms without an operating base in China to successfully buy into joint ventures and acquisitions. Fifteen years ago, an OTC traded firm of the now defunct SNLY based in California and led by a Chinese MD attempted to take control of multiple hospitals in China. It introduced a member-based discount system using TCM and western medicine, emphasizing immune system maintenance with nutraceuticals, but in the end could not raise the needed capital and bring its ambitions to fruition from an offshore base.

Another challenge for offshore investors will be to identify acquisition-worthy consolidators in healthcare. For example, both Europe and North America have extensive and efficient dialysis centers for treating diabetes that boomed in the 1990s and redirected treatment away from the congested hospital environment. China has the world's largest CKD (Chronic Kidney Disease) population at around 200 million, and also one of the most underserved with a <10 % treatment rate—due to the lack of education and service provider networks. While CHDX and CCM are currently focusing on expanding into oncology, the future may be wide open for poorly addressed opportunities such as in kidney disease and diabetes treatment.

The following tables show the main structural changes by sector:

FINANCIAL	*Banking services*	Allow qualified foreign financial institutions to set up foreign banks
		Allow qualified private capital and foreign financial institutions to establish joint venture banks.
		Allow qualified domestic banks to engage in offshore business
	Finance leasing	Remove the minimum threshold requirement of registration capital and expanding business scope
SHIPPING	*Ocean shipping*	Relax the restriction of the equity ratio between foreign funds and domestic funds for joint venture
	International ship management	WFOE allowed
COMMERCIAL	*VAT*	Foreign investment enterprises can engage in certain VAT services
	Law firms	Innovate cooperation methods between foreign and domestic law firms
	Credit investigation	Allow foreign investment
	Travel agency	Expand the business scope of the joint venture travel agency
	Headhunting services	Increase the limitation of equity ratio of foreign investors to 70 %
		Allow it to be wholly owned by HK or [illegible] investors
		Reduce the minimum threshold requirement of registered capital
	Investment management	Allow the establishment of joint-stock foreign investment companies
	Engineering design	Relax application criteria
CULTURAL	*Artists agency*	Remove restrictions of the equity ratio between foreign funds and domestic funds
		Allow WFOE to engage
	Entertainment	Allow WFOE to engage
SOCIAL	*Education*	Joint ventures allowed
	Medical service and healthcare	Allow foreign investment on health and medical insurance institutions on a pilot basis

7.3 New Opportunities for Reforms

During past years, the contribution of foreign demand to China's growth has overwhelmed other components, and it is now shrinking. As a matter of facts, it is an investment, not export that leads China's economy. The large expenditure on plant, machinery, building, and infrastructure accounted for around 48 % in country's GDP in 2011. At the same time, in the same period household consumption, supposedly the major driver of economic activity, accounts for only about a third of GDP. A disproportionate share of China's investment is made by SOEs, and more recently, by infrastructure ventures under the control of provincial and municipal authorities but not on their balance sheets. This investment has often been clunky if not burdensome and the imbalance between investment and consumption could make China's economy look precarious.

In 2007, the country's exports contributed to a growing current-account surplus, which exceed 10 % of its gross domestic product. This trend – namely the failure to import as much as it exported, spend as much as it earned or invest as much as it saved – became a unique case, generating an equally impressive surplus of commentary and explanations. Reactions came out from plenty of countries, including the U.S. However, over time, apart from U.S., China is suffering a reduction in current-account surplus with the rest of the world leading to a percentage over GDP dwarfed to 2.8 %. As shown in Chart 1, figures fall down to the level of 2002, also immediately after the WTO accession. In order for the high level of surplus to return, two major scenarios might take place.

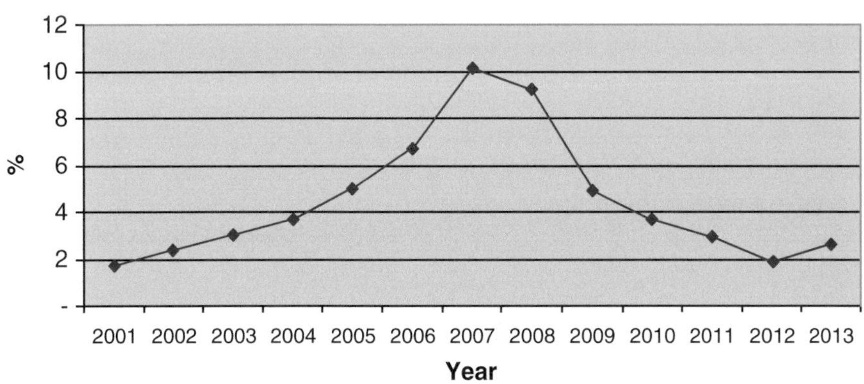

Current-account as % of GDP (Source: Trade Economics, The Economist)

First China's government could set the stage for new investment and bolster the export boom. This is exactly what occurred when China joined the World Trade Organization in 2001: the investment created an excess capacity in key industries such as cars, construction materials, and steel. For instance in less than 3 years,

China became went from being net importer to playing as the world largest exporter of steel in 2004. However, the rapid growth in post-crisis years was led by real estate investments and infrastructure, neither of them can be shipped or traded across borders. Second, given a level of investment and domestic demand, China would still rely on foreign demand to keep the economy moving. In this case risks to sustain economic growth would be higher as the world financial crisis severely hit Chinese exports.

In previous paragraph we pointed out how China can appear an "overinvested" country. Generally speaking this could mean a situation very close Asian financial crisis of 1997–1998. On the contrary, investment policy in China is far to be so reckless. In fact, figures highlight how this country is a net exported of capital, turning more savings than investments. During last years, China has always held a level of savings of some 50 %, meaning that everything cannot be invested at home, must be invested overseas.

In this system government tends to suppress consumption in favor of investment enjoyed by enterprises, usually SOEs. It comes to cheaper export and low interest rate on bank deposits. A large portion of this oversized investment capacity is devoted to two main actors: local government and SOEs. In the 1990s, China's SOEs faced a dramatic downsizing and restructuring. Thousands of them were allowed to go bankrupt, yet those that survived this bad times would have experienced a prominent feature of Chinese capitalism. Today, SOEs are responsible for about 35 % of the fixed-asset investment made by Chinese firms. They could invest so much because in a while they have become immensely big and profitable.

But glory days are over for SOEs, and returns on equity among them are substantially lower than private firms. Furthermore, their returns are artificially burst as SOEs can access cheaper inputs (land, capital, and credit), in an uncompetitive and sheltered market. Also unlike other State-participated sectors in other countries, these entities do not pay dividends to shareholders, namely the State, rather they are used to refinance SEOs. Although this big engagement in SOEs plays as reassurance of ruling party commitment in certain industries, researches show how China would have achieved a similar level of growth investing down to 21 % in private sector.

Another point raising concerns among economic analysts refers to Chinese lending. In 2010, the level of lending over GDP turned 171 % letting aside some credit item not shown in the official figures. As for investments issue, China's frenzy loan-making has traditionally been matched by equally impressive deposit taking. Even now most households have a few alternative havens for their money. This tailored system leaves China's banks shook-proof. Put it another way, they make a lot of mistakes, bet at the same time they have a lot of margin for errors. But this traditional source of strength will not last forever. Over years China's richest depositors are becoming restless, demanding better returns and seeking ways around China's regulated interest rates. The most straightforward way out could be the eventual liberalization of rates, leading to more efficiency but also to less resilience of banking system.

The real extent of China's financial exposure uncertainty is far from being explained with just a few considerations. Indeed not all "malinvestment" will results in bad loans, as many of outstanding property developments are bought by debt-free investors. By the same token, not all "bad loans" necessarily represent "malinvestmet." Rural infrastructure projects, to say one, are often "unbankable" as they fail to yield income returns from fees, charges, and tolls to service their financial obligations. However, the infrastructure will contribute more to the wider economy than it cost to provide. The main question one would raise would ask the real consequences of a financial crisis on China's financial sector. The answer could appear quite counter-intuitive. Although banking system accounts some 16 % of non-profitable loans, all the equity involved would be wiped out. However, central government could intervene long before that happens in order to recapitalize banks and prevents loans going bad. The reason lays in the fact that even though many loans do eventually sour, banks do not have to record these losses. No loan is bad until someone demands repayment. Central government by either controlling the large part of public loans or recapitalizing the equity can afford a double-way to keep control over financial system. Furthermore, banks loan rollovers give the banks time to earn their way out of troubles, setting aside the profits from good loans from losses and bad ones. This task is easier in China system as the system still remains repressed: banks can force their depositors to bear some of their losses by paying them less than market rate of interest. Government prevents banks to offer higher interest rates, substantially making households pay for their deposits. Some source explains how Chinese banks can take advantage from the oversized level of savings (around 40 % higher than loans they make).

For all these facts, China is still unlikely to be hit by a financial crisis. Due to its inherent system, this feature will remain in a chronic affliction, made on a combination of government-managed rollover, repression of interest rates and repayment. Such a combination is unfair to taxpayers and depositors, but it is also stable. However, some commentators claim that China will find it harder to repeat in the future. As depositors are no longer as docile as they were, resistance to China's financial repression seems to grow.

The ceiling over deposit rates and the floor over lending, guarantee banks a fat margin, preventing competition for deposit and allowing big banks to maintain vast pools of money cheaply. If the deposit ceiling were lifted, small banks would offer juicier rates to take market share from incumbents. Conversely, the big banks would trim their deposit base as they become more expensive. Households would be better rewarded for their saving and China's banking would be freer.

Although government is holding its feet on the liberalization track, its hesitancy may reflect the political clout of the state-owned banks. Perhaps also reflect the government fears. Most developing countries that freed-up their financial system suffered from some kind of crisis afterward. The main issue arising regards the behavior of small banks that threaten the leading position of incumbents but at the same time overextend themselves.

These are good reasons for caution but not procrastination. First repressed rates have their own dangers. To be avoided, savers have overpaid for alternative assets such as property, contributing to China's worrying speculative bubble. In some regions like Wenzhou and Zhejiang, rate ceilings have encouraged firms and individuals to make informal loans to each other, bypassing the regulated intermediation in the shadows. The negative rate over saving, make depositors prone to look for ways to circumvent the ceiling. Recently different forms of 'wealth-management products' are emerging from those with lots of money to park.

These are short-term savings instruments backed by a mix of assets that offer better returns than deposit accounts. Overall wealth-management products accounts for more than 10 % of deposits. More than a proliferating phenomenon, these new investment opportunities push toward a de-facto liberalization of interest rates.

The government may seek to formalize this liberalization, gradually, allowing banks more freedom to set rates on large long-term deposits. For instance, corporate loans did not grow at all in 2011: higher rates would help attract them back. The efficient allocation of capital would positively be affected through the establishment of a more competitive environment. In this situation, we can find big enterprises (SEOs) with a relatively low borrowing cost and credit-starved private firms which could earn potentially higher returns on investments (Fig. 7.1).

SOEs and financial system now stand as two major issues to be addressed and provide China with an up-to-date and more flexible economic framework. With respect of SOEs, the great role they have played during last two decades make them impossible to be ignored in a new stage of China's economic plan. At the same time, ruling party should reduce its sphere of influence over these giants inferring on the overall system. The slowdown occurring from 2007 on clearly requires a rethinking for SOEs, looking for a new competitive positioning aimed at not cutting resources to private sector.

Last June SASAC (the State-Owned Asset Supervision and Administration Commission) has identified six SOEs for a pilot program to attract private investment

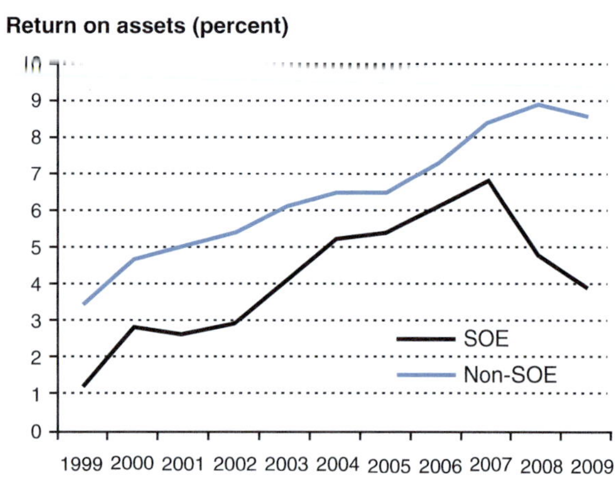

Source: NS; author's estimates.
* 2009 data is estimated by the author with the data in the first 11 months of 2009.

Fig. 7.1 Profitability of industrial SOEs and non-SOEs

and improve corporate governance, as the government pushes ahead with reforms aimed at raising economic efficiency. In a landmark blueprint for economic reform announced late last year, the ruling Communist party promised to push "mixed ownership" reform, a phrase understood to mean partial privatization, while maintaining SOEs as the backbone of the economy.

Since the financial crisis, the productivity gap between state-owned and private companies has widened, with average return on assets for state entities at around 4.6 %, compared with 9.1 % for private companies, according to several estimates published by government sources. In recent months, several provinces have announced plans to sell stakes on locally owned SOEs, but the last announcement by the SASAC is among the first concrete steps to reform central-government-owned SOEs. The six companies selected for this program are as follows:

- State Development and Investment Corporation (SDIC)
- China National Cereals, Oils and Foodstuffs Corporation (COFCO)
- China National Building Materials Group (CNBM)
- China Energy Conservation and Environmental Protection Group (CECEP)
- Xinxing Cathay International Group (XXCIG)
- China National Pharmaceutical Group (Sinopharm)

China National Building Materials Group and China National Pharmaceutical Group Corporation (Sinopharm) will start as the first two central SOEs chosen for a pilot on mixed ownership reform. The two companies, which both already have listed subsidiaries, could follow the path forged by Citic Group, the state-owned industrial conglomerate, which in May announced a plan to inject unlisted assets into its listed subsidiary Citic Pacific.

But analysts have warned that a re-run of the last round of SOE reform in the late 1990s, when the government floated minority stakes in state firms on the stock market without granting private investors management control, may do little to improve efficiency.

Indeed, the fact that only two of the six companies revealed by SASAC on Tuesday will participate in the mixed-ownership program suggests that the commission regards privatization as only one of several alternatives for SOE reform.

State Development and Investment Corp, which builds large-scale infrastructure projects, and China National Cereals, Oils and Foodstuffs Corp (COFCO) were chosen for a separate pilot scheme designed to raise efficiency without privatization.

The plan calls for transferring control of state equity to state-owned holding companies that will "focus more on capital management." The goal is to reduce political interference in the management of SOEs by designing the holding companies to focus purely on maximizing shareholder value rather than advancing the government's policy goals.

7.4 Other Provinces Are Applying for Pilot Area Status

The enthusiasm that from the establishment date of the FTZ spread over the Chinese highest ranks of politics and business world – not fully participated by Western analysts, still skeptical about the lack of clear guidelines and substantial reduction of the Negative List – caused a ripple effect of provinces applying for same fiscal benefits and Pilot Free Trade Zone status. Premier Li Keqiang, one of the main supporters of Shanghai Free Trade Zone, had previously announced that pilot projects would commence in several areas.

7.4.1 Candidates for the Next FTZ

To find out about the possible trend of Chinese FTZs development in the near future, the situation of bonded zones in two cities can be analyzed: Tianjin port and Suzhou Industry Park. The most outstanding feature of Tianjin port would be the strength support from its neighboring cities (Lee et al. 2013). Bohai bay rim occupies the land area among Chinese three economic regions, thus having the economic radiation effect on middle and western china domestically while connecting China to the eastern Europe by Eurasian Continental Bridge (Lee et al. 2013). Not only does the superior geographical location bring Tianjin convenience on facilitating transportation, but also maturely industrial structure (which also indicates a preferred GDP component proportion), high-quality labor as well as high-level market liberalization (Lee et al. 2013).

Being the fourth most important city in terms of export volume in 2002, Suzhou is also one of the representatives of cities that grow up from an export-oriented economy just as Yang and Hsia (2007) concluded. Suzhou has been enjoying the foreign enterprises' preference (Yeung 2000) for its special location. As one of the prosperous municipality, Suzhou locates in the Yangtze river district anchored by Shanghai 100 km to the east and has an ascendant economic structure. From 1985 to 2004, Suzhou primary industry GDP share declined to 2.2 %, while the share of other two sectors GDP increased from 61.6 % to 65.7 % and from 18.7 % to 32.1 % respectively (Beijing: China Statistical Press, 2005). To date, the tertiary sector composed more than 44.2 % to the whole GDP which meant that Suzhou owned the largest nonagricultural population (38.3 %) of all YRD prefectural municipalities with the exception of the extra large cities of Shanghai and Nanjing (Suzhou statistic yearbook 2013).

Although Suzhou seems to have the potential to go further, it never replaces Shanghai's position as the functional gateway to the YRD. Historically, from the early 1980s to the early 1990s, many Shanghai industries relocated to YRD cities such as Suzhou because that state-owned industrial enterprises were given autonomy for central government decentralization reforms, which made secondary cities such as Suzhou depend on Shanghai for technology transfer as well as a gateway for product exports. Now, the pilot FTZ program enhances Shanghai's leadership in trading magnification and economic restructure step further, meanwhile complicates the relationship between the two cities.

Airries (2008) analyzed the competitiveness of Suzhou, claiming that it was vacillated by the contribution from the Suzhou Industrial Park (SIP) as a joint venture between Chinese and Singaporean national and local authorities. The park is composed of an IT park, an international technology park, a life science park, and a national software park, within which Singaporean firms provided the infrastructure design and management functions under the well-recognized Singapore "brand name" (Pereira 2004). Instead of simply looking for cheap land and labor, Singaporean firms were engaged in the government-induced program with local firms.

By the end of 2012, 15,138 foreign companies were attracted to set up in SIP along with over 9,164,900 USD of FDI were actually used in 2012 (Suzhou statistic yearbook 2013). Consequently, SIP is experienced in dealing with foreign capital and meanwhile optimizes the economic structure. It means that typically, Taiwanese IT companies represent the classic corporate patterns which establish a Suzhou-based platform to serve multinational brand name clients but outsource higher value production chain manufacturing to Suzhou. But for the last decade, Suzhou's local Taiwanese branches have gradually become responsible for both material purchases and R&D functions of the production chain (Yang and Hsia 2007), as some industries have moved their assembly functions to less expensive and smaller YRD cities, and retained their R&D functions in Suzhou, thus having enabled the city to gain economic benefits.

7.4.2 Future Trends of Chinese FTZs

Indicators used to judge whether shanghai FTZ would be successful should be laid not only on performance of Shanghai FTZ itself, but also whether the regulations are applicable for other regions on China mainland. Furthermore, effects on surrounding cities of Shanghai FTZ should be assessed. For instance, reforming benefits of Shanghai FTZ might have symphonic effects on foreign capitals in other YRD cities such as Suzhou, which is harmful to Suzhou economic development if foreign enterprises transfer their core business to Shanghai but only left the manufacturing activities. The pilot program is not supposed to succeed at the cost of sacrificing the other region's benefit. Instead, trade spillover effect should be adapted to stimulating the economic development of the surrounding regions.

Economic indicators of four cities in 2012

Items	Shanghai	Shenzhen	Tianjin	Suzhou
GDP(billion CNY)	2010.133	1295	1,289.39	1201.165
GDP components (billion CNY)				
Primary industry	12.78	0.63	17.16	33.772
Secondary industry	791.277	573.86	666.382	3452.8
Tertiary industry	1206.076	720.61	605.846	531.432
FDI(billion USD)	22.338	5.23		9.165
Export volume(billion USD)	138.68	271.36	32.814	174.689
Import volume(billion USD)	151.235	195.47	44.621	131.003

Source: China statistic yearbook, Shanghai statistic yearbook, Shenzhen statistic yearbook and Suzhou statistic yearbook, 2012

As discussed earlier, the choice of FTZ locations in Shanghai is considerable to embrace seaport, airport, and inland bonded zones. However, data in McCalla (1990)'s report suggested that there was one mode that all FTZs follow while the FTZs locating on both maritime ports and remote areas. Brown (1981) and Abler et al. (1971) also claimed that the spread of port free zones was a diffusion process. Shanghai is not the earliest bench of cities that available to market-based economy, but it has abundant experience dealing with foreign investment and global trading in well-developed bonded zones. Combined with McCalla (1990)'s opinion that ports were the natural place for free-zone development, the next Chinese FTZ would locate on the east coastal cities associated with port. For the early phase, as it shows in Table 4, with close GDP numbers, Tianjin and Shenzhen are the possible options for their superior seaports conditions and strong hinterland supporting. And the feasible administrative plans from Shanghai pilot program would need more inspection and need to be enhanced. Therefore, the next FTZ are probably consisted with the similar components like Shanghai FTZ. Coastal cities like Tianjin and Shenzhen has an intact system of infrastructure as seaports, airports, and inland transportation networks are integrated with each other. More importantly, these two cities have a long history of opening and have the economic capabilities to ascend the world trading. Besides, Shenzhen owns a bigger possibility to become the next FTZ of china, not only because of the outperformance in export-import volume but also for the reason that although Tianjin port has stronger hinterland support, it locates closely to Chinese political center and complex political issues would limit the level of market liberalization.

For the next phase, Suzhou Industry Park seems to outperform other southeast cities on dealing with foreign capitals as well as sophisticated administration environment directly introduced from Singapore. Despite that Suzhou itself is not a seaport city, designation of FTZ could take advantages of geographical proximity of cities in east china (as the map shows), the FTZ could be designed as combining Suzhou industry park, the city-controlled district Zhangjiagang and Wuxi Shuofang airport, which could format intercity synergy effect. This could be meaningful for the remote areas to promote their hinterland functions. Special cases such as Chinese west bonded zones like Xinjiang Bole Alashankou district is limited by its economic aggregate and international trading partners would probably be the last part of opening.

The provincial authorities in Fujian province are considering teaming up the cities of Xiamen, Fuzhou, and the Pingtan Comprehensive Pilot Zone in its application for the province's first free trade zone (FTZ).

The idea was first brought up at a recent provincial working conference, according to Zhang Chanmin, vice-mayor of Xiamen on February 20. Insiders revealed that the Fujian Commerce Department will be responsible for organizing the co-application of Haixi (West Coast of Taiwan Straits) Free Trade Zone. The news came as a surprise to many as Pingtan and Xiamen submitted FTZ applications separately to the State Council last year. The Haixia FTZ application means the two areas will have to retract their previous applications and make a joint one with Fuzhou. Fujian has been moved backward and forward in its FTZ blueprint. In mid December, it applied to set up the Xiamen FTZ to central authorities. And in January, the plan of Fuzhou-Pingtan FTZ was put forward at an annual session of the Fuzhou People's Congress; while on February 12, Fuzhou government officials told media that Pingtan and Fuzhou had reached consensus in their joint application. Shanghai became China's first FTZ in August 2013. As of February 21, the State Council hadn't approved any other FTZs. No progress in reviewing either Pingtan or Xiamen's FTZ applications have been reported.

The joint FTZ application by Fuzhou, Xiamen, and Pingtan comes with both pros and cons, according to experts.

Combing Xiamen and Pingtan into one FTZ will have large enough space to accommodate a number of enterprises. During their own FTZ applications, Xiamen and Pingtan both highlighted their links with Taiwan, which is larger than either of the two, economically and geographically. So either Pingtan or Xiamen faces huge challenges in independently introducing Taiwan's enterprises, said Tang Yonghong, director of the Taiwan economic research center of Xiamen University. With Fuzhou, Xiamen, and Pingtan joining hands, there will be a bigger chance of being approved and that will boost the regional economy of Fujian province but the difficult part of a joint FTZ application lies in how to connect the trio as they are relatively independent in their economies and culture and have imbalanced development.

Moreover, located in southwest Sichuan, Chengdu is China's fifth most populous city with a total population of about 11 million. It is also one of the most important economic, transportation, and communication hubs in western China. For decades, Chengdu has made great efforts to attract foreign investment, offering various incentives such as preferential tax policies and financial support for foreign investors. Recently, three pilot areas of Chengdu – the Chengdu High-tech Industrial Development Zone, Longquanyi District, and Tianfu New District – released the details of their respective negative lists governing foreign investment into the city. Following the precedent of the Shanghai Free Trade Zone (FTZ) and the Pingtan Comprehensive Pilot Zone (PCPZ), Chengdu is now the third city in China to adopt a negative list approach to foreign investment. Under this system, foreign investors enjoy equal treatment as Chinese domestic enterprises in any industry not explicitly restricted or prohibited on the list. Different from that implemented in the Shanghai FTZ, however, Chengdu has issued a "supervision list" and "permission list" alongside its "negative list" to further clarify the corporate establishment procedure and encouraged industries within the zone. Matthew Zito of Asia Briefing comments, "This may be in response to the governmental ban on additional free trade zones issued in June of this year. Prior to this, some 20 cities were said to have submitted applications for approval by the Central Government. Chengdu's negative lists may be an attempt to create a watered-down version of a free trade zone that attracts foreign investment while nominally avoiding the ban." Details of the negative lists released by the three pilot areas are as follows: Chengdu High-tech Industrial Development Zone established in 1988, Chengdu High-tech Industrial Development Zone (CHIDZ) was approved as one of the first national high-tech development zones. It ranks 5th among the 53 national high-tech development zones in China in terms of comprehensive strength. By the end of June, 2014, over 1,000 foreign-invested enterprises (FIEs) have been established within the zone. The zone's negative list includes two parts, domestic investors and foreign investors, respectively; the latter covers the following 17 industries in six sectors, including 69 management measures for foreign investment: New information technology, bio-pharmaceuticals, high-end equipment manufacturing, green technology, service industry and other supporting industries (e.g., construction and real estate). Compared with the newly revised negative list introduced in the Shanghai FTZ, the number of industries restricted for foreign investment has been substantially reduced by 50 %. The list contains no restrictions on the agriculture and mining sectors and reduces prohibited items in education, manufacturing, and transportation. Meanwhile, foreign investors are restricted from the catering industry, including cafeterias that might produce smoke or harmful gases (permitted in the Shanghai FTZ), based on Chengdu's regulations on air pollution. Foreign investors are also compelled to abide by the "Catalogue of Prohibited Industries for Foreign Investment (2011 Revision, released by the Chinese Government)," according to a CHIDZ official. Longquanyi District (Economic Development Zone), situated in southwest Chengdu, is one of the most prosperous areas of Chengdu. In 2013, the area's GDP ranked first in Sichuan. The district's negative list is divided between "non-manufacturing" and "manufacturing" industries and subdivided into "leading industries (e.g., automotive and high-end equipment)," "developing industries (e.g., construction materials and pharmaceuticals)," and "restricted industries (e.g., petrochemicals and coal)." The list covers 44 industries in 16 sectors, including 157 management measures. Tianfu New District aiming to become the Sichuanese equivalent to Pudong, the Tianfu New District is focused on the modern manufacturing and services industries. The district's negative list covers 16 industries including 120 management measures (41 prohibited items and 79 restricted items). Notably, the negative list for domestic investment is longer than the one for foreign investment, with the former containing 164 management measures.

To conclude, although a strand of literature suggested that the geographical spread is irregular on a worldwide basis, factors of geography, economy, polity, and history should be taken into consideration in the case of China. Generally, from the historical point, the opening momentum would march in concentric of Shanghai, then go down to south coastal areas and then up to north seaport based cities (e.g. Tianjin, Qingdao and Dalian etc.). As for Chinese west border trade ports, there are both domestic and transfrontier constrains on cross-border trading so that economic reformation required an appropriate time. The other inland cities locates in the middle of China would be powerful supports to the special economic zones.

7.4.3 Skepticism and Brakes

As requests from regions to be approved as Pilot Free Trade Zones came into a rash, public declarations from the government came as a cold shower to put a brake on rumors and contagious enthusiasm. Beijing has publicly declared that applications received to date have tended to overemphasize the proposed zones as a way to generate tax dollars and had failed to grasp their wider economic significance. Local governments are suggested to have wanted to secure licensing for such zones solely as means to secure funding for land redevelopment. China's Central Government has suspended the approval of any further Free Trade Zones (FTZ). This reveals an obvious disconnection between local Provincial Governments and the Central Government when it comes to strategic planning. Many local officials seem mired in the mindset that land is everything and that wealth is created only through land redevelopment and the easy State funding that comes with it. There appears to have occurred a breakdown of longer-term economic sensibility in many of China's major cities and provinces The ban, to take immediate effect, affects some 20 cities believed to have submitted applications for FTZs. Included among these is the much-anticipated Guangdong Free Trade Zone, which had already received approval yet has now been caught up in the blanket ban. Proposals for new Economic and Technology Development Zones (ETZ) have also been suspended. At present, it remains unclear when the ban will be lifted. In the meantime, previously submitted applications have been sent back for revisions.

This is cause for concern, China's brightest contemporary economists are clearly not making it into the political and strategic planning channels of the country's provincial governments, yet this is where future economic growth is supposed to be coming from. China needs to overhaul the quality of the people responsible for economic reform at the provincial and municipal government levels. At the end of January of this year, Economic Information Daily (EID), a news agency directly supervised by the state-owned Xinhua News Agency, reported that China's State Council had approved 12 more regional free trade zones (FTZs). It further announced that Guangdong Province and Tianjin had completed the finalizing investigations of their detailed FTZ schemes while most of the other approved proposals were at the beginning of this process.

However, shortly after, an officer from the Department of International Trade and Economic Affairs of China's Ministry of Commerce (MOFCOM) didn't hesitate to clarify that thus far the State Council has not approved any FTZs except for the Shanghai FTZ. The officer did confirm that some provinces and cities have submitted their application for building FTZs and they are "currently conducting research and demonstrations."

References

Abler R, Adams JSA, Gould P (1971) Spatial organization: the geographer's view of the world. Pretice-Hall, Englewood Cliffs

Airries C (2008) The geographies of secondary city growth in a globalized China: comparing Dongguan and Suzhou. J Urban Hist 35:134–149

Brown LA (1981) Innovation diffusion: a new perspective. Methuen, London

Lee B, Zhou F, Sun (2013) Construction Of China Free Trade Zones. China Machine Press

Ma C, Zhao X (2008) Why did China's energy intensity increase during 1998–2006: decomposition and policy analysis. Energy Policy 38:1379–1388

Mccalla R (1990) The geographical spread of free zones associated with ports. Geoforum 21(1):121–134

Pereira (2004) The Suzhou industrial park experiment: the case of China–Singapore governmental collaboration. Routledge, pp 173–193

Suzhou Statistic Yearbook (2013) by Su Zhou Shi Tong Ji Ju. Guo Jia Tong Ji Ju Su Zhou Diao Cha Dui (Author)

Yang YR, Hsia CJ (2007) Local clustering and organizational governance of trans-border production networks: a case study of Taiwanese IT companies in the Greater Suzhou Area, China. Environ Plan A 39

Yeung HWC (2000) State intervention and neoliberalism in the globalising world economy: lessons from Singapore's regionalisation programme. Pac Rev 13(1):133–162

Appendixes

In order to offer a full guide of the new China (Shanghai) Pilot Free Trade zone, we selected and attached here some institutional reports (regulations, opinions, circulars) that we consider the basis of the new Shanghai Free Trade Zone. We analyzed deeply them during our exposure, but we prefer to report here for completeness of their original text. They are:

1. Regulations of China (Shanghai) Pilot Free Trade Zone
2. Opinions of the People's Bank of China on Financial Measures to Support the China (Shanghai) Pilot Free Trade Zone
3. Notice of the Shanghai Headquarters of the People's Bank of China on Issuing Implementation Opinions on Cross-border RMB Payment Service by Payment Institutions in Shanghai
4. Circular of the Shanghai Headquarters of the People's Bank of China on Supporting Expanded Cross-Border Use of RMB in the China (Shanghai) Pilot Free Trade Zone
5. Notice of the Shanghai Headquarters of the People's Bank of China on Effectively Combating Money Laundering and Terrorist Financing in the China (Shanghai) Pilot Free Trade Zone
6. Circular of the Shanghai Headquarters of the People's Bank of China on Lifting the Upper Limit on Small-amount Foreign Currency Deposit Rates in the China (Shanghai) Pilot Free Trade Zone
7. Implementation Regulations concerning Foreign Exchange Administration to Support the Construction of the China (Shanghai) Pilot Free Trade Zone
8. Circular of the State Council on the Framework Plan for the China (Shanghai) Pilot Free Trade Zone

L. Riccardi, *Investing in China through Free Trade Zones*,
DOI 10.1007/978-3-662-47354-2

Appendix 1

Regulations of China (Shanghai) Pilot Free Trade Zone

(Adopted at the 14th Session of the Standing Committee of the 14th Shanghai Municipal People's Congress of Shanghai on July 25, 2014)

Chapter I General Provisions

Article 1 – For the purposes of pushing forward and ensuring the construction of China (Shanghai) Pilot Free Trade Zone, giving full play to its role of "experimental plot" in advancing reforms and raising the level of open economy, these Regulations are formulated in accordance with the Decision of the Standing Committee of the National People's Congress on Authorizing the State Council to Temporarily Adjust the Relevant Administrative Approval Items Prescribed in Laws in the China (Shanghai) Pilot Free Trade Zone, the Framework Plan for China (Shanghai) Pilot Free Trade Zone (hereinafter referred to as the "Framework Plan") approved by the State Council, the Decision of the State Council on Adjusting Temporarily Administrative Approval Items or Special Administrative Measures for Access Prescribed by Related Administrative Regulations and the State Council's Documents and other related laws and administrative regulations.

Article 2 – These Regulations apply to the China (Shanghai) Pilot Free Trade Zone (hereinafter referred to as the "PFTZ") established with approval of the State Council.

Article 3 – To push forward the construction of the PFTZ, it is imperative to focus on the national strategic requirements and the building of Shanghai international financial center, international trade center, international shipping center and international economic center, follow the principles of taking the lead in making the first try, putting risks under control, advance by stages and make gradual perfection, combine the expanded opening and the institutional reform, combine the cultivating function and policy innovation, accelerate the transformation of government functions, establish the basic institutional system and surveillance mode in line with the common international investment and trade rules, cultivate an internationalized, market-driven and law-based business environment, and build up a pilot free trade zone up to the international standards with convenient investment and trade, highly active and efficient supervision and standardized legal administration.

Article 4 – To push forward the construction of the PFTZ in this Municipality, it is imperative to focus on key fields and links of institutional innovation, make full use of the existing legal regime and policy resources, reform the system and mechanism that hamper the institutional innovation, constantly motivate the initiative and enthusiasm in institutional innovation so as to build up a good atmosphere of independent reform and proactive attitude.

Article 5 – The vitality of market subjects shall be motivated fully and in respect of matters not prohibited by laws, rules and regulations; citizens, legal persons and other organizations shall be encouraged to actively conduct activities of reform and innovation in the PFTZ.

Chapter II Administrative System

Article 6 – As required for deepening reforms of the administrative system, it is necessary to streamline administration and delegate powers to the lower levels, combine the delegation and supervision, actively promote the notification-promise system and others, and establish an administrative management system in the PFTZ with scientific division of powers and efficient, unified management and open, transparent operation.

Article 7 – The Municipal People's Government shall, under the leadership of the State Council and with the guidance and support of relevant state departments, in accordance with the target location and first-try tasks prescribed in the Framework Plan, organize the implementation of pilot reforms, draw up according to law rules and policy measures relating to the construction and management of the PFTZ.

This Municipality shall establish a coordination mechanism for the construction of the PFTZ, advance the pilot reforms and organize relevant departments to draw up and carry out phase targets and every measure.

Article 8 – China (Shanghai) Pilot Free Trade Zone Administration (hereinafter referred to as the "Administrative Committee") is the agency of the Municipal People's Government, specifically carrying out the pilot reforms in the PFTZ, making overall management and coordination of administrative affairs relating to the PFTZ and performing the following duties under these Regulations:

1. Taking charge of organizing the implementation of the development plan and policy measures of the PFTZ and drawing up the relevant administrative management system.
2. Taking charge of such administrative management work such as the investment, trade, financial services, planning and land resources, construction, transportation, greening and city appearance, environmental protection, human resources, intellectual property rights, statistics, housing, civil defense, water affairs and municipal works.
3. Exercising leadership over the administrative management work of the departments of industry and commerce, quality and supervision, taxation and public security in the zone; coordinating the administrative management work of the departments of finance, customs, inspection and supervision, maritime affairs and frontier inspection in the zone.
4. Organizing the implementation of the sharing work of credibility management and surveillance information in the PFTZ, performing duties relating to examination of national security and examination of anti-monopoly according to law.

5. Making overall guidance to the industrial layout and development construction activities in the zone, coordinating in pushing forward the construction of major investment projects.
6. Releasing public information, providing guidance, consultation and services for enterprises and relevant institutions.
7. Performing other duties entrusted by the Municipal People's Government.

The Municipal People's Government shall establish in the PFTZ a system and mechanism for comprehensive examination and relatively concentrated administrative penalty, and the Administrative Committee shall exercise this Municipality's power of relevant administrative examination and approval and administrative penalty in a concentrated manner. The specific matters under the administrative examination, approval and penalty to be exercised by the Administrative Committee shall be determined and promulgated by the Municipal People's Government.

Article 9 – The departments of customs, inspection and quarantine, maritime affairs, frontier inspection, industry and commerce, quality supervision, taxation and public security shall set up agencies in the PFTZ (hereinafter referred to as the "Zone-stationed Agencies"), which shall perform relevant administrative management duties according to law.

The Municipal People's Government and other relevant departments and the people's government of Pudong New Area (hereinafter referred to as the "Relevant Departments") shall, according to their respective duties and functions, support all the work of the Administrative Committee and assume other administrative affairs in the PFTZ.

Article 10 – The Administrative Committee shall, in conjunction with the Zone-stationed Agencies and the Relevant Departments, establish a working mechanism of cooperation, coordination and joint law enforcement to raise the efficiency of law enforcement and the level of administration.

Article 11 – The Administrative Committee and the Zone-stationed Agencies shall publish the powers of administrative examination and administrative penalty and the list of relevant administrative powers and operation procedures to be exercised by law and shall update them in time in case of adjustment.

Chapter III Investment Opening

Article 12 – The PFTZ shall expand the opening in the fields such as the financial service, shipping service, commercial and trade service, professional service, cultural service, social service and general manufacturing, suspend, cancel or relax the qualification requirements of investors, restrictions in share ratio of foreign investment and business scope and other special management measures for access.

Article 13 – The special management measures for access in the PFTZ prescribed by the State in respect of foreign investment shall be stated in the negative list released by the Municipal People's Government and shall be adjusted in time according to the development practice.

The PFTZ shall exercise the management mode of national treatment plus negative list before foreign investment access. As for fields outside of the negative list, according to the principle of no difference between the domestic and overseas investment, foreign-funded projects are subject to the filing system, except for approval reserved for inbound investment projects as prescribed by the State Council; the establishment and alteration of foreign-funded enterprises are subject to filing administration. In respect of fields within the negative list, foreign-funded projects are subject to the approval system, except for those subject to the filing as prescribed by the State Council; the establishment and alteration of foreign-funded enterprises are subject to examination and approval administration.

The filing procedures for foreign investment projects and foreign-funded enterprises shall be formulated by the Municipal People's Government.

Article 14 – The PFTZ shall facilitate the enterprise registration system, exercising according to law the registered capital subscription registration system.

The administration for industry and commerce shall organize the setting up of enterprise access single-window working mechanism for such administrative affairs as the approval (filing) of foreign investment projects, and the examination (filing) of establishment and alteration of enterprises, accepting the application submissions and serving relevant documents in a unified manner. The investors who establish foreign-funded enterprises in the PFTZ may arrange on their own the business term, except that laws and regulations provide for otherwise.

The enterprises established with registration in the PFTZ (hereinafter referred to as "the enterprise in the zone") may make reinvestment or launch business outside the zone. Where special provisions require for handling relevant formalities, such provisions shall apply.

Article 15 – The enterprise in the zone, after obtaining the business license, may conduct general production and business activities; as for those in need of examination and approval, application may be made to the relevant department after obtaining the business license.

In respect of production and business activity in need of pre-examination and approval as required by laws, administrative regulations or decisions of the State Council, approval formalities shall be completed according to law before application for the business license.

Article 16 – The investors in the PFTZ may make diversified overseas investments. General overseas investment projects are subject to the filing administration. And overseas investment in enterprise running is subject to administration mainly under the filing system, the Administrative Committee accepting the application submissions and serving the relevant documents in a unified manner.

The filing procedures for overseas investment projects and overseas investment in enterprise running shall be formulated by the Municipal People's Government.

Article 17 – In respect of dissolution and bankruptcy of an enterprise in the zone, liquidation shall be made according to law and registration canceling formalities shall be handled.

In respect of an enterprise in the zone subject to the registered capital subscription system according to law, shareholders shall take responsibility for debts of the enterprise limited by their capital or share subscription.

Chapter IV Trade Facilitation

Article 18 – The administration between the PFTZ and overseas is "front-line" administration, and that between the PFTZ and the place inside the border and outside the zone is "back-line" administration; according to the principles of "opening at front-line, exercising efficient control over the back-line, and free circulation within the zone", a supervision mode shall be set up in the PFTZ in line with the development demands of international trade and other business.

Article 19 – As required by the clearance facilitation, security and efficiency, the innovation in customs supervision system shall be conducted in the PFTZ, to promote the development of new trade business mode.

The customs shall institute the supervision system of goods status classification in the PFTZ, conduct the electronic seine management, and carry out paper-free clearance and low-risk rapid clearance.

Goods entering the zone from abroad may enter the zone by presentation of import manifest first and then go through the entry declaration formalities step by step. The export goods at the port are subject to declaration first and then entry.

The goods entry and exit between the zone and the place inside the border and outside the zone are subject to the check of entry-exit filing bills, enterprise account book management, electronic information networking and such other supervision system.

There is no storage term for bonded storage goods in the zone. The procedure for circulation of goods within the zone shall be streamlined; separate distribution, centralized declaration and transportation under self-control shall be allowed, so as to make goods circulate in an efficient and rapid manner between the zone and other special areas under customs supervision.

Article 20 – According to the principles of making entry quarantine, relaxing appropriately export inspection, facilitating entry and exit, taking strict precaution against quality safety risk, the innovation in the supervision system for inspection and quarantine shall be conducted in the PFTZ.

The inspection and quarantine department shall employ the means of information technology in the PFTZ to establish a risk management mechanism for entry-exit quality safety and epidemic situation, exercise paper-free declaration, visa and clearance, carry out the collection, analysis, notification, and application of information on risks, and provide inquiry service of information on entry-exit goods inspection and quarantine.

Goods entering the zone from abroad, if falling in the quarantine scope, are subject to the entry quarantine; except for key sensitive goods, other goods are exempt from inspection.

In respect of goods in the zone to leave the zone, the pre-inspection system shall be practiced depending on the application by enterprises, one-time centralized inspection and clearance being made by verification in batches. Bonded goods for display entering and leaving the PFTZ are exempt from inspection.

Goods under storage and interflow between enterprises in the zone are exempt from inspection and quarantine.

The administration system in favor of the development and standardization of the third-party inspection and appraisal institutions shall be established in the PFTZ, and the inspection and quarantine department shall admit the third-party test results according to the international prevailing rules.

Article 21 – The single window for international trade shall be set up in the PFTZ to form a comprehensive management service platform for trans-department trade, transportation, processing, storage and other business in the zone, and realize the inter-department exchange of information, mutual recognition of supervision and mutual aid in law enforcement.

Enterprises may, through the single window, make one-time submissions of standardized electronic information as required by different administrations, and the feedback of handling outcome shall be given through the single window.

Article 22 – In the PFTZ, the integrated development of domestic and foreign trade shall be carried out, and the enterprise in the zone shall be encouraged to make overall plan for conducting international and domestic trade, cultivate the trade new business mode and function, and form the competition edge with technology, brand, quality and service as the core.

The PFTZ shall support the transformation and upgrading of basic businesses of international trade, storage and logistics, processing manufacture and the development of service trade. Encourage shall be given to the development of offshore trade, international bulk commodity transaction, financing lease, bonded delivery of futures, trans-border e-commerce and other new trade, promoting the development of outsourcing businesses such as biomedical R&D, software and information service and data processing.

Transnational companies are encouraged to establish headquarters in the zone, setting up the operation center that consolidates trade, logistics, settlement and such other functions.

Article 23 – The PFTZ shall strengthen the linkage with the seaport and airport hub, enhance the coordinated development with shipping industry clusters outside of the zone, and explore and form the shipping development system and operation mode with international competition edge.

The PFTZ shall support the development of international transshipment, consolidation (LCL) and distribution as well as container transfer business and air cargo international transshipment. Eligible shipping enterprises may conduct cabotage incidental business of foreign trade export–import containers between domestic coastal ports and Shanghai port.

The shipping service development environment shall be improved, with industries of shipping finance, international shipping transport, international ship management, international seamen service and international shipping brokerage to be developed and with shipping freight index derivative trading business to be expanded and with functional agencies of shipping service to be clustered in the PFTZ.

In the PFTZ the international ship registration system with China Yangshan Port as the port of registry shall be carried out with efficient ship registration procedures to be set up.

Article 24 – In the PFTZ the examination formalities for employment permit to the foreign employees of enterprises in the zone shall be simplified, with visa and valid term of residence permit to be relaxed and with entry, exit and residence to be facilitated.

To foreigners who conduct commercial trade at the invitation of enterprises in the zone, the entry-exit administration shall, pursuant to regulations, give visa waiver and easy temporary entry.

For Chinese employees of enterprises in the zone who need to go abroad or outside the border frequently, the entry-exit administration shall provide easy process of exit papers.

Chapter V Financial Service

Article 25 – Under the premise of risk under control, conditions shall be created in the PFTZ for steadily conducting the first try of RMB capital account convertibility, market-driven interest rate of financial market, RMB cross-border use and foreign exchange reform and such other aspects.

The financial factor market and financial institutions shall be encouraged to conduct innovation in financial products, business, services, and risk management in the PFTZ pursuant to the State provisions. Relevant departments of this Municipality shall provide support and facility for financial innovation in the PFTZ.

This Municipality shall establish the PFTZ financial work coordination mechanism with participation of Shanghai-stationed agencies of the national financial management department, the municipal financial service department and the Administrative Committee.

Article 26 – The PFTZ shall establish a free trade account system in favor of risk management and exercise separate accounting management. Residents in the zone may open resident free trade accounts pursuant to regulations; non-residents may open non-resident free trade accounts in the banks in the zone, and accept relevant financial service on the principle of pre-access national treatment; financial institutions in Shanghai areas may, through setting up separate accounting units, provide financial service relating to free trade accounts.

Funds may be transferred freely between free trade accounts and between free trade accounts and overseas accounts and domestic outside-the-zone non-resident institution accounts. Free trade accounts may, pursuant to regulations, handle cross-border financing and guarantee business. Fund flow between resident free trade accounts and domestic outside-the-zone bank settling accounts shall be deemed as cross-border business management. The resident free trade accounts in the same non-financial institution subject may, pursuant to regulations, handle fund transfer to other bank settling accounts.

Article 27 – The cross-border fund flow in the PFTZ shall be under management on the financial macro-prudential principle. The cross-border direct investment remittance formalities shall be simplified in the PFTZ, the PFTZ cross-border direct investment, disconnected from the pre-approval, may directly handle the involved cross-border payment and remittance business at the bank. Various subjects in the zone may, pursuant to regulations, conduct relevant cross-border investment or financing remittance business.

Individuals in the zone may, pursuant to regulations, handle current-account cross-border RMB receipt and payment business and conduct various cross-border investments including securities investment. Individual businessmen in the zone may, depending on business needs, provide cross-border loan to their overseas business subjects.

Financial institutions and enterprises in the zone may, pursuant to regulations, enter the securities and futures trading place to make investment and transaction. Overseas parent companies of the enterprises in the zone may, pursuant to regulations, issue RMB bonds in the domestic capital market. Enterprises in the zone may, pursuant to regulations, conduct overseas securities investment and derivatives investment business.

Enterprises, non-bank financial institutions and other economic organizations may, pursuant to regulations, borrow domestic and foreign currency funds from overseas, and conduct the hedge risk management in the zone or overseas.

Article 28 – Pursuant to relevant provisions of China People's Bank, all policy measures hammered out by the State for encouraging and supporting the expanded RMB cross-border use apply to the PFTZ.

The cross-border use of RMB under the current accounts and direct investment in the PFTZ shall be simplified. Financial institutions and enterprises in the zone may borrow RMB funds from overseas. Enterprises in the zone may, according to their business needs, conduct cross-border two-way RMB fund pool and current-account cross-border RMB concentrated receipt and payment business. The banking industry financial institutions in Shanghai areas may cooperate with eligible payment institutions in providing cross-border e-commerce RMB settlement service.

Article 29 – The building of an interest-rate market-driven system is to be pushed forward in the PFTZ, with the monitoring mechanism of free trade account domestic and foreign currency funds interest rate market-driven pricing to be improved, and eligible financial institutions in the zone may have priority in issuing negotiable certificates of deposits (NCDS), with the interest-rate ceiling to be opened for foreign-currency deposit in the zone.

Article 30 – A foreign exchange management system shall be established in line with the development demands of the PFTZ. The current account document check and direct investment foreign exchange registration formalities shall be simplified. External debt claims management is to be relaxed. The centralized operation management of transnational corporation's headquarters foreign exchange fund and the foreign exchange management of foreign currency fund pool and the international trade settlement center shall be improved. The foreign exchange settlement and sale management shall be perfected to facilitate the counter transactions of bulk commodity derivatives.

Article 31 Depending on the needs of the PFTZ and upon approval by the financial administration, support shall be given to financial institutions at different levels, with different functions, in different types and with different ownerships to let them enter the PFTZ; non-government capital shall be guided and encouraged to invest in the financial industry in the zone; the Internet financial development in the PFTZ shall be supported; support is given to the building of a platform geared to international financial transaction and service so as to provide registration, trusteeship, transaction, liquidation and other services; support is also given to the building and improving of a trust registration platform to explore the transfer mechanism of the beneficial right of the trust.

Article 32 – This Municipality shall, in cooperation with the financial administration, perfect the financial risk monitoring and evaluation, and establish a risk prevention mechanism in line with the financial business development in the PFTZ.

Financial institutions and specified non-financial institutions in Shanghai areas that conduct business in the PFTZ shall, pursuant to regulations, submit relevant information to the financial administration, discharge obligations of anti-money laundering, anti-terrorist financing, and anti-tax evasion, cooperate with the financial administration to pay attention to cross-border abnormal capital flow and carry out the responsibility for protection of financial consumers and investors.

Chapter VI Taxation Management

Article 33 – The PFTZ shall, pursuant to the state's provisions, implement taxation policy relating to promoting investment and trade; Shanghai Waigaoqiao bonded area, Shanghai Waigaoqiao bonded logistic park, Yangshan bonded port area and Shanghai Pudong airport comprehensive bonded area under its jurisdiction shall execute the corresponding taxation policy of special areas under customs supervision.

It is imperative to follow the direction of tax reform and international conventions, actively study and perfect the tax policy that does not cause the profit transfer, the tax base erosion but adapts to overseas equity investment and offshore business development.

Article 34 – The tax department shall establish a convenient tax service system in the PFTZ, exercise the tax professional concentrated examination, gradually cancel prior examination, carry out the working pattern of first examination and then verification, separating examination from verification; pursue online tax, provide online services of tax payment consultation and tax-involved matters handling inquiry, and gradually realized the cross- regional tax process.

Article 35 – The tax department shall conduct the pilot modernization of tax collection in the PFTZ, raise tax revenue efficiency, and build up a tax environment in favor of enterprise development and fair competition.

The tax department shall conduct tax risk monitoring by using the tax information system and the supervision information sharing platform in the PFTZ to raise the level of tax administration.

VII Comprehensive Supervision

Article 36 – It is imperative to innovate in the administrative management mode in the PFTZ, push forward the government administration from paying attention to prior examination to paying attention to mid- and post-event supervision, increase the participation in supervision, and promote the institution of a comprehensive supervision system of administrative supervision, industrial self-discipline, social supervision and public participation.

Article 37 – The PFTZ shall establish a working mechanism of national security examination involving foreign investment. As for foreign investment under the scope of national security examination, the investor shall apply for national security examination; relevant administrations, trade associations, enterprises in the same industry and upstream and downstream firms may propose suggestions on the national security examination.

The party concerned shall cooperate in the national security examination, providing necessary material and information and accept relevant inquiry.

Article 38 – The PFTZ shall establish an anti-monopoly working mechanism.

Involving the agglomeration of operators of the enterprises in the zone and reaching the declaration standard as prescribed by the State Council, the operator shall make prior declaration, and shall not carry out agglomeration without declaration. In respect of monopoly agreements, abuse of market-dominating positions and competition elimination and restriction by abusing administrative power, and such other behaviors, investigation and law enforcement shall be conducted according to law.

Article 39 – The Administrative Committee, the zone-stationed agencies and the relevant departments shall record information on credit of enterprises and relevant persons in charge thereof, and, according to the public credit information catalogue, send to the PFTZ sub platform of the municipal public credit information service platform for integration.

The Administrative Committee, the zone-stationed agencies and the relevant departments may, in the work of market access, goods clearance, government purchase and bids and bid invitations, inquire about the relative credit record and use credit products to grant convenience to enterprises and individuals with good credit and impose restriction and punishment on those who break their promise.

The PFTZ shall encourage credit service institutions to use all sides' credit information to develop credit products and provide credit service for administrative supervision and market transactions; enterprises and individuals are encouraged to use credit products and service.

Article 40 – The PFTZ shall exercise the publication system of enterprises' annual reports and the system of directory of enterprises with abnormal operation.

The enterprises in the zone shall, pursuant to regulations, submit enterprise's annual reports and be responsible for the truth and legality of information thereon. The enterprise's annual report shall be published to society as prescribed except for contents involving state secrets, business secrets and personal privacy.

The administration for industry and commerce shall conduct supervisory inspection on submission of annual reports by the enterprises in the zone. If finding out that any enterprise failed to discharge the obligation of publishing its annual report, the said administration shall record the enterprise in the directory of enterprises with abnormal operation and make it known to the public.

Every citizen, legal person and other organization may get access to the enterprise's annual report and the directory of enterprises with abnormal operation and such publication information, and the administration for industry and commerce and other departments shall provide convenience for inquiry.

The procedures for management of publication of enterprise annual reports and the directory of enterprises with abnormal operation shall be formulated by the municipal administration for industry and commerce.

Article 41 – A unified supervision information sharing platform shall be built in the PFTZ to promote the collection, exchange and sharing of supervision information. The Administrative Committee, zone-stationed agencies and relevant departments shall provide information on their initiative and in time, participating in information exchange and sharing.

The Administrative Committee, zone-stationed agencies and relevant departments shall rely on the supervision information sharing platform to consolidate supervision resources, promote full dynamic supervision and raise efficiency of combined supervision and coordinated service.

The procedures for collection, exchange and sharing of supervision information shall be formulated by the Administrative Committee, zone-stationed agencies and relevant departments.

Article 42 – The professional institutions of law firms. accounting firms, certified tax agents offices, IP right service institutions, customs inspection institutions, inspection and testing institutions, certification authorities, ship and crew agencies, notarization institutions, forensic appraisal institutions and credit service institutions are encouraged to conduct business in the PFTZ.

The Administrative Committee, zone-stationed agencies and relevant departments shall, by institutional arrangement, refer the matters in the zone that fit for handling by professional institutions thereto, or adopt the competition mechanism or purchase of service to guide and cultivate the development of professional institutions.

Article 43 – The PFTZ shall establish a mechanism of social participation composed of enterprises and representatives of relevant organizations, to guide enterprises and relevant organizations to lodge claims for interests and participate in pilot policy evaluation and market supervision.

Trade associations and chambers of commerce are supported to participate in the construction of the PFTZ, and they are urged to draw up the trade management standard and trade convention to strengthen trade self-discipline.

The enterprises in the zone engaged in business activities shall observe social morality, business ethics and accept supervision of the general public.

Article 44 – In the PFTZ it is imperative to speed up the development of E-government, promote electronic official documents with electronic signature that have force of law, and carry out electronic documents filing and electronic archives management. Electronic records and paper files have the same legal effect.

Article 45 – This Municipality shall establish a comprehensive evaluation mechanism for the PFTZ. The municipal development and reform department shall, in conjunction with the Administrative Committee and relevant departments, conduct, by themselves or by a third party they entrust, evaluation of the innovation in the supervision system, the whole industry, the implementation of pilot policy on industrial businesses and risk prevention, and propose policy-related suggestions for promoting, improving and expanding the opening fields, pilot reform tasks and measures for institutional innovation.

Chapter VIII Law-Based Environment

Article 46 – It is imperative to adhere to applying the thought and mode of rule by law to innovate in every reform in the PFTZ, so as to build a good environment of rule by law for the construction of the PFTZ.

Where there are adjustments to the pilot reform measures provided for by the State for investment, trade, finance, and tax in the PFTZ or where the pilot reform measures in other regions provided for by the State apply to the PFTZ, the implementation shall be done according to relevant provisions.

Where this Municipality's local bylaws do not adapt to the development of the PFTZ, the Municipal People's Government may request the Municipal People's Congress and its standing committee to make relevant provisions on the application thereof in the PFTZ; where this Municipality's regulations do not adapt to the development of the PFTZ, the Administrative Committee may request the Municipal People's Government to make relevant provisions on the application thereof in the PFTZ.

Article 47 – The equal positions and rights to development of various market subjects in the PFTZ shall be protected by law. Various market subjects in the zone shall enjoy equal treatment in terms of supervision, tax and government purchase.

Article 48 – The enterprise, equity, intellectual property right, profit and other property and business interests owned legally by the investors in the PFTZ shall be protected by law.

Article 49 – The rights of workers in the PFTZ in terms of equal employment, vocational choice, labor remuneration, rest and holiday, labor safety and health protection, vocational skill training, social insurance and benefits, and participation in democratic management shall be protected by law.

In the PFTZ it is imperative to carry out a mechanism of collective consultation between the enterprise and workers, promote the equal consultation between both parties on labor remuneration, labor safety and health and relevant matters. It is imperative to give play to the role of trade unions in maintaining the rights and interests of employees and promoting the harmonious and steady labor relationship.

In the PFTZ it is imperative to perfect the mechanism of conducting fair, open, efficient and convenient labor and social security inspection and labor dispute settlement so as to protect legitimate rights and interests of workers and employers.

Article 50 – It is imperative to strengthen the environmental protection work in the PFTZ, explore and conduct the classified management of EIA, and raise the level and efficiency of environmental protection management.

The enterprises in the zone shall be encouraged to apply for international prevailing certification of environment and energy management system standard, adopt advanced production techniques and technologies, save energy and reduce the emission of pollutants and greenhouse gases.

Article 51 – It is imperative to strengthen the intellectual property right protection work in the PFTZ, and improve the mechanism of linking the administrative protection and judicial protection.

This Municipality's relevant departments shall strengthen cooperation with relevant State departments, carry out the coordinated management and law enforcement of IP entry-exit protection and domestic protection, explore and establish the system and mechanism of unified management and law enforcement of intellectual property rights in the PFTZ.

It is imperative to perfect the multiple settlement mechanism of IP disputes in the PFTZ, encourage trade associations and institutions of mediation, arbitration and IP intermediary service to play their role in the coordinated settlement of IP disputes.

Article 52 – When formulating local regulations, government rules and normative documents regarding the PFTZ, this Municipality shall publish the draft contents on its initiative to solicit opinions from the general public, relevant industrial organizations and enterprises; and after passage and promulgation thereof, explanation shall be given for disposition of opinions from all sides of society; in the period between the promulgation and implementation, a rational term shall be reserved for preparation for implementation, and however, with an exception of need for prompt formulation and implementation due to emergency and for other reasons.

The local regulations, government rules and normative documents regarding the PFTZ formulated by this Municipality shall, after passage thereof, be published in time, with interpretation and explanation.

Article 53 – Every citizen, legal person and other organization, if having any objection to the normative documents drawn up by the Administrative Committee, may request the Municipal People's Government for review. The review rules shall be formulated by the Municipal People's Government.

Article 54 – This Municipality shall establish the release mechanism of PFTZ information, releasing in time the information relating to the PFTZ through the press conference, regular meeting of information notification or release in writing or in other way.

The Administrative Committee shall collect information on laws, regulations, rules, policies and administrative procedures relating to the PFTZ provided for by the State and this Municipality, publish on the portal website of China (Shanghai) Pilot Free Trade Zone to facilitate inquiry by all sides.

Article 55 – The system of relatively concentrated administrative reconsideration right is exercised in the PFTZ.

Every citizen, legal person or other organization, if disagreeing with the specific administrative act made in the PFTZ by the Administrative Committee, the working department and the zone-stationed agency of the Municipal People's Government, or the Pudong New Area people's government, may apply for administrative reconsideration to the Municipal People's Government; if disagreeing with the specific administrative act made by the working department of the Pudong New Area people's government, they may apply for administrative reconsideration to the Pudong New Area people's government. The major, complex and difficult administrative reconsideration case shall be reviewed by the administrative reconsideration committee.

Article 56 – The judicial organ shall be established according to law in the PFTZ to safeguard the legitimate rights and interests of Chinese and foreign parties in a just and efficient manner.

The arbitration institution established according to law in this Municipality shall, pursuant to laws and regulations and by using for reference international arbitration conventions, perfect the arbitration rules to adapt to the characteristics of the PFTZ, raise the internationalized level of business dispute arbitration and, based on their own choice of the clients, provide independent, just, professional and efficient arbitration service.

The trade associations, chambers of commerce, and professional mediation institutions for business disputes established in this Municipality may take part in the mediation of business disputes in the PFTZ and give play to their role in dispute settlement.

Chapter IX Supplementary Provision

Article 57 – These Regulations shall be effective as of August 1, 2014. The Regulations of Shanghai Waigaoqiao Bonded Area adopted at the 32nd session of the 10th Shanghai People's Congress on December 19, 1996 shall be repealed at the same time.

Appendix 2

Opinions of the People's Bank of China on Financial Measures to Support the China (Shanghai) Pilot Free Trade Zone

2nd December 2014

The PBC has released the following opinions in order to implement the important strategic decision of the CPC Central Committee and the State Council on establishing the China (Shanghai) Pilot Free Trade Zone, support the development of the FTZ and the real economy development in the FTZ, deepen financial sector reform, and promote opening-up.

I. General Principles

1. The principle of financial sector serving the real economy will be followed to further facilitate trade and investment, promote the opening of financial sector and facilitate the FTZ to compete internationally on a higher platform.
2. The principle of continuing reform and innovation, and leading the way in experiment will be followed to promote the cross-border use of RMB, the move towards capital account convertibility, market-based interest rate reform and foreign exchange administration reform.
3. The principle of keeping risks within controllable ranges and making steady progress will be followed to organize experiments in an orderly manner whenever the conditions for an experiment are mature.

II. Innovations in Account Management System That Facilitates Risk Management

4. Residents in the FTZ can open local and foreign currency free trade accounts (hereinafter referred to as a resident free trade account) to realize separate accounting for their transactions and to conduct innovative investment and financing activities specified in Part III of the *Opinions*; non-residents can open local and foreign currency free trade accounts with banks that operate in the FTZ (hereinafter referred to as a non-residesnt free trade account) and receive financial services based on the principle of pre-access national treatment.
5. Fund can be transferred freely between a resident free trade account on the one hand, and an overseas account, or a non-resident account opened in China but outside of the FTZ, or a non-resident free trade account, or a free trade account of another resident on the other. Fund can be transferred between a resident free trade account and other bank settlement accounts held by the same non-financial company or agency for the purpose of current account transactions, loan repayment, investment in the real economy and other cross-border transactions that comply with relevant regulations. The fund transfer between a resident free trade account and a bank settlement account opened within China but outside the FTZ is to be regulated as cross-border business.
6. A resident free trade account and non-resident free trade account can be used for cross-border financing and guarantee transactions. When conditions are mature, the foreign currency and local currency fund can be converted freely within a free trade account. An RMB exchange and remittance monitoring mechanism will be established covering the resident free trade accounts and non-resident free trade accounts in the FTZ.
7. Financial institutions in Shanghai can establish a separate accounting system for the FTZ in accordance with the PBC regulations, open free trade accounts for eligible clients in the FTZ, and provide financial services.

III. Explorations to Facilitate Exchange and Remittance for Investment and Financing

8. Measures will be taken to facilitate cross-border direct investment by enterprises. In the FTZ, cross-border direct investment can be conducted and delinked from the upfront verification as required by the regulations of the Shanghai municipal government, i.e., the cross-border payment, receipt, and exchange involved in the investment can be directly processed by banks.
9. Measures will be taken to facilitate cross-border investment by individuals. Eligible individuals who are employed in the FTZ can make various kinds of overseas investment including securities investment. The income that an individual has legally obtained within the FTZ can be used for payment to overseas recipients after tax payment obligations are honored. The businesses established by self-employed individuals in the FTZ can provide cross-border loans to its overseas operations based on the need of the business operations. Overseas individuals who are employed in the FTZ can open non-resident specialized account for personal investment within China and make various kinds of investments in China including securities investment.
10. Measures will be taken to steadily open up the capital market. Financial institutions and enterprises in the FTZ can make investment and trading on the securities and futures markets in Shanghai in accordance with relevant regulations. The overseas parent company of an enterprise located in the FTZ can issue RMB-denominated bonds in China's domestic bond market in accordance with relevant regulations. Based on market demand, explorations will be made to conduct international financial asset trading in the FTZ.
11. Measures will be taken to facilitate overseas financing. According to operational needs, Chinese- and foreign-funded enterprises, non-bank financial institutions and other economic units registered in the FTZ (hereinafter referred to as units in the FTZ) can borrow domestic and foreign currency-denominated funds from overseas markets according to relevant regulations. Efforts will be made to improve macro-prudential regulation over all kinds of foreign debts, and effective measures will be taken to prevent foreign debt risks.
12. A variety of risk hedging instruments will be provided. Based on authentic demand for managing currency and maturity mismatch, units in the FTZ can hedge risk in the FTZ or overseas markets in accordance with relevant regulations. Eligible enterprises in the FTZ are allowed to conduct overseas securities investment and derivative investment. Financial institutions shall square or hedge the open positions in the FTZ separate accounting system that arise from providing domestic and foreign currency exchange and remittance service to other institutions in the FTZ or overseas institutions in the FTZ or overseas markets. Based on the demand for risk management, separate accounting units in the FTZ can conduct derivative transactions in overseas markets in accordance with relevant regulations. Upon approval, a separate accounting unit can borrow, lend or conduct repo transactions in the domestic interbank market within a prescribed quota.

IV. Measures to Promote Cross-Border Use of RMB

13. Based on the three principles of "know your customer", "know your business" and "due diligence", banking institutions located in Shanghai can directly process cross-border RMB settlement for current account transactions and direct investment after the units in the FTZ (with the exception of the enterprises who are on the list of focused supervision of RMB settlement of export trade in goods) and individuals in the FTZ submit receipt and payment orders.
14. Financial institutions located in Shanghai can work together with payment institutions that hold payment business license and that include internet payment in the range of business to provide RMB settlement service for cross-border e-commerce (trade in goods and services) in accordance with the regulatory policy applicable to payment institutions.
15. Financial institutions and non-financial companies located in the FTZ can borrow RMB fund from overseas but the borrowed money must not be used for investment in securities or derivatives, nor for entrusted lending.
16. Enterprises located in the FTZ can conduct two-way RMB fund pooling business within their enterprise group based on the need of business operation to provide centralized receipt and payment service for current account transactions of their affiliated enterprises located in China and overseas.

V. Measures to Steadily Promote Market-Based Interest Rate Reform

17. Establishment of a market-based interest rate system in the FTZ will be promoted based on the availability of basic conditions.
18. The market-based interest rate pricing monitor mechanism will be improved covering the RMB and foreign currency fund in resident FTA and non-resident FTA accounts.
19. Eligible financial institutions in the FTZ will be included in the list of institutions that will lead the way in issuing inter-bank CDs so that the FTZ will be the test ground for inter-bank CD issuing.
20. When the conditions are available, the foreign currency interest-rate ceiling applicable to the small-value fund in the general accounts in the FTZ will be lifted.

VI. Measures to Deepen Foreign Exchange Administration Reform

21. The FTZ's efforts to develop a CBD and promote new trade will be supported. More enterprises will be included in the pilot program of foreign currency fund centralized management by multinational company headquarters, the regulation of foreign currency fund pooling will be further simplified, and the foreign exchange administration pilot program covering international trade settlement center will be deepened to facilitate trade and investment.

22. Foreign exchange registration procedure for direct investment will be simplified. The foreign exchange registration and alteration registration for direct investment will be delegated to the banks and ex-post surveillance will be strengthened. Under the precondition of ensuring authentic transactions and integrity of collected data, the foreign exchange fund involved in an FDI project in the FTZ may be sold to the banks on a voluntary basis.
23. Overseas and domestic leasing services will be supported in the FTZ. The case-by-case approval applicable to overseas leasing and other overseas claim businesses of financial leasing companies will be replaced by registration-based management. After being approved, financial leasing companies and Chinese-funded leasing companies are allowed to receive rents in a foreign currency for their domestic leasing business. The procedure of prepayment for goods purchase will be simplified for large-scale leasing projects involving aircrafts and ships.
24. The verification and approval procedure will be removed for payment of guarantee fees by units in the FTZ to overseas recipients so that these units may go directly to bank counters to purchase foreign exchange and pay guarantee fees.
25. Foreign exchange surrender management will be improved to support commercial banks to conduct OTC trading of commodity derivatives with their clients.

VII. Monitoring and Regulation

26. Financial institutions and designated non-financial institutions located in the FTZ shall earnestly honor anti-money laundering, counter-terrorism financing and tax evasion prevention obligations in compliance with relevant laws and regulations, report to the PBC and other financial regulatory agencies their balance sheet and other business operation information in a timely and accurate manner, ensure the integrity of data, go through BOP statistics declaration procedures in accordance with relevant regulations, and cooperate with financial regulatory agencies to closely watch the anomalies in cross-border fund flow.
27. The Shanghai Municipal Government can establish an FTZ comprehensive information oversight platform to regulate non-financial institutions, evaluate the non-financial institutions on an annual basis, and divide them into different groups based on the evaluation outcome to exercise oversight.
28. The business recorded in the FTZ separate accounting system shall be included by a legal person bank in the calculation of capital adequacy ratio. The liquidity management of the FTZ outlets should follow the principle of seeking a balance on their own while liquidity can be provided by the outlet at the next higher level when necessary.
29. Macro-prudential regulation will be applied to the FTZ. The PBC may strengthen regulation over short-term speculative capital flow in the FTZ based on its assessment of the situation, and may even take temporary control measures. The communication and coordination with other financial regulatory agencies will be strengthened to ensure the prompt and adequate sharing of information.

30. The PBC will formulate detailed implementation rules, organize the implementation based on the principle of keeping risks within a controllable range and making steady progress, and set up good arrangements to coordinate with the macro-prudential requirements of other financial regulatory agencies.

Appendix 3

Notice of the Shanghai Headquarters of the People's Bank of China on Issuing Implementation Opinions on Cross-Border RMB Payment Service by Payment Institutions in Shanghai

February 18, 2014

State-owned commercial banks; joint-stock commercial banks; Shanghai Branch of Postal Savings Bank of China; Bank of Shanghai; Shanghai Rural Commercial Bank; foreign banks in Shanghai operating RMB business; payment institutions with legal person status in Shanghai; and Shanghai branches of payment institutions that are not based in Shanghai:

In accordance with the Opinions of the People's Bank of China on Financial Sector Support for the China (Shanghai) Pilot Free Trade Zone, the Administrative Measures for the Payment Services Provided by Non-financial Institutions and other relevant regulations, a notice entitled Implementation Opinions on Cross-border RMB Payment Service by Payment Institutions in Shanghai is issued upon the approval and authorization of the People's Bank of China (PBC), with an aim to facilitate the cross-border e-commerce, expand the cross-border use of RMB, standardize and promote the cross-border RMB services by payment institutions in Shanghai, and enhance the development of the FTZ. In case of any emerging questions during the implementation of this notice, please notify the Shanghai Headquarters of the People's Bank of China (PBS) – Financial Services Department (I).

Implementation Opinions on Cross-Border RMB Payment Service by Payment Institutions in Shanghai

These Implementation Opinions are formulated in accordance with the Opinions of the People's Bank of China on Financial Sector Support for the China (Shanghai) Pilot Free Trade Zone, the Administrative Measures for the Payment Services Provided by Non-financial Institutions and other relevant regulations, with an aim to facilitate the cross- border e-commerce, expand the cross-border use of RMB, and standardize and promote the cross-border RMB services by payment institutions in Shanghai.

I. General Principles

1. Supporting the construction of the China (Shanghai) Pilot Free Trade Zone (referred to hereafter as "the PFTZ"), further expand the scope of opening up, and building up replicable and widely applicable experience as soon as possible.
2. Developing real economy in the financial service sector in a consistent manner, striving to meet the need of domestic and foreign markets, and strengthening efforts to promote the cross-border use of RMB.
3. Focusing on risk control in a consistent manner and developing cross-border RMB payment services in an active, progressive and stable manner.

II. Eligible Entities

The following entities are eligible to provide cross-border RMB payment service:

- Payment institutions which are registered in Shanghai and possess the Online Payment Service License, including payment institutions registered in the PFTZ and those registered outside the PFTZ but within Shanghai;
- Shanghai branches of the payment institutions registered outside Shanghai which possess the Online Payment Service License (Institutions aforementioned are referred to hereafter as "payment institutions").

The branches set up in the PFTZ by payment institutions registered outside Shanghai shall submit a report to the PBS (or PBC Shanghai Branch) as required by the Administrative Measures for the Payment Services Provided by Non-financial Institutions and other relevant regulations.

III. Eligibility Criteria

Eligible entities shall:

1. Be legally authorized to provide payment services, including online payment services;
2. Develop robust internal control systems and risk management measures for the operation of cross-border RMB payment business;
3. Possess adequate infrastructure and facilities, including technological support for online cross-border RMB payment business operation;
4. Develop specific mechanisms and measures for anti-money laundering, counter-terrorist financing and anti-tax evasion in the operation of cross-border RMB business;
5. Be in business in compliance with laws and regulations since the acquisition of the Payment Service License, possess strong risk-control capability, and engage in no severe violation of rules and laws in the last two years;
6. Meet other requirements stipulated by PBC.

IV. Required Filing Documents

Payment institutions eligible to provide cross-border RMB payment services shall provide the following filing documents to the Anchor PBS (or PBC Shanghai Branch) within 7 days as of the launch of the services:

1. Filing reports;
2. A copy of Payment Service License;
3. Details about the procedures of the cross-border RMB payment business operation;
4. Details about the internal control schemes and risk management measures for the operation of cross-border RMB payment services, including those concerning payment, technology support and anti-money laundering;
5. Business cooperation agreements signed with reserve banks;
6. Declaration of authenticity of the submitted documents.

V. The Scope of Business

Payment institutions are authorized to provide payment services through internet for payers and payees both at home and abroad, and make RMB transfers according to the actual need by non-FTAs. Cross-border RMB payment services include both outbound payment from China and inbound payment to China. Payment netting is prohibited.

Payment institutions are prohibited to provide cross-border RMB payment services for the following transactions or entities:

1. Those involving commodities or services without actual transaction request;
2. Those involving trade in commodities or services that fails to meet China's import and export management regulations;
3. Enterprises which are not qualified to operate import and export business under the item of tangible goods trade;
4. Enterprises whose import and export settlement of tangible goods trade is identified by the six relevant ministries and committees under the State Council, including PBC, as requiring special attention and supervision;
5. The object of transaction under the item of trade in services involving goods with no market-recognized consideration, or other intangible goods with ambiguous pricing scheme or potential risks;
6. Transactions under the item of capital;
7. Business projects or operations which might bring harm to the country, social security and public interests of the society;
8. Business projects prohibited or not permitted by relevant laws and regulations, including rules and regulations stipulated by PBC and the State Administration of Foreign Exchange.

VI. The Management of Reserves

The payment institutions' management of the reserves of cross-border RMB clients shall be subject to the Measures for the Custody of the Reserves of Payment Institutions' Clients and other relevant supervision requirements of PBC for the clients' reserves.

Payment institutions shall effectively identify domestic and cross-border RMB payment services by adding new business types and other measures, and report information in this respect according to relevant requirements of Anchorthe PBS (or PBC Shanghai Branch).

VII. Risk Management

1. Before submitting an application to reserve banks for providing cross-border RMB payment services, payment institutions shall sign the Cooperative Agreement on Handling Cross-border RMB Payment Business, including but not limited to the following clauses:

   (a) Payment institutions shall open a specialized cross-border RMB account within the designated reserve account system so as to use the reserves separately without occupying or misappropriating the client's reserves in any form;
   (b) Payment institutions shall establish and implement a sound identity recognition mechanism, avoid providing cross-border RMB payment services for transactions without a real trade background, and keep all the proof of the authenticity of the trade for inspection;
   (c) Payment institutions shall establish a monitoring model targeting suspicious transactions such as those involving large sum and split operations, and include relevant clients in the focus list for inspection. Where a transaction is determined as abnormal after inspection, the payment institution concerned shall stop providing payment services for the relevant client;
   (d) Payment institutions shall agree with reserve banks on the transaction details, including the information on transactions, logistics and funds, and submit in a timely manner these details to reserve banks. Reserve banks shall inspect whether the details are complete and meet the requirements;
   (e) After finishing the cross-border RMB payment transactions for the payment institutions, reserve banks shall report to the RMB cross-border receipt and payment information management system in an accurate, complete and timely manner, and shall process relevant information for corresponding international payment statistics reporting in accordance with the requirements of the PBS (or PBC Shanghai Branch); and
   (f) Payment institutions and reserve banks shall specify the approaches to handle errors, disputes and accidents as well as measures to guarantee the clients' rights and interests; identify risks and responsibilities; and clearly state the termination of the agreement and liability for breach of agreement.

2. Payment institutions shall inspect the authenticity of the trade based on the information available on the transaction, logistics and funds, and avoid providing cross-border RMB payment services for transactions without a real trade background.
3. Payment institutions shall select the right transaction type according to the real situation of the trade, correctly record the transaction information, ensure that the information is complete, authentic and traceable, and keep all the proof of the authenticity of the trade for inspection and verification.
4. Payment institutions shall establish and implement a sound identity recognition mechanism. Payment institutions shall adopt a real-name system and access verification system for contractual merchants; inspect whether the commodities and services provided by such merchants and their terms of service comply with relevant laws and regulations; and check their background, status and credibility. Payment institutions shall record the information of their clients, including the name, gender, nationality, occupation, address, contact information as well as the type, number and validity period of their effective identity documents. They shall also verify the authenticity of such basic information as the name, gender and the type and number of effective IDs.
5. Payment institutions shall strictly follow the requirements of PBC on the limit of cross- border RMB payment services.
6. Payment institutions shall include clients dealing with suspicious transactions such as those involving large sum and split operations in the focus list for inspection. Where a transaction is determined as abnormal after inspection, the payment institution concerned shall stop providing payment services for the relevant client.
7. After finishing the cross-border RMB payment transactions for the payment institutions, reserve banks shall report to the RMB cross-border receipt and payment information management system in an accurate, complete and timely manner, and shall process relevant information for corresponding international payment statistics reporting in accordance with the requirements of the PBS (or PBC Shanghai Branch).
8. Payment institutions shall provide cross-border RMB payment services in line with relevant laws and regulations. In case any payment institution is found to have violated relevant laws and regulations, the PBS (or PBC Shanghai Branch) shall take legal action against the institutions concerned.

Appendix 4

Circular of the Shanghai Headquarters of the People's Bank of China on Supporting Expanded Cross-Border Use of RMB in the China (Shanghai) Pilot Free Trade Zone

Bank Headquarters Publication [2014] No. 22
February 20, 2014

To the Shanghai branches of the China Development Bank, policy banks, state-owned commercial banks, joint-stock commercial banks, and China Postal Savings Bank; Bank of Communications, Shanghai Pudong Development Bank, Bank of Shanghai, and Shanghai Rural Commercial Bank; the Shanghai branches of other urban commercial banks; foreign banks in Shanghai; and non-banking financial institutions in Shanghai:

According to the *Opinions of the People's Bank of China on Financial Sector Support for the China (Shanghai) Pilot Free Trade Zone* (referred to hereafter as the "*Opinions*") and other relevant provisions, as approved by the headquarters of the People's Bank of China ("PBC"), the *Circular on Supporting Expanded Cross-border Use of RMB in the China (Shanghai) Pilot Free Trade Zone* ("PFTZ") is published as follows:

I. All Policies and Measures Issued by the State Government to Encourage and Support Expanded Cross-Border Use of RMB Shall Apply to the PFTZ

II. Cross-border RMB Settlement under Current Accounts and Direct Investment in the PFTZ

Banking institutions in Shanghai may, based on the three principles of "knowing your clients, knowing your business, and due diligence, directly process cross-border RMB settlement under current accounts and under direct investment for entities (excluding those on a monitoring list for cross-border RMB settlement) or individuals in the PFTZ according to their receipt/payment instructions.

1. When conducting settlement under direct investment for the aforesaid parties, banks shall, according to the negative list management requirements for investment in the PFTZ, require them to produce approval documents issued by competent authorities if the settlement business is subject to negative list management.
2. The Shanghai Headquarters of the People's Bank of China ("PBC Shanghai") and the Administration Committee of the PFTZ shall establish a direct investment information sharing system through the comprehensive information management system of the PFTZ and provide relevant information services for commercial banks.

III. Bank Settlement Accounts of Individuals in the PFTZ

To facilitate individuals in conducing cross-border RMB settlement under current accounts, individuals working in the PFTZ as employees or business practitioners may, according to the *Administrative Measures for RMB Bank Settlement Accounts* (The People's Bank of China Decree [2003] No. 5) and other relevant rules governing bank settlement accounts, open individual bank settlement accounts or institutional bank settlement accounts for individual business owners, and use them for cross-border RMB receipt and payment. In particular, an overseas individual who wishes to open a RMB bank settlement account shall also produce a residence permit valid for one year or more as issued by the exit-entry administrative division of the public security authorities.

IV. Overseas RMB Borrowing in the PFTZ

Financial institutions and enterprises in the PFTZ may borrow RMB funds from overseas (excluding trade credits and intercompany operational financing) to use in the fields that are consistent with national macro-control programs. It is not allowed for the time being to use such funds in investing in negotiable securities (including wealth management products and other asset management products) or derivative products, or in entrusted loans.

1. The upper limit of the size (balance) of overseas RMB funds that enterprises in the PFTZ may borrow must not exceed the paid-up capital * 100 % * the macro-prudential policy parameters, where: the paid-up capital shall be that as indicated in the latest capital verification report, and the term of loan shall be longer than one year (not inclusive). Such borrowers in the PFTZ may, according to the *Administrative Measures for RMB Bank Settlement Accounts*, open special deposit accounts at banks in Shanghai to exclusively deposit RMB funds borrowed outside China. Such funds may only be used inside the PFTZ or outside China for the purposes including production and operation inside the PFTZ, and project construction inside the PFTZ or outside China.

   Foreign enterprises established in the PFTZ before the launch of the PFTZ may use their own discretion to elect to follow the previous method to determine the quota (i.e., the ceiling amount is calculated as the difference between the total investment and the registered capital), or to observe the rules as set forth by this *Circular* when borrowing RMB funds outside China, and file their decisions with PBC Shanghai through banks with which their accounts are opened. Once an election has been made, no change shall be made.
2. The upper limit of the size (balance) of overseas RMB funds borrowed by non-banking institutions in the PFTZ must not exceed the paid-up capital * 150 % * the macro-prudential policy parameters. The term of loan shall be longer than one year (not inclusive). The borrowed funds may be transferred back and deposited into their special deposit accounts opened with banks in Shanghai, and may only be used inside the PFTZ or outside China for the purposes including production and operation inside the PFTZ, and project construction inside SHFTZ or outside China.
3. The interest of the RMB funds borrowed from overseas and then retained in the dedicated deposit account opened by the enterprises and non-banking financial institutions in the PFTZ shall be calculated at the rate of current deposit.

4. The RMB funds borrowed outside China by banks in the PFTZ shall be subject to separate accounting in the PFTZ, and shall be used within the PFTZ, for real economy development purposes.
5. The macro-prudential policy parameters as mentioned in the above formulas shall be determined by PBC Shanghai, and may be adjusted in light of the need for nationwide credit control.

V. Cross-Border Two-Way RMB Capital Pooling in the PFTZ

1. Enterprises in the PFTZ may, in light of their operating and management needs, engage in cross-border two-way RMB capital pooling inside their own group. A group shall mean a multinational group of companies mainly linked by means of capital and composed of the parent company, subsidiaries, companies with capital participation and other members with investment relationships, including enterprises (and financial management companies) in the PFTZ. The cross-border two-way RMB capital pooling shall refer to the two-way capital pooling among the domestic- and overseas-based enterprises within the group. It shall be regarded as an operational financing activity within the group.
2. To engage in the cross-border two-way RMB capital pooling inside its own group, the headquarters of a group must designate a member enterprise (including a financial management company) registered, formed and actually engaged in business operation or investment in the PFTZ and select a bank in Shanghai to open a special RMB deposit account to be exclusively used for cross-border two-way RMB capital pooling inside the group. The said account may not be used for other funds. All parties inside and outside China that participate in the capital pool operations shall enter into agreements to specify their respective responsibilities and obligations for anti-money laundering, counter-terrorist financing and anti-tax evasion.
3. The flow of funds from parties whose cash is pooled to parties pooling the cash is considered as the "upstream flow"; while the flow of funds from parties pooling the cash to parties whose cash is pooled is considered as the "downstream flow". The RMB funds in the upstream and downstream flows shall be the cash generated from production and operation, as well as industrial investment by enterprises. Cash flows generated by financing activities shall not be pooled for now.

VI. Centralized Payment and Receipt of Cross-Border RMB Under Current Account in the PFTZ

1. Based on operating and management needs, enterprises in the PFTZ may receive and make current account payments of cross-border RMB receipts and payments under current accounts, on behalf of its domestic and foreign related parties on a centralized basis. Domestic and overseas related parties include member

companies connected mainly by capital, and by investment-based relationships, as well as the non-group members that have supply-chain and close business relationships with the group.
2. The group headquarters shall designate an operating or investing member enterprise (including a financial management company) which is incorporated in the PFTZ, and choose a bank to open one RMB dedicated deposit account for centralized payment and receipt of cross-border RMB under current account on behalf of its domestic and overseas related parties.
3. The enterprise in the PFTZ shall enter into agreements of centralized payment and receipts under current account with each party that is making such arrangement with them, defining respective responsibilities in respect of the trade authenticity.

VII. Cross-Border E-Business RMB Settlement

1. Banks in Shanghai are encouraged to directly provide cross-border RMB settlement services for actual e-Business transactions to the PFTZ-registered institutions that are engaged in cross-border e-Business.
2. Banks in Shanghai are supported to cooperate with the PFTZ-based payment service institutions (and their branches) holding an Internet Payment Business Permit, to provide cross-border RMB settlement services for actual e-Business transactions, including transactions by individuals and entities engaged in cross-border e-Business exports.
3. Banks shall enter into agreements with payment service institutions in respect of processing cross-border e-Business RMB settlement, and shall file the agreement with PBC Shanghai. The banks shall verify the authenticity and compliance status of the underlying transaction of the cross-border RMB settlement business processed through payment service institutions. The cross-border RMB settlement business forwarded to the banks by the payment service institutions shall have a cross-border e-Business transaction background, and shall be in accordance with the relevant state laws and regulations. The payment service institutions shall perform verification duties concerning anti-money laundering, counter-terrorist financing and keep corresponding transaction record, and shall coordinate with relevant state authorities to conduct inspections.
4. Payment service institutions shall conform to the *Administrative Measures for the Payment Services Provided by Non-financial Institutions* (The People's Bank of China Decree [2010] No. 2), the *Measures for the Custody of the Reserves of Payment Institutions' Clients* (The People's Bank of China Announcement [2013] No. 6) and other relevant regulations.

VIII. Cross-Border RMB Settlement Service

1. The China Foreign Exchange Trade System (CFETS) (also being the National Interbank Funding Center) shall provide RMB- denominated financial services in the PFTZ for assets transactions between the PFTZ and offshore markets to expand the cross-border use of RMB.
2. The Shanghai Gold Exchange (SGE) shall provide RMB- denominated services in the PFTZ for precious metal trading, delivery and settlement between the PFTZ and offshore markets, promoting the use of RMB in international precious metal market.

IX. Information Reporting and Submission

All cross-border RMB business, as well as receipt and payment information, shall be reported and submitted to the RMB cross-border receipt and payment information management system in an accurate, complete and timely manner, and shall be processed for corresponding international payments statistics reporting.

X. Anti-money Laundering, Counter-Terrorist Financing and Anti-tax Evasion

When providing relevant cross-border RMB services for financial institutions and enterprises in the PFTZ, banks shall specify in the service agreements that each party shall (i) fulfill the obligations and duties concerning anti-money laundering, counter-terrorist financing and anti-tax evasion as stipulated in relevant regulations; (ii) keep relevant transaction records and vouchers to ensure that the transaction can be retraced; and (iii) coordinate with the relevant authorities to conduct inspections.

Appendix 5

Notice of the Shanghai Headquarters of the People's Bank of China on Effectively Combating Money Laundering and Terrorist Financing in the China (Shanghai) Pilot Free Trade Zone

Bank Headquarters Publication [2014] No. 24

February 27, 2014

Bank of Communications; Shanghai Pudong Development Bank; China Development Bank; policy banks, state-owned commercial banks, and joint-stock commercial banks; Shanghai Branch of Postal Savings Bank of China; Bank of

Shanghai; Shanghai Rural Commercial Bank; Shanghai branches of other banks with legal person status; village or township level banks in Shanghai; foreign banks in Shanghai; trust companies, financial asset management companies, financial management companies, financial leasing companies, auto finance companies, and currency brokerage companies in Shanghai; securities companies, futures companies, and fund management companies in Shanghai; insurance companies and insurance assets management companies in Shanghai; and payment institutions in Shanghai:

In order to facilitate the construction of China (Shanghai) Pilot Free Trade Zone (referred to hereafter as "the PFTZ") and avoid potential risks, and in accordance with the *Anti-Money Laundering Law* and other relevant laws and regulations, as well as the *Opinions of the People's Bank of China on Financial Sector Support for the China (Shanghai) Pilot Free Trade Zone*, you are hereby notified of the following issues about effectively combating money laundering and terrorist financing in the PFTZ:

I. Fully Understanding the Importance of Effectively Combating Money Laundering and Terrorist Financing

The establishment of the PFTZ is an important decision made by the CPC Central Committee and the State Council of China in the new context of China's reform and opening up. According to the *Opinions of the People's Bank of China on Financial Sector Support for the China (Shanghai) Pilot Free Trade Zone*, financial institutions and specific non-financial institutions in the PFTZ shall adhere to the relevant laws and regulations and fulfill their due obligations in terms of anti-money laundering, counter-terrorist financing and anti-tax evasion. The effective implementation of anti-money laundering and counter- terrorist financing is beneficial to fostering in the PFTZ an internationalized market strictly subject to the rule of law; the application of anti-money laundering control measures helps to adequately assess and effectively control potential money laundering risks in the PFTZ's operation; the risk-based nature and indirect involvement of anti-money laundering supervision and management are conducive to improving supervisory authority's capability to tackle issues based on intermediary and post-establishment supervision, while ensuring that the PFTZ's vigorous drive for development remains unhindered. All financial institutions and payment institutions (referred to hereafter as "obligatory institutions") shall fully understand that anti-money laundering and counter-terrorist financing are crucial to the PFTZ's stable and healthy development, and therefore shall implement schemes and measures for anti-money laundering and counter-terrorist financing, take proactive actions to seek innovative solutions, and build up the PFTZ's anti-money laundering experience which is replicable and widely applicable.

II. Fully Implementing Schemes and Measures for Anti-money Laundering and Counter-Terrorist Financing

1. Obligatory institutions shall fully implement the *Anti-Money Laundering Law*, the *Regulations on Combating Money Laundering by Financial Institutions* and other relevant laws and regulations, fulfill due obligations of anti-money laundering, set up a robust internal control scheme to combat money laundering related to the PFTZ's operation, apply strict procedures to client identification and verification, submit reports on large and suspicious transactions as required, and properly preserve clients' information and transaction records, so as to prevent potential risks of money laundering and terrorist financing.
2. During the design and development process of the separate accounting system for Free Trade Accounts (referred to hereafter as "FTAs"), obligatory institutions shall consider embedding into the system anti-money laundering requirements or modules, keep an accurate record of the transaction parties' basic information, type of account, transaction amount, customs declaration form number, tax clearance certificate number and other relevant information, and make sure that the transaction information and client information are transmitted in a complete manner, so as to provide support for the system to carry out cash flow monitoring and analysis and allow efficient and accurate information retrieval for large and suspicious transactions.
3. When building and maintaining business relationship with PFTZ entities, obligatory institutions shall clearly identify the actual controller of the client or the actual beneficiary of the transaction. Also, obligatory institutions shall take into consideration various factors of different clients, including locations, characteristics, scopes of business, and business sectors, so as to properly determine the level of risk to a client. When all other things being equal, clients from the PFTZ shall be viewed as potentially involving higher risk. And for those determined as high-risk clients, obligatory institutions shall conduct more in-depth due diligence investigation. Upon approval of relevant authorities, obligatory institutions are entitled to refuse building business relationship with the following clients from the PFTZ: (1) clients who refuse to provide basic information; (2) clients who are reasonably suspected of involvement in money laundering, terrorist financing and other crimes; (3) clients who come from countries/areas with poor regulation on anti-money laundering and counter-terrorist financing; and (4) high-risk clients who are assessed to be beyond the obligatory institution's risk governance capacity.
4. Obligatory institutions shall strengthen the monitoring and analysis of FTAs and PFTZ entities, conduct adequate background investigation of FTAs' fund transfer, and make accurate judgment on the types and trends of trade-based money laundering. When a transaction or a client is, based on effective analysis of client information, transaction information and other relevant information, reasonably

suspected of involvement in money laundering or other crimes, the obligatory institutions shall submit a suspicious transaction report as required to China Anti-Money Laundering Monitoring & Analysis Center as well as to Shanghai Headquarters of the People's Bank of China (referred to hereafter as "PBC Shanghai").

The suspicious transaction reports submitted to PBC Shanghai by obligatory institutions shall meet the following requirements: (1) comprehensive investigation and collection is carried out to identify client information and transaction information related to the suspicious transaction reports, including information from the internal system of the bank and publicly available information; (2) it is believed that, through relevant analysis, identification and verification, the transaction or the client is involved in money laundering, terrorist financing or other crimes; and (3) a complete suspicious transaction report is completed as required, which keeps a detailed record of the due diligence investigation, suspicious transaction investigation analysis and other relevant information.

1. Obligatory institutions shall establish a money-laundering risk assessment scheme for the PFTZ's innovative business. The obligatory institutions' anti-money laundering departments shall be fully engaged in the design, development and operation of innovative business, and assess the associated risk of money laundering. The PFTZ's innovative business is allowed to be launched only when it is subject to the above-mentioned assessment and control measures that match the level of risk.

The report on the money laundering risk of the PFTZ's innovative business shall include the following elements: (1) details about the money laundering risk assessment, including the specific part of the process that involves risk, the level of risk and possible penalties for the money laundering that has taken place; (2) money laundering risk control measures, including control measures for different parts of the process that involves risk and the effectiveness of the control measures; and (3) comments and conclusion.

2. Obligatory institutions shall strengthen the anti-money laundering risk management for the whole process of PFTZ cross-border business, keep a complete record of cross-border remittances, and make sure that background information related to the trade is transmitted in a transparent and complete manner throughout the business process. The watch list for money laundering shall be updated in a timely manner and the timeliness of cross-border business monitoring shall be improved via technical support. Meanwhile, anti-money laundering monitoring on the cash flow between FTAs and domestic accounts outside the PFTZ shall also be enhanced.

The following PFTZ cross-border business shall be subject to investigation by anti-money laundering departments of the obligatory institutions: (1) a cross-border transaction involving more than two million RMB (or its equivalent in foreign currency) processed through accounts owned by legal persons, other organizations or individual business, or a cross- border transaction involving more than 200,000

RMB (or its equivalent in foreign currency) processed through accounts owned by natural persons; (2) a transaction involving one or more parties that come from countries/areas with poor supervision on money laundering and terrorist financing; (3) a transaction involving one or more parties whose names are identical to those identified by the relevant departments and bodies of the State Council or judicial authorities as crime suspects or people involved in money laundering and terrorist financing who require investigation or special attention from the part of obligatory institutions; (4) a transaction involving one or more parties who have been reported to be involved in suspicious transaction or whose name is identical to those contained in the risk warning list issued by relevant authorities; (5) a transaction related to countries/areas with poor supervision on money laundering and terrorist financing; (6) other high-risk cross- border business.

III. Improving the Organization and Leadership in Anti-money Laundering and Counter- Terrorist Financing

1. Obligatory institutions shall build a robust anti-money laundering management system for the PFTZ-related business, improve their internal control scheme to combat money laundering related to the PFTZ business, and submitted reports to PBC Shanghai on the their anti-money laundering management framework and internal control system for the PFTZ-related business.
2. Obligatory institutions shall clearly designate senior management members to be responsible and accountable for anti-money laundering activities, and provide sufficient staff to implement anti-money laundering for the PFTZ-related business. It shall be ensured that the senior management members responsible for anti-money laundering are capable of doing so, and adequate resources are provided to facilitate their work. Obligatory institutions shall promote training to personnel responsible for anti-money laundering and other relevant business operations so as to enhance their knowledge about international trade, trade-based money laundering and other relevant issues, and strengthen their awareness and skills of identifying and preventing the risks of trade-based money laundering.
3. A communication and cooperation mechanism on anti-money laundering between People's Bank of China (referred to hereafter as "PBC") and the Administrative Committee of the PFTZ shall be established, in order to enhance information sharing among relevant departments, including the customs, tax administrations and industrial and commercial administrative authorities, and strengthen the capability of back-end monitoring for the trade and cash flow within the PFTZ. The obligatory institutions shall also join hands with tax administrations and police authorities to improve research on the types of crimes that may occur in the PFTZ, and strengthen efforts to combat trafficking and tax-related crimes.
4. PBC shall promote specific training on anti-money laundering related to the PFTZ business operations, disseminate knowledge about anti-money laundering laws and regulations, and create a better legislative environment for the development

of the PFTZ. Meanwhile, PBC shall adhere to the risk-based approach, and enhance supervision and effectiveness evaluation on the construction and operation of the obligatory institutions' internal control scheme for anti-money laundering. PBC shall also publish in a timely manner warning notices concerning money laundering risks related to the PFTZ business operations, and conduct targeted anti-money laundering investigation against the obligatory institutions with poor internal control against money laundering or high risks of money laundering.

Appendix 6

Circular of the Shanghai Headquarters of the People's Bank of China on Lifting the Upper Limit on Small-amount Foreign Currency Deposit Rates in the China (Shanghai) Pilot Free Trade Zone

Bank Headquarters Publication [2014] No. 23

The Shanghai Headquarters of the People's Bank of China

February 25, 2014

To Shanghai branches of the China Development Bank, policy banks, state-owned commercial banks, joint-stock commercial banks, and China Postal Savings Bank; Bank of Shanghai, and Shanghai Rural Commercial Bank; Shanghai branches of other urban commercial banks; foreign banks in Shanghai; village or township-level banks in Shanghai; and financial management companies, financial leasing companies, and auto finance companies in Shanghai:

According to the *Opinions of the People's Bank of China on Financial Sector Support for the China (Shanghai) Pilot Free Trade Zone* (referred to hereafter as the "*Opinions*"), as approved by the headquarters of the People's Bank of China ("PBC"), the Shanghai Headquarters of the People's Bank of China ("PBC Shanghai") has decided to remove the ceiling on small-amount foreign currency deposit rates in the China (Shanghai) Pilot Free Trade Zone ("PFTZ"), effective March 1, 2014, to support the steady liberalization of interest rates in the PFTZ. The decision is as follows:

I. Financial institutions shall reinforce the interest rate pricing mechanism for foreign currency deposits, and improve relevant management systems in accordance with the *Opinions on Lifting the Upper Limit on Small-amount Foreign Currency Deposit Rates in the China (Shanghai) Pilot Free Trade Zone* (see Annex).

II. Financial institutions shall establish risk prevention and management mechanisms, and file with the Currency and Credit Management Department of PBC their letters of commitment to risk prevention, risk self-assessment reports, risk management measures, and relevant supporting systems they have developed.

III. Financial institutions shall, apart from managing their foreign currency deposits in the PFTZ, establish a daily interest rate quotation system for foreign currency deposits; and fill in and submit to PBC Shanghai's interest rate management system a monitoring form for their foreign currency deposit business on time. They shall promptly report to the PBC major adjustments to foreign currency deposit rates, substantial funds transfers, and any other major changes in connection with foreign currency deposits.
IV. Financial institutions shall make efforts to prevent and control risks and make sure that their operations are consistent with policy requirements. PBC Shanghai shall establish a dynamic monitoring and inspection mechanism for better inspection of their operations. Any financial institution that fails to observe the aforementioned requirements shall be subject to an internal warning, a notice of criticism, forced rectification, punishment through macro prudential management tools, or even cancellation of business.

Annex: *Opinions on Lifting the Upper Limit on Small-amount Foreign Currency Deposit*

Annex

Opinions of the Shanghai Headquarters of the People's Bank of China on Lifting the Upper Limit on Small-amount Foreign Currency Deposit Rates in the China (Shanghai) Pilot Free Trade Zone

Promulgated on February 25, 2014 Effective on March 1, 2014

Article 1 – According to the *Opinions of the People's Bank of China on Financial Sector Support for the China (Shanghai) Pilot Free Trade Zone* (referred to hereafter as the "*Opinions*") and the general requirements of the People's Bank of China ("PBC"), the Shanghai Headquarters of the People's Bank of China ("PBC Shanghai") has decided to remove the ceiling on small-amount foreign currency deposit rates in the PFTZ, to support the steady liberalization of interest rates, promote the development of interest rate pricing mechanisms for foreign currency deposits, and improve the market-based interest rate setting system in the PFTZ. This pilot program for interest rate liberalization is designed to accumulate some replicable experience for further reforms.

Article 2 – Following the removal of the upper limit on small-amount foreign currency deposit rates, financial institutions in Shanghai may exercise discretion in setting interest rates for foreign currency deposits made by the PFTZ-based residents. The PFTZ-based residents shall refer to enterprises and institutions (including financial institutions) incorporated in the PFTZ by foreign or Chinese legal persons in accordance with law; organizations that are registered in the PTFT but that have not yet obtained any legal person status; business units set up by overseas institutions in the PFTZ; and Chinese individuals that have been employed in the PFTZ for over a year.

Article 3 – Financial institutions shall focus on building and improving their capacity for independently setting proper interest rates for foreign currency deposits based on market supply and demand, impose more rigid financial restrictions, and provide further differentiated services. They shall establish sound and appropriate strategies and models for the setting of interest rates, and develop management measures accordingly. Their interest rate setting models shall adequately reflect the cost of capital, operating expenses, customer profitability, as well as risk premiums, so as to provide an effective basis for differentiated and refined pricing.

Article 4 – Financial institutions shall establish an interest rate risk management system for foreign currency deposits in the PFTZ. The system shall include risk management goals, methods for assessing interest rate risks, interest rate risk limits, stress test tools and risk management measures.

Article 5 – Financial institutions shall closely monitor the movements of interest rates and exchange rates in domestic and international financial markets; properly predict the trends of foreign currency interest rates; make sound assessment of the potential impacts of changing spreads of interest rates inside and outside the PFTZ on foreign currency capital movement; and prepare response plans for interest rate fluctuations.

Article 6 – To open an account, resident enterprises in the PFTZ shall present valid registration documents, while the PFTZ-based individuals shall provide in-service certificates issued by their employers. Financial institutions shall establish detailed rules for screening the qualifications of potential customers, as well as strict standards for opening accounts, to prevent illegal fund transfers and arbitrage through accounts under false identities in the PFTZ.

Article 7 – Financial institutions shall establish mechanisms for the monitoring and analysis of foreign currency deposit rates in the PFTZ; fill in the *Monitoring Form for Foreign Currency Transactions in the PFTZ* available at the interest rate management system of PBC Shanghai and upload the completed form onto the same system without any delay; track and analyze any suspicious transactions; and submit monitoring reports accordingly.

Article 8 – Financial institutions shall file with PBC Shanghai their management measures in a timely manner, including measures for setting foreign currency interest rates, risk management systems, and risk monitoring and analysis mechanisms.

Article 9 – PBC Shanghai shall closely track and analyze the movements of foreign currency interest rates inside and outside the PFTZ, predict market trends, and use a combination of tools for risk prevention, to protect the reform from systemic risks.

Article 10 – Financial institutions shall make efforts to prevent and control risks and make sure that their operations are consistent with policy requirements. PBC Shanghai shall establish a dynamic monitoring and inspection mechanism for better inspection of their operations. Any financial institution that fails to observe the aforementioned requirements shall be subject to an internal warning, a notice of criticism, forced rectification, punishment through macro prudential management tools, or even suspension of business.

Appendix 7

Implementation Regulations concerning Foreign Exchange Administration to Support the Construction of the China (Shanghai) Pilot Free Trade Zone

Shanghai Branch of the State Administration of Foreign Exchange
February 28, 2014

Chapter I – General Provision

Article 1 – To support the construction of the China (Shanghai) Pilot Free Trade Zone ("Pilot FTZ"), and implement "*The Framework Plan for the China (Shanghai) Pilot Free Trade Zone*" (Guo Fa [2013] No. 38) and "*Opinions of People's Bank of China to Support China (Shanghai) Pilot Free Trade Zone in Financial Sector*" (Yin Fa [2013] No. 244, hereinafter as "Opinions"), the following implementation regulations are hereby set.

Article 2 – Pilot FTZ banks (which include banks registered in the Pilot FTZ and other banks in Shanghai that conduct banking business relating to the Pilot FTZ, the same below), domestic and overseas enterprises, non- banking financial institutions and individuals (hereinafter collectively as "Pilot FTZ principals") shall apply these implementation regulations.

Article 3 – The Shanghai Branch of the State Administration of Foreign Exchange (hereinafter as "foreign exchange bureau") will be in charge of supervision and administration of Pilot FTZ-related foreign currency account opening, funds transfer, purchase and sale of foreign exchange, as well as relevant data statistics of RMB and foreign currency, etc.

Article 4 – Pilot FTZ principals should fulfil data reporting and submission obligations in respect of international balance of payment, purchase and sale of foreign exchange, transfer of domestic funds, accounts etc., and ensure its accuracy, timeliness and completeness.

Article 5 – Pilot FTZ banks shall adhere to KKD principles (i.e. "Know your customer", "Know your business" and "Due diligence") and perform examination of authenticity and compliance of Pilot FTZ-related foreign exchange business according to these implementation regulations, as well as establish sound internal control management system which shall be filed with the foreign exchange bureau.

Article 6 – The innovated foreign exchange business stipulated in these regulations dealt with by the enterprises, non-banking financial institutions and individuals etc. in the Pilot FTZ, shall be based on genuine and legitimate transaction and processed through accounts. No false agreement shall be used and transactions shall not be made up when dealing with relevant business.

Chapter II – Current Account Transactions

Article 7 – For transactions under current account items between Pilot FTZ principals and overseas, article 5 of these regulations shall be followed in the relevant purchase/payment or receipt/sale of foreign exchange. If the nature of the funds is unclear, the Pilot FTZ bank shall require the relevant enterprises, non-banking financial institutions and individuals to provide relevant documents.

Foreign exchange income derived from goods trade by "A ranking" enterprises in the Pilot FTZ does not need to diverted to "to-be-verified" accounts. Where a single outbound payment is above USD 50,000 (or its equivalent) in relation to trade in service, income and current account transfer, the tax filing form shall be submitted according to relevant regulations.

Article 8 – Qualifying enterprises in the Pilot FTZ may process foreign exchange funds centralized receipt and payment and "netting balance" settlement under current account items, through a Domestic foreign exchange funds master account.

Article 9 – Financial leasing companies (which are approved by the China Banking Regulatory Commission), foreign invested leasing companies (which are approved by the commercial authorities) as well as domestic- funded finance leasing companies (which are jointly approved by the commercial and tax authorities) in the Pilot FTZ (hereinafter collectively as "finance leasing companies") are permitted to receive rental in foreign currency when undertaking finance lease business with domestic lessees. Special foreign exchange supervision and administration in respect of trade in goods shall be carried out for large-scale finance leasing companies in the Pilot FTZ.

Chapter III – Capital Account Transactions

Article 10 – The foreign exchange registration and alternation registration under direct investment account items are delegated to banks.

Article 11 – Foreign invested enterprises in the Pilot FTZ may freely convert its foreign exchange capital into RMB as they wish. The foreign invested enterprise shall open a dedicated RMB deposit account in the bank where it opens a foreign exchange capital account. The RMB deposit account shall be used to deposit the RMB funds converted from foreign exchange capital. Various payments from the RMB deposit account shall be dealt with based on genuine trade or business needs.

The bank shall refer to the requirements stipulated in the Appendix IV of "*Notice of the State Administration of Foreign Exchange (SAFE) on work relating to capital item information system pilot and relevant data reporting and submission*" (Hui Fa [2012] No. 60) (i.e. "*Foreign exchange account data collecting rules (version 1.1)*"), when reporting and submitting information regarding opening/closing account, fund receipt/payment and balance of the dedicated RMB deposit accounts; the account nature coding for such dedicated RMB deposit account is 2113, with descriptive name of account nature as "capital items – converted and to be paid". The bank shall refer to the requirements stipulated in the "*Notice of the SAFE on work concerning adjusting domestic bank outbound receipt and payment voucher and preparation for relevant information reporting"* (Hui Fa [2011] No. 49), when reporting and submitting the receipt/payment information between the dedicated RMB deposit account and other domestic RMB accounts based on relevant domestic receipt/payment vouchers.

Article 12 – The foreign exchange capital of the foreign invested enterprise and the RMB funds converted from the capital shall not be used for the following purposes:

1. directly or indirectly spent as expenditures beyond business scope or prohibited by laws and regulations;
2. directly or indirectly used for security investment, unless otherwise stipulated;
3. directly or indirectly used for RMB entrust loan purpose (unless business scope permits), or repaying loans among enterprises (including third party cash advance) or repaying bank RMB loans that are sub-lent to third parties; and
4. used for paying expenses relating to purchase of non-self-use properties, except for foreign invested real estate enterprises.

Article 13 – The ceiling amount for an enterprise in the Pilot FTZ to extend foreign exchange loans offshore will be raised to 50 % of the enterprise's shareholders equity; if an enterprise needs to apply for a higher ratio due to its actual needs, the foreign exchange bureau shall review and determine on case-by-case basis.

Article 14 – An enterprise in the Pilot FTZ may sign a guarantee agreement and provide guarantee to overseas parties at its own discretion, without pre-approvals from the foreign exchange bureau.

When an enterprise in the Pilot FTZ provides guarantee to overseas parties, no restriction shall be imposed in respect of the guarantor and/or guarantee's ratio of net assets, profitability of the guarantee, as well as the shareholding relationship between the guarantor and guarantee.

When an enterprise in the Pilot FTZ enters into guarantee agreement with overseas parties, it shall, according to relevant regulations, perform guarantee registration formalities and apply for pre-approvals before it fulfills the guarantee (in case the guarantee defaults its relevant contractual obligations); the enterprise shall also comply with the restrictive rules regarding the use scope of funds under guaranty.

Article 15 – With a payment notice, an enterprise or non-banking institution in the Pilot FTZ may directly apply to the relevant bank for the purchase of foreign exchange and then use the foreign exchange to pay guarantee fees to overseas parties without pre-approvals from the foreign exchange bureau.

When the bank is arranging the purchase and payment of foreign exchange, it shall verify that relevant regulations from the foreign exchange bureau have been complied with in the guarantee arrangement.

Article 16 – The transaction-based approval requirement is removed in respect of the receivables arising from finance leasing services provided by a finance leasing company in the Pilot FTZ to overseas parties, and is replaced with a registration administration.

Article 17 – The following foreign exchange pilot schemes will be integrated: centralized operation and management scheme of foreign exchange by multinational headquarters, domestic foreign currency cash pooling scheme, and foreign exchange reform pilot scheme for international trade settlement center. The special accounts set up under the above schemes (i.e. "Domestic foreign currency cash pooling account" and "International trade settlement center dedicated account") by enterprises in the Pilot FTZ will be integrated into "Domestic foreign exchange funds master account", which will inherit the functions of the existing accounts.

In addition to the business allowed under article 8 and international trade settlement center business, a centralized management of domestic group members' funds from capital injection, foreign debts, disposal of assets etc. may also be performed through Domestic foreign exchange funds master accounts.

According to its operation needs, a qualifying enterprise in the Pilot FTZ may open an International foreign exchange funds master account. The flow of funds between the International foreign exchange funds master account and overseas is free of foreign exchange restrictions and controls. Funds may be freely transferred between the entity's Domestic foreign exchange funds master account and International foreign exchange funds master account, subject to a quota prescribed by the foreign exchange bureau.

The relevant administrative approval requirement shall be changed to filing procedure for various pilot business processed through Domestic foreign exchange funds master accounts and International foreign exchange funds master accounts by qualifying enterprises in the Pilot FTZ.

Chapter IV – Foreign Exchange Market Business

Article 18 – when banks dealing with commodity derivative transactions for enterprises in the Pilot FTZ, the following rules shall be adhered to when processing concerned purchase/selling of foreign exchange:

1. The relevant parties must fulfill requirements in regulations issued by relevant finance supervision and administration departments, including obtaining necessary business qualification in advance, going through necessary procedures for product information reporting etc.; bank branches that run this business must follow bank internal management rules, including obtaining necessary pre-authorization etc.
2. The bank or its general head office must qualify as an market maker in the inter-bank foreign exchange market; or alternatively, this bank has been ranked as A class for more than once, and not been ranked below B class, in foreign exchange management examinations in Shanghai during the latest three years.
3. Banks shall file with the foreign exchange bureau before they may conduct the business of purchase/sale of foreign exchange in respect of commodity derivative transactions.
4. When banks provide service to enterprises in respect of commodity derivatives, they shall verify whether the enterprise has background of genuine commodity trades, follow the proper hedging principle, and honestly disclose information and reveal risk to clients, and let the enterprise bear relevant risk independently.

5. In respect of exchange rate exposure or foreign exchange gain/loss resulting from closing positions in overseas by banks under commodity derivative transaction service to enterprises, the bank may arrange the corresponding purchase/selling of foreign exchange, and have it incorporated into the bank's overall closing positions; the foreign exchange bureau shall impose restrictions on the annual accumulated amounts of such foreign exchange purchase/sale.
6. Banks shall include the aforementioned purchase/sale of foreign exchange into the bank's statistics, categorizing the transaction under "240/440 other investment" catalogue and mark the transaction party as "Bank itself" for statistics purpose.
7. Banks shall regularly report and submit relevant information regarding commodity derivative transactions and relevant purchase/sale of foreign exchange to the foreign exchange bureau.

Chapter V – Supplementary Articles

Article 19 – The foreign exchange bureau shall perform off-site supervision and monitoring over foreign exchange receipt/payment in goods trade of enterprises in the Pilot FTZ, carry out on-site inspection under any abnormal or suspicious circumstances, and conduct different administrations according to the on-site inspection results respectively.

Article 20 – The foreign exchange bureau may take relevant temporary measures when serious imbalance arises or may arise in international receipt/payment.

Article 21 – The foreign exchange bureau may gradually improve innovated business according to the State macro-control policy, position of foreign exchange receipt and payment as well as performance of the innovated business.

Article 22 – The foreign exchange bureau shall monitor, inspect and investigate Pilot FTZ principals according to relevant laws and regulations. Permissions on innovated business will be suspended for relevant parties if they violate the "*Foreign exchange administration rules*" or these regulations, and penalties will be imposed accordingly.

Article 23 – These implementation regulations shall take effect on day of promulgation. Any uncovered issues shall be dealt with according to other existing foreign exchange administration regulations such as foreign exchange administration measures in the areas under special customs supervision etc.

Appendix 8

Circular of the State Council on the Framework Plan for the China (Shanghai) Pilot Free Trade Zone

The State Council
September 18, 2013

To People's Government of all provinces, autonomous regions and municipalities directly under the Central Government and all ministries and commissions of and institutions directly under the State Council:

The State Council has approved and promulgated the *"Framework Plan for the China (Shanghai) Pilot Free Trade Zone"* (the "Framework Plan").

1. The establishment of China (Shanghai) Pilot Free Trade Zone is a strategic decision by the Central Government, and is a significant measure to boost China's reform and opening up under the new circumstances. The China (Shanghai) Pilot Free Trade Zone is critically meaningful and aims to expedite the functional transformation of the government, explore administrative innovation, stimulate trading and investment facilitation, and accumulate experience on achieving a more open China economy.
2. The Shanghai Municipal People's Government shall be responsible for the implementation of the Framework Plan. The China (Shanghai) Pilot Free Trade Zone shall explore the administration approach of "National Treatment" on investment permission and "Negative List", deepen the reform on administrative approval system, expedite the functional transformation of the government, and enhance the follow up supervision. The Shanghai Municipal People's Government shall expand the opening up of service industry, boost the opening up and innovation in financial sector, and establish a new pilot free trade zone with international standards in providing business and investment convenience, highly effective and efficient supervision and investor-friendly regulatory environment. The China (Shanghai) Pilot Free Trade Zone will serve as a "role model" nationwide in national system reforms and further opening up of the Chinese economy; if successful it will likely be expanded, and thus will contribute to the overall development of the economy. All governmental bodies shall support the coordination, guidance and evaluation entailed.
3. According to *"The Decision of the Standing Committee of the National People's Congress on Authorizing the State Council to Temporarily Adjust the Administrative Examination and Approval of Relevant Laws in China (Shanghai) Pilot Free Trade Zone"*, relevant laws and regulations shall be temporarily adjusted. Further details will be announced by the State Council under separate cover.

The Shanghai Municipal People's Government shall report to and consult the State Council on significant issues arising during the implementation of the Framework Plan.

Framework Plan for the China (Shanghai) Pilot Free Trade Zone

The China (Shanghai) Pilot Free Trade Zone is established based on the strategic decision by the Central Government, and is a significant measure to boost China's reform and opening up under the new circumstances. This Framework Plan provides detailed guidance on initiatives and their respective implementation measures.

1. General Requisition

The China (Shanghai) Pilot Free Trade Zone is a national strategy aiming to expedite the functional transformation of government, explore administrative innovation, stimulate trading and investment facilitation, and accumulate experience on achieving a more open Chinese economy.

(a) Guiding principles
We should hold high the great socialism banner with Chinese characteristics, take Deng Xiaoping Theory, "Three Represents" important thought and scientific development approach to guide this national strategy. We should further unleash our minds, dare to pilot, and promote reform and development by opening up the economy. The China (Shanghai) Pilot Free Trade Zone will create a regulatory environment on cross border investment and trading that is in line with international practices, enhance China's economic position globally, and contribute to achieving the revival of the Chinese People's China Dream.

(b) *Overall objectives*
During the course of two to three years of piloting reforms, the China (Shanghai) Pilot Free Trade Zone shall expedite the functional transformation of government, expand the opening up of service sectors and promote the reform of the foreign investment administrative system, and develop headquarter economy and new trade forms; shall explore RMB convertibility under capital account items and opening up of financial services; shall explore to improve Customs' supervision efficiency; and shall create a framework to support investment and innovation activities to cultivate an internationalized business environment. The China (Shanghai) Pilot Free Trade Zone shall pilot a free trade zone, as measured by international standards, with convenient investment and trading procedure, full convertibility of currencies, effective and efficient goods supervision, and investor-friendly regulatory environment. As such, experience hence gained shall serve nationwide with the new ideas and approaches for opening up of the economy and deepen the reform further.

(c) *Scope of implementation*
The China (Shanghai) Pilot Free Trade Zone is comprised of the four customs supervision areas, including *Shanghai Waigaoqiao Bonded Zone*, *Waigaoqiao Bonded Logistics Zone*, *Yangshan Bonded Port* and *Shanghai Pudong Airport Free Trade Zone*, and based on the ongoing results of the implementation, as well as to develop industry and the need to spur the radiating effect, the scope of implementation and the scope of the pilot measures will be progressively expanded, forming a supporting mechanism for building Shanghai as an international economic, finance, trade and transportation center.

2. Major Tasks and Measures

Based on the unity of openness expansion and system reform, and the unity of functional development and policy innovation, the China (Shanghai) Pilot Free Trade Zone aims to develop a framework in line with international norms for investment and trade. To do so, one needs to bear in mind the strategic requirements of going to the world and serving the nation, as well as the strategic task of building "The Four Centers" of Shanghai, and take actions to experiment step by step with risks under control.

1. *Accelerate the functional transformation of government*

   (a) *Deepened reform in administration system.* The China (Shanghai) Pilot Free Trade Zone will accelerate the functional transformation of government and governmental administrative management innovation. An administrative management system meets and fits with international trade and investment standards will be established. The focus of administrative management procedures will shift from prior approval to mid-event control and subsequent supervision. A service pattern will be set up to materialize one-off acceptance, integrated examination and approval, and efficient operation. An online information platform will be established to consolidate information and improve information sharing amongst various departments. A comprehensive assessment mechanism of industry information tracking, supervision and collection will be established, to strengthen the tracking, administration and supervision of activities outside of the zone conducted by entities registered in the China (Shanghai) Pilot Free Trade Zone. A joint supervision and enforcement system will be implemented to cover the areas of quality and technical supervision, food and drug supervision, intellectual property, industry and commercial administration, and tax administration to enhance efficiency. In addition to relevant administrative authorities, the social forces are also encouraged to take an active part in market supervision. Transparency in administrative management will be enhanced, and the information disclosure mechanism that reflects the participation of investors and is in line with international norms will be established. To protect the interests of investors, various administration reforms will be put in place, for instance enhancing fair competition, and allowing qualified foreign investors to remit investment gains at their discretion. An intellectual property related dispute resolution and assistance system will be established.

2. *Opening up of investment sectors*

   (b) *Opening up of service sectors.* The financial services, transportation services, commerce and trade services, professional services, cultural services, and public services sectors are selected to be enlarged and opened (for a detailed list please refer to the Appendix 9), and market access restrictions such as requirements concerning the qualification of investors, limitations on foreign participation, restrictions concerning business scope, etc., (except in respect of banks, information and communication services) will be suspended or cancelled, in order to create an environment of equal market access for the benefit of all investors.

(c) *Explore the "Negative List" administrative approach.* The China (Shanghai) Pilot Free Trade Zone will reform the administrative approach of foreign investment based on international norms. Trial national treatment on investment permission and a "Negative List" mechanism will be implemented within the zone. For the projects that are not stated in the "Negative List", foreign investors and domestic investors will receive the same treatment, by going through filing procedures instead of approving requirements (with the exception of areas specifically defined by the State Council). Shanghai Municipal People's Government will be in charge of the project filing procedures. The approving requirement on foreign investment contracts and Articles of Association will be replaced by a filing procedure with Shanghai Municipal People's Government, with the same follow up procedures finished according to the current laws and regulations. The registration process with the Administration of Industry and Commerce will be aligned with the business registration system reform, and the process will be optimized. National security review system will be improved, and pilot national security review on foreign investment projects will be trialed in the China (Shanghai) Pilot Free Trade Zone to constitute a safe and efficient open economic system. A foreign investment administrative system that is aligned with international standard will be set up.

(d) *Set up a system to support outbound investment.* The China (Shanghai) Pilot Free Trade Zone is aiming at the reform of outbound investment administration by principally implementing the filing system on the setup of overseas companies and on the general outbound investment projects. The Shanghai Municipal People's Government will be in charge of the filing procedure on general outbound investment projects to facilitate the convenience on outbound investment. A new investment service enhancement mechanism will be created to strengthen the post outbound-investment administration and service, and to set up an information-monitoring platform shared by multiple government departments for statistics and annual inspection purposes. Various types of investors in the China (Shanghai) Pilot Free Trade Zone are encouraged to conduct outbound investment in different forms. SPVs specializing in overseas equity investment are encouraged to be set up in the China (Shanghai) Pilot Free Trade Zone, and qualified investors are encouraged to establish fund of funds for making offshore equity investments.

3. *Promote the transformation of trade development approach*

(e) *Promote the transformation and upgrading of trade.* The China (Shanghai) Pilot Free Trade Zone is cultivating new trading types and functions, aiming to increase China's competitive advantage and enhance their position in the global trade value chain by focusing on the development of technology, brands, quality and service. Multinational companies are encouraged to set up Asia-Pacific regional headquarters and/or operation centers with comprehensive functions of trading, logistics, settlement, etc. More efforts will be made to promote Shanghai as the international trade settlement center, and to expand the function of the special account on cross-border receipt or payment and financing under trade in service. Enterprises in the China (Shanghai) Pilot Free Trade Zone will be supported to develop offshore business. Enterprises are encouraged to employ an overall plan in international and domestic trade to integrate the development of domestic and foreign trading business. International commodity trading and resource configuration platform will be explored to trade energy products, basic industrial raw materials and agriculture commodities. The ongoing pilot bonded futures delivery will be expanded and improved and the warehouse receipt financing and other functions will be extended. The establishment of outbound cultural trade bases will be accelerated. The outsourcing service sectors include bio-pharmaceuticals, software and information, management consulting, data services etc. will be encouraged. Financial leasing companies will be allowed and encouraged to set up project companies in the China (Shanghai) Pilot Free Trade Zone and to carry out domestic and international leasing business. Third-party inspection and appraisal institutions are encouraged to set up with appraisal results be acceptable in accordance with international standards. High-tech and value-added maintenance services will be trialed in the China (Shanghai) Pilot Free Trade Zone. Cross border e- business service function will be cultivated, and a system covering customs, inspection & quarantine, tax refunds, cross-border payment and logistics will be set up to support cross-border e-business.

(f) *Elevate the capacity of the shipping service.* The China (Shanghai) Pilot Free Trade Zone will leverage on the Waigaoqiao Port, Yangshan Deep-Water Port and Pudong International Airport to form a shipping development system and operation model that will have strong global competitive advantages. Shipping related services such as shipping financing, international ship transportation, international ship management, and international ship brokerage, will be proactively encouraged. Additionally, the development of freight index derivatives will be accelerated. Transition and LCL businesses will be further promoted. Foreign ships owned or indirectly owned by Chinese invested companies are allowed to pilot the coastal shipping between domestic coastal ports and Shanghai port. Pudong International Airport is encouraged to increase the number of flights for cargo transition. By utilizing the geographic advantages of Shanghai and the preferential taxation on Chinese "flag of convenience" ships, qualified ships will be encouraged to register in Shanghai. The China (Shanghai) Pilot Free Trade Zone will implement the international ship registration policy as piloted in Tianjin. The application process on permitting international shipping will be simplified to create a more efficient ship registration system.

4. *Deepen innovation and opening up of financial services*

(g) *Accelerate the innovation of the financial system.* Under proper risk control, the China (Shanghai) Pilot Free Trade Zone will pilot RMB capital account convertibility, interest rate liberalization, and the cross-border use of RMB. In China (Shanghai) Pilot Free Trade Zone, the assets by the financial institutions will be at market rate. The China (Shanghai) Pilot Free Trade Zone will explore the trial of a foreign exchange administrative system that is in line with international practice to better facilitate trade and investment. Enterprises are encouraged to leverage on both domestic and international market resources to liberalize cross-border financing. Administration on foreign debt will be further reformed to facilitate cross-border financing. Foreign exchange centralized operation by multinational companies' headquarters will be enhanced to encourage the setup of regional or global treasury centers in Shanghai. A mechanism needs to be established to associate financial reforms in the China (Shanghai) Pilot Free Trade Zone and Shanghai's development into an international financial center.

(h) *Enhance the financial service function.* The finance sector will be fully opened to private investors and foreign invested financial institutions. Foreign-invested and Sino-foreign equity joint venture banks will be allowed to incorporate in the China (Shanghai) Pilot Free Trade Zone. Platforms for international transactions will also be permitted to be established in the China (Shanghai) Pilot Free Trade Zone by financial markets. The oversea companies will gradually be allowed to engage in commodity futures trading. Financial market innovations are encouraged. Equity escrow institutions will be supported to setup comprehensive financial service platform in the China (Shanghai) Pilot Free Trade Zone. The cross-border RMB reinsurance business is also encouraged to cultivate reinsurance market.

5. *Improve regulatory supporting systems*

(i) *Strengthen protection through regulatory system enhancements.* A regulatory system of high standard investment and trade rules will be developed rapidly to serve the needs of the China (Shanghai) Pilot Free Trade Zone. In regard to the content of the pilot, some administrative regulations and provisions in the State Council's documents will be terminated according to the prescribed procedures. Among these regulations and provisions, certain administrative examination and approval requirements under "Law of the People's Republic of China on Wholly Foreign Owned Enterprises", "Law of the People's Republic of China on Sino-Foreign Equity Joint Venture Companies", "Law of the People's Republic of China on Sino-Foreign Cooperative Joint Venture Companies" will be temporarily adjusted and such adjustment will be tentatively implemented in the next three years started from 1 October 2013. The government departments shall support the expansion and opening of service industry in the China (Shanghai) Pilot Free Trade Zone, the deepening of pilot reforms on the implementation of "National Treatment" on investment permission and "the Negative List" management approach, and solve the problems in regulatory protection during the pilot period. The Shanghai Municipal People's Government will establish an administrative system through local legislation in correspondence to the demands of the China (Shanghai) Pilot Free Trade Zone.

3. Establish an Appropriate Regulatory Environment for Supervision and Tax

In order to establish a service system for investment and trade with international standard, an innovative supervision model will be created to facilitate smooth transactions for all goods and services under a highly transparent administrative system within the China (Shanghai) Pilot Free Trade Zone and to promote opening up in service sectors and further development in goods trade. Meanwhile, under the premise of keeping a fair, consistent and standardized current tax system, related policies for the purpose of functional development will be improved.

1. *Create new mode of supervision*
    (a) *Simplify the import supervision model to realize "Frontier Opening".* Enterprises are allowed to bring goods into the China (Shanghai) Pilot Free Trade Zone with import manifests before completing the customs declaration formalities with entry and exit record list. The simplification on entry and exit record list as well as the formalities on international transit, LCL and distribution business will be explored. The supervision techniques and approaches will be improved to pilot the model of "import quarantine and relaxed import/export inspection". The construction of relatively separated goods trading area (focusing on trade facilitation) and service trade area (focusing on opening up of service sectors) will be explored. Under the condition of ensuring effective supervision, a categorized supervision model will be explored to monitor goods based on their import status. With respect to exploration on function expansion, under the condition of strict implementation of tax collection on imported and exported goods, exhibition and trading platforms for bonded goods may be set up within specified areas of China (Shanghai) Pilot Free Trade Zone.
    (b) *Strictly enforce "Second-tier Effective and Efficient Control".* The Customs administration process will be optimized while the administration of "frontier" (i.e. goods flow between overseas and the zone) and "second-tier" (i.e. goods flow between the zone and other domestic areas) will be coordinated by improvement on e-information network, entry and exit record lists cross check, accounting books management, physical verification, and risk analysis. An inspection and quarantine model of "easily import and export, with

strict quality and safety risk control" will be promoted. Actions will be taken to strengthen the management of electronic Customs books and facilitate the smooth flow of goods moving between the China (Shanghai) Free Trade Zone and other domestic places in the charge of different Customs offices. Enterprises within the China (Shanghai) Pilot Free Trade Zone in principle will be allowed to re-invest and conduct business outside of the zone without geographic restriction, unless specific procedures required under the applicable laws and regulations. The government will enhance the connection of enterprises' operation information and the government's supervision system, through which effective supervision can be realized through risk monitoring, third-party management and security deposits etc. The government will, through the development and utilization of Shanghai's credit system, accelerate the formulation of policies and mechanism in respect of enterprises' business credit management and exclusive jurisdiction of business activities.

(c) *Enhance cooperation among authorities.* Under the principle of protecting national security and fair competition in the market, collaboration will be strengthened between the relevant departments and the Shanghai Municipal People's Government to improve the capability to protect the economic and social security. The China (Shanghai) Pilot Free Trade Zone will collaborate with relevant departments of the State Council to strictly implement the provisions in respect of anti-monopoly investigations. In order to streamline supervision, cooperation among various government bodies will be enhanced, including that between the Customs, Inspection & Quarantine, Industry & Commerce, Taxation, Foreign Exchange and other administrative authorities. The China (Shanghai) Pilot Free Trade Zone will set up a port supervision institution with integrated functions, and explore the feasibility of applying an electronic monitoring system and setting up of effective risk management system.

2. *Explore a supporting tax regime*

(d) *Implement tax policies to boost investment.* For enterprises or individual shareholders registered in the China (Shanghai) Pilot Free Trade Zone that carry out investment using non-monetary assets, the income tax payable due to the increase in asset valuation can be paid by installments within a five-year period. Where enterprises within the China (Shanghai) Pilot Free Trade Zone award highly-skilled employees or employees in short supply by means of shares or capital contributions, the relevant individual income tax may be paid by installments as same as the policies piloted in Zhongguancun.

(e) *Implement tax policies to promote trade.* Financial leasing companies registered or project companies set up by financial leasing companies with registration in the China (Shanghai) Pilot Free Trade Zone may enjoy the pilot policies of export tax refund for qualified financial leasing business. A domestic leasing company registered or its project companies with registration in the Pilot Free Trade Zone may enjoy reduced import VAT on an aircraft with empty weight no less than 25 tons, provided that such aircraft is to be leased to a domestic airline with approval from competent authorities. Import VAT and consumption taxes will be applicable in accordance with relevant laws and regulations, on the products manufactured or processed by a company within the China (Shanghai) Pilot Free Trade Zone but sold to the Mainland China outside of the China (Shanghai) Pilot Free Trade Zone. Enterprises will be provided with the option of calculating import duty according to the duty rates applicable to the finished goods or the imported parts. Currently, the imported machines, equipment and other goods required by manufacturing enterprises as well as manufacturing service companies that are set up in the China (Shanghai) Pilot Free Trade Zone, may be exempt from import taxes, other than those imported by consumer services companies or those which cannot enjoy import taxes exemption as stipulated in laws and regulations. Tax refund policies on the port-of-departure will be improved, and the expansion on pilot scope (e.g. departure ports, carriers and means of transport) will be studied.

Additionally, in line with the direction of tax reform and international practice, tax policies will be studied to support the development of overseas equity investment and offshore business, under the condition that such tax polies do not lead to base erosion or profit shifting.

4. Organize and Implement Effectively

The State Council will lead and coordinate the promotion of the China (Shanghai) Pilot Free Trade Zone. The Shanghai Municipal People's Government is responsible for organizing implementation, improving the working mechanism, and allocating detail responsibilities. Based on the targets which were clearly set out in the Framework Plan and pilot tasks, in accordance with the principle of "go ahead with the matured ones and follow by perfection", the Shanghai Municipal People's Government can create a practical implementation plan and enforce without delay. During the implementing, the Shanghai Municipal People's Government shall study new cases, resolve new problems and report to the State Council in a timely fashion on significant issues. All relevant departments need to support actively, provide cooperation, guidance and evaluation feedbacks, work together to promote the innovation on relevant system, mechanism and policy, and construct and well-manage the China (Shanghai) Pilot Free Trade Zone.

Appendix 9

Measures to Open Up the Service Sectors in the China (Shanghai) Pilot Free Trade Zone

1. Financial Services

1. Banking service (Classification of National Economic Industries: J Finance industry – 6620 Monetary banking service)	
Opening up measures	(1) Qualified foreign financial institutions will be allowed to set up wholly foreign-owned banks and Sino-foreign equity joint venture banks with eligible private capital within the China (Shanghai) Pilot Free Trade Zone. Restricted license banks will be allowed to be incorporated under certain conditions. (2) Qualified Chinese banks will be allowed to conduct offshore business under the condition of improving related regulations and enhancing supervision.
2. Specialized health and medical insurance (Classification of National Economic Industries: J Finance industry – 6812 Health and accident insurance)	
Opening up measures	Setup of foreign invested specialized health and medical insurance institutions will be allowed.
3. Financial leasing (Classification of National Economic Industries: J Finance industry – 6631 Finance leasing service)	
Opening up measures	(1) The minimum registered capital requirements for a project company (i.e. single-ship/aircraft company) set up by financial leasing companies within the China (Shanghai) Pilot Free Trade Zone will be removed. (2) Financial leasing companies will be allowed to conduct commercial factoring that are related to its primary businesses.

2. Transportation Services

4. Ocean transportation (Classification of National Economic Industries: G Transportation, warehousing and postal industry – 5521 Ocean transportation)	
Opening up measures	(1) Limitations on foreign participation in Sino-foreign equity joint venture and Sino-foreign cooperative joint venture international shipping enterprises will be relaxed. The transport administrative authorities of the State Council shall be in charge of the rulemaking. (2) Foreign ships owned or indirectly owned by Chinese-invested companies are allowed to pilot the coastal shipping between domestic coastal ports and Shanghai port.
5. International ship management (Classification of National Economic Industries: G Transportation, warehousing and postal industry – 5539 Other water transportation auxiliary service)	
Opening up measures	Incorporation of wholly foreign-owned ship management enterprises will be allowed.

3. Commerce and Trade Services

6. Value-added telecommunications (Classification of National Economic Industries: I Information transmission, software and information technology service – 6319 Other telecommunication service, 6420 Internet information service, 6540 Data processing and storage service, 6592 call centre)	
Opening up measures	Subject to the network information security, qualified FIEs will be allowed to engage in specific value-added telecommunication services. Approval by the State Council is required if the limitations exist in administrative regulations.
7. Entertainment and gaming consoles sales and service (Classification of National Economic Industries: F Wholesale and retailing – 5179 Wholesale of other mechanical and electronic products)	
Opening up measures	FIEs will be allowed to engage in the manufacturing and sales of entertainment and gaming consoles. The consoles with content passing the censorship by the culture administrative authorities will be allowed to be sold in the domestic market.

4. Professional Services

8. Lawyer service (Classification of National Economic Industries: L Leasing and business service – 7221 Lawyers and related legal service)	
Opening up measures	Cooperative mechanism between Chinese and foreign law firms will be explored.
9. Credit inquiry (Classification of National Economic Industries: L Leasing and business service – 7295 Credit service)	
Opening up measures	Incorporation of foreign invested credit information companies will be allowed.
10. Tourism companies (Classification of National Economic Industries: L Leasing and business service – 7271 Travel agency service)	
Opening up measures	Sino-foreign equity joint venture tourism companies registered in the China (Shanghai) Pilot Free Trade Zone will be allowed to engage in overseas tourism business activities, with the exception of Taiwan.
11. Human resources service (Classification of National Economic Industries: L Leasing and business service – 7262 Professional intermediary service)	
Opening up measures	(1) Setup of Sino-foreign equity joint venture human resources agencies will be allowed with the foreign participation at 70 % or below. Investors from Hong Kong and Macau will be allowed to set up wholly foreign-owned human resources agencies. (2) The minimum registered capital for foreign invested human resources agencies will be reduced from USD300,000 to USD125,000.
12. Investment management (Classification of National Economic Industries: L Leasing and business service – 7211 Headquarters management)	
Opening up measures	Incorporation of foreign-invested joint-stock holding companies will be allowed.

13. Engineering design (Classification of National Economic Industries: M Scientific research and technology service company – 7482 Engineering investigation and design)	
Opening up measures	Foreign-invested engineering design (excluding engineering survey) companies registered in the China measures (Shanghai) Pilot Free Trade Zone may be waived from the requirement to provide the investor's previous project records on initial application of the relevant qualifications for those applicants providing services in Shanghai.
14. Construction service (Classification of National Economic Industries: E Construction industry – 47 Housing construction industry, 48 Civil Engineering Construction, 49 Construction and Installation, 50 Building decoration and other construction)	
Opening up measures	Wholly foreign-owned construction enterprises registered within the China (Shanghai) Pilot Free Trade Zone will be allowed to conduct Sino-foreign joint construction projects in Shanghai regardless of the extent of foreign participation in the project.

5. Cultural Services

15. Entertainment artist agency (Classification of National Economic Industries: R Culture, sports and entertainment – 8941 Culture and entertainment agency)	
Opening up measures	The limitation on foreign participation in entertainment artist agencies will be removed. A wholly foreign-owned entertainment artist agency will be allowed to set up to provide service in Shanghai.
16. Entertainment facilities (Classification of National Economic Industries: R Culture, sports and entertainment – 8911 ballroom recreation activities)	
Opening up measures	Wholly foreign-owned entertainment facilities will be allowed to set up and provide service in the China (Shanghai) Pilot Free Trade Zone.

6. Public Services

17. Education and training, vocational skills training (Classification of National Economic Industries: P Education – 8291 Vocational skills training)	
Opening up measures	(1) Establishment of Sino-foreign cooperative joint venture education and training institutions will be allowed. (2) Establishment of Sino-foreign cooperative joint venture vocational skills training institutions will be allowed.
18. Medical service (Classification of National Economic Industries: Q Health and social work – 8311 General hospital, 8315 Specialized hospital, 8330 Out-patient department)	
Opening up measures	Establishment of wholly foreign-owned medical institutions will be allowed.

Note: The opening up measures above are only applicable to the enterprises registered within the China (Shanghai) Pilot Free Trade Zone.

References

Institutional Sources Regarding the Establishment of the New China (Shanghai) Pilot Free Trade Zone

China Banking Regulatory Commission (2013a) Circular of China banking regulatory commission on issues concerning banking supervision in China (Shanghai) Free Trade Zone (Yin Jian Fa [2013] No. 40)
China Securities Regulatory Commission (2013) Polices and measures on capital market for supporting and promoting China (Shanghai) Pilot Free Trade Zone
China State Council (2013a) Decision of the state council on temporary adjustments to the administrative approval items or special administrative measures on access prescribed in relevant administrative regulations or state council's documents in the China (Shanghai) Pilot Free Trade Zone
China State Council (2013b) Circular of the state council on the framework plan for the China (Shanghai) Pilot Free Trade Zone (Guo Fa 2013 No. 38)
Chinese General Administration of Customs (2014a) Several measures of general administration of customs on supervising and supporting safely and effectively and promoting the construction of China (Shanghai) Pilot Free Trade Zone
Chinese General Administration of Customs (2014b) Notice of the general administration of customs on printing and distributing the reform plan of the customs supervision service mode in China (Shanghai) Pilot Free Trade Zone
Chinese Ministry of Culture (2013) Circular of the Ministry of Culture on implementing the policies of cultural market administration for the China (Shanghai) Pilot Free Trade Zone (Wen Shi Fa [2013] No. 47)
Chinese Ministry of Finance (2014) Notice on supporting accounting firms to establish a branch and carry out pilot work in China (Shanghai) Free Trade Pilot Zone
Chinese Ministry of Finance, General Administration of Customs, State Administration of Taxation (2013) Circular on import tax policies for the China (Shanghai) Pilot Free Trade Zone
Chinese Ministry of Industry and Information Technology and Shanghai Municipal People's Government (2014a) Procedures for administration of pilot value-added telecom business with foreign investment in the China (Shanghai) Pilot Free Trade Zone
Chinese Ministry of Industry and Information Technology and Shanghai Municipal People's Government (2014b) Suggestions of Ministry of Industry and information technology and Shanghai municipal people's government on further opening up value-added telecommunication business to foreign investors in China (Shanghai) Pilot Free Trade Zone

L. Riccardi, *Investing in China through Free Trade Zones*,
DOI 10.1007/978-3-662-47354-2

Chinese Ministry of Justice (2014) Official reply of ministry of justice on approving the pilot program of exploring the close cooperation mode and mechanism of Chinese and foreign law firms in China (Shanghai) Pilot Free Trade Zone

Chinese Ministry of Transport (2014a) Announcement of ministry of transport on trial coastal transportation incidental in Shanghai by Chinese non-Five-Star-Flag international navigation ships

Chinese Ministry of Transport (2014b) Opinions of the general office of the ministry of transport on promoting the transformation, upgrading and healthy development of the shipping industry

Chinese Ministry of Transport (2014c) Announcement of the ministry of transport on trial implementation of coastal carriage of Chinese-invested non-Five-Star Flag Ships Of International Voyages In Shanghai

Chinese Ministry of Transport and Shanghai Municipal People's Government (2013) Implementation opinions of the ministry of transport and Shanghai municipal people's government on implementing the "framework plan for the China (Shanghai) Pilot Free Trade Zone" and accelerating the construction of the Shanghai International Transport Center (Jiao Shui Fa [2013] No. 584)

Chinese National Tourism Administration (2014) Suggestions of the national tourism administration on tourism supporting the construction of China (Shanghai) Pilot Free Trade Zone

Chinese Standing Committee of the National People's Congress (2013) Decision of the standing committee of the national people's congress on authorizing the state council to temporarily adjust the relevant administrative approval items prescribed in laws in the China (Shanghai) Pilot Free Trade Zone

Chinese Standing Committee of the National People's Congress (2014) Interpretation of the standing committee of the national people's congress on Article 158 and Article 159 of criminal law of the people's republic of China

Chinese State Administration for Industry and Commerce (2013a) Reply of the State Administration for industry & commerce to approval of plan for trial implementation of new business license in China (Shanghai) Pilot Free Trade Zone

Chinese State Administration for Industry and Commerce (2013b) Notice of state administration for industry & commerce on granting administrative rights of registration of enterprises with foreign investment to Shanghai municipal administration for industry & commerce Pilot Free Trade Zone Sub-Bureau

Chinese State Administration for Industry and Commerce (2013c) Circular of the state administration for industry and commerce on authorizing the administrative authority of foreign-invested enterprises registration to the branch of shanghai administration for industry and commerce in The Free Trade Zone

Chinese State Administration for Industry and Commerce (2013d) Policy Interpretation of the Opinions of the State Administration for Industry and Commerce on Supporting the Construction of the China (Shanghai) Pilot Free Trade Zone

Chinese State Administration for Industry and Commerce (2013e) Opinions of the state administration for industry and commerce on supporting the construction of the China (Shanghai) Pilot Free Trade Zone (No. 147 [2013] of the State Administration for Industry and Commerce)

Chinese State Administration for Industry and Commerce (2013f) Reply of the state administration for industry and commerce on approving the trial implementation plan of new business licenses in the China (Shanghai) Pilot Free Trade Zone

Chinese State Administration of Foreign Exchange (2014) Implementation regulations concerning foreign exchange administration to support the construction of the China (Shanghai) Pilot Free Trade Zone

General Office of Shanghai Municipal People's Government (2014) Notice of the general office of Shanghai municipal people's government on printing and distributing the implementation rules on cultural services opened to foreign investment in the China (Shanghai) Pilot Free Trade Zone Formulated By Five Departments Including The Municipal Administration Of Culture, Radio, Film & TV

Lawyers Working Committee of Pudong New Area (2014) Interpretation of the provisions on registration administration of enterprises in the China (Shanghai) Pilot Free Trade Zone

People's Bank of China (2013a) Opinions of People's Bank of China to Support China (Shanghai) Pilot Free Trade Zone In Financial Sector

People's Bank of China (2013b) Notice of the Shanghai head office of the people's Bank of China to promote cross-border use of Renminbi in the China (Shanghai) Pilot Free Trade Zone

People's Bank of China (2014a) Circular of the Shanghai headquarters of the people's Bank of China on lifting the upper limit on small-amount foreign currency deposit rates in the China (Shanghai) Pilot Free Trade Zone

People's Bank of China (2014b) Notice of the Shanghai headquarters of the people's Bank of China on effectively combating money laundering and terrorist financing in the China (Shanghai) Pilot Free Trade Zone

People's Bank of China (2014c) Notice of the Shanghai headquarters of the people's Bank of China on issuing implementation opinions on cross-border RMB payment service by Payment Institutions in Shanghai

Shanghai Customs (2013a) Announcement of Shanghai customs on developing futures bonded delivery business in China (Shanghai) Pilot Free Trade Zone

Shanghai Customs (2013b) Announcement of Shanghai customs on developing financing lease business in China (Shanghai) Pilot Free Trade Zone

Shanghai Customs (2013c) Announcement of Shanghai customs on establishing a customs service window in the China (Shanghai) Pilot Free Trade Zone

Shanghai Court (2013) Suggestions of Shanghai court on serving and guaranteeing the construction of China (Shanghai) Pilot Free Trade Zone

Shanghai Customs (2014a) Announcement of Shanghai customs on handling networked supervision formalities by enterprises in China (Shanghai) Pilot Free Trade Zone

Shanghai Customs (2014b) Announcement of Shanghai customs on implementing the operation mode of goods flow by "Transportation under self-control" in China (Shanghai) Pilot Free Trade Zone

Shanghai Customs (2014c) Announcement of Shanghai customs on implementing the operation mode of goods entering the zone from abroad by "First Entering and then Declaring" in China (Shanghai) Pilot Free Trade Zone

Shanghai Customs (2014d) Announcement of Shanghai customs on developing cross-border trade e-commerce import business

Shanghai Customs (2014e) Announcement of Shanghai customs on developing bonded display trade business in China (Shanghai) Pilot Free Trade Zone

Shanghai Customs (2014f) Announcement of Shanghai customs on developing domestic and overseas maintenance service in China (Shanghai) Pilot Free Trade Zone

Shanghai Customs (2014g) Announcement of Shanghai customs on implementing the processing trade work-order write-off mode in China (Shanghai) Pilot Free Trade Zone

Shanghai Administration for Industry and Commerce (2013) Circular of the Shanghai administration for industry and commerce on issuing the provisions on registration administration of enterprises in the China (Shanghai) Pilot Free Trade Zone

Shanghai Administration for Industry & Commerce (2014) Notice of Shanghai administration for industry & commerce on promulgating the procedures for publication of annual reports by enterprises in China (Shanghai) Pilot Free Trade Zone (For trial implementation) and procedures for administration on directory of enterprises with abnormal operation in China (Shanghai) Pilot Free Trade Zone (For Trial Implementation)

Shanghai Branch of the State Administration of Foreign Exchange (2014) Notice of Shanghai branch of the state administration of foreign exchange on issuing the detailed rules for the implementation of regulations on foreign exchange management in the China (Shanghai) Pilot Free Trade Zone

Shanghai Municipal Administration for Industry and Commerce (2013) Notice of Shanghai municipal administration for industry and commerce on Promulgation of the Provisions on Administration of Enterprise Registration in China (Shanghai) Pilot Free Trade Zone

Shanghai Municipal Commission of Commerce, Shanghai Municipal Office of Financial Service and the Administrative Committee of the PFTZ (2014) Interim provisions on the supervision over trading business on commodity spot markets in China (Shanghai) Pilot Free Trade Zone

Shanghai Municipal Commission of Commerce, Shanghai Municipal Commission of Economy and Informatization, Shanghai Customs, Shanghai Entry-Exit Inspection and Quarantine Bureau, and China (Shanghai) Pilot Free Trade Zone Administration (2013) Notice of Shanghai municipal commission of commerce, shanghai municipal commission of economy and informatization, Shanghai Customs, Shanghai Entry-Exit Inspection and Quarantine Bureau, and China (Shanghai) Pilot Free Trade Zone Administration on Issuing the Implementation Opinions on Carrying Out Global Maintenance Services in China (Shanghai) Pilot Free Trade Zone.

Shanghai Municipal Commission of Health and Family Planning, Shanghai Municipal Commission of Commerce, Shanghai Municipal Administration for Industry and Commerce (2013) Interim Procedures for Administration of Wholly-Foreign–Funded Medical Institutions in China (Shanghai) Pilot Free Trade Zone

Shanghai Municipal Commission, Shanghai Municipal Commission of Commerce, Shanghai Municipal, Human Resources and Social Security Bureau, Shanghai Municipal Administration for Industry and Commerce (2013) Interim procedures for administration of China-foreign cooperative training institutions of business nature in China (Shanghai) Pilot Free Trade Zone

Shanghai Municipal People's Government (2013a) Administrative measures for the China (Shanghai) Pilot Free Trade Zone (Shanghai Municipal People's Government Decree No. 7)

Shanghai Municipal People's Government (2013b) Circular of Shanghai municipal people's government on printing and distributing "Filing administrative measures for foreign investment projects in China (Shanghai) Pilot Free Trade Zone" (Hu Fu Fa 2013 No. 71)

Shanghai Municipal People's Government (2013c) Circular of Shanghai municipal people' government on printing and distributing the "Filing administrative measures for outbound investment in setting up enterprises by China (Shanghai) Pilot Free Trade Zone Enterprises"

Shanghai Municipal People's Government (2013d) Circular of Shanghai municipal people's government on printing and distributing the "Filing administrative measures for outbound investment projects by China (Shanghai) Pilot Free Trade Zone Enterprises"

Shanghai Municipal People's Government (2014a) Regulations of China (Shanghai) Pilot Free Trade Zone (Adopted at the 14th session of the standing committee of the 14th Shanghai municipal people's congress of Shanghai on July 25, 2014)

Shanghai Municipal People's Government (2014b) Interim procedures for the administration of commercial factoring in the China (Shanghai) Pilot Free Trade Zone

Shanghai Municipal People's Government (2014c) Special administrative measures (Negative List) on foreign investment access to the China (Shanghai) Pilot Free Trade Zone (2014 Amended Version)

Shanghai Municipal Office, Chinese State Administration of Taxation, Shanghai Municipal Bureau of Taxation (2013) Notice on printing and distributing the operating rules of filing matters of enterprise income tax policy on nonmonetary asset investment asset evaluation increment of enterprises in the China (Shanghai) Pilot Free Trade Zone

The Chinese General Administration of Quality Supervision, Inspection and Quarantine (2013) Opinions of the general administration of quality supervision, inspection and quarantine on supporting establishment of the China (Shanghai) Pilot Free Trade Zone (Guo Zhi Jian Tong [2013] No. 503)

Other Sources

Bhattasali D (2002) Accelerating financial market restructure in China. World Bank Mimeo, Washington, DC

China Statistics Office (2013a) China statistical year book. China Statistics Press, Beijing

China Statistics Office (2013b) Shenzhen statistical year book. China Statistics Press, Beijing

Chinese State Administration of Taxation (2009a) Guoshuihan [2009] No. 81. State Administration of Taxation, Shanghai, China
Chinese State Administration of Taxation (2009b) Guoshuihan [2009] No. 601. State Administration of Taxation, Shanghai, China
Chinese State Administration of Taxation (2010) Chongqing Bureau of SAT implements DTT to defend interest of the state. State Administration Of Taxation, China
Chinese State Administration Of Taxation (2012) Sat public notice [2012] No.59. State Administration Of Taxation, China
Chinese State Administration Of Taxation (2013) Interpretation of sat public notice [2012] No.59. State Administration Of Taxation, China
Chiu RH et al (2011) An evaluation of free trade port zone in Taiwan. Asian J Shipp Logist 27(3):423–446
Department of Foreign Investment Administration of Mofcom (2013a) Statistics on FDI in China 2013. Department of Foreign Investment Administration of Mofcom, China
Department of Foreign Investment Administration of Mofcom (2013) 2013 report on foreign investment in China
Fink C, Mattoo A, Rathindran R (2003) An assessment of telecommunications reform in developing countries. Inf Econ Policy 15(4):443–466
Fisher JM (2014) Fairer shores: tax havens, tax avoidance, and corporate social responsibility. Boston Univ Law Rev 94:337
Goldstein M, Lardy NR (2008) China's exchange rate policy: an overview of some key issues. Am Econ Rev 96(2):422–426
Ho MY (2002) Ho Taiwan's free port plan, CEPD, Executive Yuan
Hodjera Z (1978) The Asian currency market: Singapore as a regional finance center. Int Monet Fund Staff Pap 25(2):221–253
Hryck D, Andreoli B (2005) Foreign tax strategies can boon to multinationals. Financial Exec 21(7):56
Ianchovichina E, Mcdougall RA, Hertel TW (1999) A disequilibrium model of international capital mobility. Paper presented at the second annual conference on global economics analysis, Denmark, 20th–22nd June
Iras (2007) Iras circular-one-tier corporate tax system. Inland Revenue Authority Of Singapore, Singapore
Iras (2010) Taxable income. Inland Revenue Authority Of Singapore, Singapore
Iras (2012) Iras E-tax guide-income tax: certainty of non-taxation of companies' gains on disposal of equity investments. Inland Revenue Authority Of Singapore, Singapore
Iras (2013a) Tax exemption scheme for new start-up companies. Inland Revenue Authority Of Singapore, Singapore
Iras (2013b) Corporate income tax rebate for years of assessment 2013 to 2015. Inland Revenue Authority Of Singapore, Singapore
Iras (2013c) Exemption of foreign sourced income. Inland Revenue Authority Of Singapore, Singapore
Janeba E (1996) Foreign direct investment under oligopoly: profit shifting or profit capturing? J Public Econ
Jin NK (1996) Singapore as a financial center: new development, challenges and prospects. In: Ito T, Krueger AO (eds) Financial deregulation and integration in east asia. University of Chicago Press, Chicago
Karen Sun Ying W (2013) Offshore financial centres and offshore business structures. Aust Tax Forum 28(4):787
Lardy NR (2003) trade liberalization and its role in Chinese economic growth. In: Tseng WA, Cowen D (eds) A tale of two giants: India's and China's experience with reform and growth. Palgrave Macmillan, New York
Lin JY (2001) WTO accession and financial reform in China. Source, Cato J 21(1):13–18

Mattoo A (2002) China's accession to the WTO: the services dimension. World Bank Press, Washington, DC

Mckibbin WJ, Tang KK (1998) The global economic impacts of trade and financial reform in China. Brookings discussion paper in international economics No.137, vol 22, The Bookings Institution, Washington DC: World Economy

Mui, M. & Wong, R. (2008), Tax Regime change. China Busi Rev

Naughton B (2007) The Chinese economy, transitions and growth. The Mit Press, Cambridge, MA

Ng E, Whalley J (2003) Geographical expansion as trade liberalization. Mimeo, UWO, London

Oestreicher A, Koch R (2012) Taxation and corporate group structure – evidence from a sample of European multinationals, Schmalenbach Business Review (SBR)

Palan R, And MR, Chavagneux C (2010) Tax havens: how globalization really works. Cornell University Press, Ithaca

Riccardi L, Riccardi G (2014) Gli Investimenti in Asia Orientale. Maggioli Editore

Sassen S (1999) Global financial centers. Foreign Aff 78(1):75–87

Shanghai Social Sciences Union (2013) 150 questions about Shanghai Ftz. Shanghai People's Publisher, Shanghai

Sharman JC (2012) chinese capital flows and offshore financial centers. Pacific Review 25(3):317–337

Singapore Department of Statistics (2014) Singapore's investment abroad 2012

van der Hoek MP, Kong S, Li Z (2008) The dual corporate income tax in China: the impact of unification. Publ Finance Manage 8(4):655–677

Wang Z (2001) The impact of China's WTO accession on trade and economic relations cross the Taiwan Strait. Econ Trans 9:743–785

Wei Liu (2004) China's free trade zones: a study of their economic effects. China Rep 40:431–444

Wilson P, Tat KC (2001) Exchange rates and the trade balance: the case of Singapore 1970 to 1996. J Asian Econ 12:47–63

Yang YC (2009) A comparative analysis of Free Trade Zone Policies in Taiwan and Korea based on a port hinterland perspective. Asian J Shipp Logist 25(2):273–303

Useful Websites

Official website of the New China (Shanghai) Pilot Free Trade Zone http://en.shftz.gov.cn/

Official website of the People's Bank of China http://www.pbc.gov.cn/publish/english/963/index.html

Official website of the Shanghai Municipal Government http://www.shanghai.gov.cn/

Official website of the State Council of the People's Republic of China http://english.gov.cn/

MIX
Papier aus verantwortungsvollen Quellen
Paper from responsible sources
FSC® C105338

If you have any concerns about our products,
you can contact us on
ProductSafety@springernature.com

In case Publisher is established outside the EU,
the EU authorized representative is:
Springer Nature Customer Service Center GmbH
Europaplatz 3, 69115 Heidelberg, Germany

Printed by Libri Plureos GmbH
in Hamburg, Germany